# Meet Your King

## WARREN W. WIERSBE

This book is designed for your personal
reading pleasure and profit. It is also
designed for group study. A leader's guide
with helps and hints for teachers and
visual aids (Victor Multiuse Transparency
Masters) is available from your local book-
store or from the publisher.

# VICTOR BOOKS

a division of SP Publications, Inc.

WHEATON, ILLINOIS 60187

Offices also in Fullerton, California • Whitby, Ontario, Canada • Amersham-on-the-Hill, Bucks, England

## Other Victor Books by Warren Wiersbe

*Be Complete* (Colossians)
*Be Faithful* (1, 2, Timothy, Titus)
*Be Free* (Galatians)
*Be Joyful* (Philippians)
*Be Mature* (James)
*Be Real* (1 John)
*Be Ready* (1 and 2 Thessalonians)
*Be Rich* (Ephesians)
*Be Right* (Romans)
*Meet Yourself in the Parables*
*Meet Your King* (Matthew)

*Third printing, 1981*

Most of the Scripture quotations in this book are from the King James
Version. Other quotations are from *The New International Version* (NIV),
©1978 by The New York International Bible Society; the *New American
Standard Bible* (NASB), ©1960, 1962, 1963, 1968, 1971, 1972, 1973 by
the Lockman Foundation, La Habra, California; and *The New Scofield
Reference Bible* (SCO), ©1967 by the delegates of the Oxford University
Press, Inc., New York. Used by permission.

Library of Congress Catalog Card Number: 79–92552
ISBN: 0–88207–799–6

©1980 by SP Publications, Inc. All rights reserved
Printed in the United States of America

VICTOR BOOKS
A division of SP Publications, Inc.
P. O. Box 1825 • Wheaton, Illinois 60187

Dedicated to some gifted friends
whose keyboard ministries have greatly
enriched my own life:
David Brackley
Merrill Dunlop
Bill Fasig
John Innes

# CONTENTS

# PREFACE

"The Gospel According to Matthew" has been called by many Bible scholars the most important single document of the Christian faith. Historians tell us that this book was the most widely read, and the most quoted, in the early church. While all four Gospels are important to us, it is not without reason that Matthew stands first.

This book is an expository survey of Matthew, presenting Jesus Christ as the King. It is not a detailed commentary, although I have tried to cover all the important passages and the "problem areas." The limitations of space have prevented me from arguing the pros and cons of various views. I have tried to present what I feel Matthew wanted to convey to us about Jesus Christ and His ministry. If I should disagree with your position, at least I trust I have not been disagreeable!

May our study of this important book lead all of us into a deeper love for, and loyalty to, Jesus Christ, the King of kings.

WARREN W. WIERSBE

# 1

# HERE'S GOOD NEWS!

Twenty or thirty years after Jesus had gone back to heaven, a Jewish disciple named Matthew was inspired by the Spirit of God to write a book. The finished product is what we know today as "The Gospel According to Matthew."

Nowhere in the four Gospels do we find a single recorded word that Matthew spoke. Yet in his Gospel, he gives us the words and works of Jesus Christ, "the Son of David, the Son of Abraham" (Matt. 1:1). Matthew did not write to tell us about himself. But let's get acquainted with him and the book he wrote. Then we can learn all that he wanted us to know about Jesus Christ.

The Holy Spirit used Matthew to accomplish three important tasks in the writing of his Gospel.

**The Bridge-Builder:** He Introduced a New Book
That book was the New Testament. If a Bible reader were to jump from Malachi into Mark, or Acts, or Romans, he would be bewildered. Matthew's Gospel is the bridge that leads us out of the Old Testament and into the New Testament.

The theme of the Old Testament is given in Genesis 5:1: "This is the book of the generations of Adam." The Old Testament gives the history of "the Adam family," and it is a sad history indeed. God created man in

His own image, but man sinned—thus defiling and deforming that image. Then man brought forth children "in his own likeness, after his image" (Gen. 5:3). These children proved themselves to be sinners like their parents. No matter where you read in the Old Testament, you meet sin and sinners.

But the New Testament is, "The book of the generation of Jesus Christ" (Matt. 1:1). Jesus is the last Adam (1 Cor. 15:45), and He came to earth to save the "generations of Adam." (This includes you and me, by the way.) Through no choice of our own, we were born into the generations of Adam, and this made us sinners. But by a choice of faith, we can be born into the generation of Jesus Christ and become the children of God!

When you read the genealogy in Genesis 5, the repeated phrase *and he died* sounds like the tolling of a funeral bell. The Old Testament illustrates the truth that "the wages of sin is death" (Rom. 6:23). But when you turn to the New Testament, that first genealogy emphasizes *birth* and not death! The message of the New Testament is that "the gift of God is eternal life through Jesus Christ our Lord" (Rom. 6:23).

The Old Testament is a book of promise, while the New Testament is a book of fulfillment. (To be sure, there are many precious promises in the New Testament. But I am referring to the emphasis of each half of the Bible.) Beginning with Genesis 3:15, God promised a Redeemer; and Jesus Christ fulfilled that promise. *Fulfilled* is one of the key words in the Gospel of Matthew, used about 15 times.

One purpose of this Gospel is to show that Jesus Christ fulfilled the Old Testament promises concerning the Messiah. His birth at Bethlehem fulfilled Isaiah 7:14 (Matt. 1:22-23). Jesus was taken to Egypt for safety, and this fulfilled Hosea 11:1 (Matt. 2:14-15). When Joseph and the family returned and decided to settle in Nazareth, this fulfilled several Old Testament prophecies (Matt. 2:22-23). Matthew used at least 129 quotations or allusions to the Old Testament in this Gospel. He wrote primarily for Jewish readers to show them that Jesus Christ was indeed their promised Messiah.

**The Biographer:** He Introduced a New King

None of the four Gospels is a biography in the modern sense of the word. In fact, the Apostle John doubted that a complete biography of Jesus could ever be written (John 21:25). There are many details about the earthly life of Jesus that are not given in any of the Gospels.

Each of the four Gospels has its own emphasis. Matthew's book is called, "the Gospel of the King." It was written primarily for Jewish readers. Mark's book, the Gospel of the Servant, was written to instruct Roman readers. Luke wrote mainly to the Greeks and presented Christ as the perfect "Son of man." John's appeal is universal, and his message was, "This is the Son of God." No one Gospel is able to tell the whole story as God wants us to see it. But when we put these four Gospel accounts together, we have a composite picture of the person and work of our Lord.

Being accustomed to keeping systematic records, Matthew gives us a beautifully organized account of our Lord's life and ministry. The book can be divided into 10 sections in which "doing" and "teaching" alternate. Each teaching section ends with, "When Jesus had ended these sayings" or a similar transitional statement. The chapters can be divided like this:

| Narrative | Teaching | Transition |
|---|---|---|
| 1—4 | 5—7 | 7:28 |
| 8:1—9:34 | 9:35—10:42 | 11:1 |
| 11:2—12:50 | 13:1-52 | 13:53 |
| 13:53—17:27 | 18:1-35 | 19:1 |
| 19:1—23:39 | 24:1—25:46 | 26:1 |
| 26:1—28:20 (the Passion narrative) | | |

Matthew described Jesus as the *Doer* and the *Teacher*. He recorded at least 20 specific miracles and 6 major messages: the Sermon on the Mount (chaps. 5—7), the charge to the apostles (chap. 10), the parables of the kingdom (chap. 13), the lesson on forgiveness (chap. 18), the denunciation of the Pharisees (chap. 23), and the prophetic discourse on the Mount of Olives (chaps. 24—25). At least 60 percent of this book focuses on the teachings of Jesus.

Remember, Matthew focuses on the *kingdom.* In the Old Testament, the Jewish nation was God's kingdom on earth: "And you shall be unto Me a kingdom of priests, and an holy nation" (Ex. 19:6). Many people in Jesus' day were looking for the God-sent Deliverer who would release them from Roman bondage and reestablish the glorious kingdom of Israel.

The message of the kingdom of heaven was first preached by John the Baptist (Matt. 3:1-2). The Lord Jesus also preached this message from the very beginning of His ministry (Matt. 4:23). He sent out the Twelve Apostles with the same proclamation (Matt. 10:1-7).

However, the Good News of the kingdom required a moral and spiritual response from the people, and not simply the acceptance of a ruler. John the Baptist called for repentance. Likewise, Jesus made it clear that He had not come to overcome Rome, but to transform the hearts and lives of those who trusted Him. Before He could enter into the glory of the kingdom, Jesus endured the suffering of the cross.

At this point, let's look at a suggested outline of the Gospel according to Matthew. This outline will help us see the biography of Jesus Christ, the King, as presented in this Gospel.

I.  THE REVELATION OF THE KING—chapters 1—10
    A.  His person—1—4
    B.  His principles—5—7
    C.  His power—8—10
    (Note: The message during this period of His ministry was, "The kingdom of heaven is at hand" [3:2, 4:17, 10:7].)

II.  THE REBELLION AGAINST THE KING—chapters 11—13
    A.  His messenger rejected—11:1-19
    B.  His works denied—11:20-30
    C.  His principles refused—12:1-21
    D.  His person attacked—12:22-50
    E.  Result: the "mysteries of the kingdom"—13

III.  THE RETIREMENT OF THE KING—chapters 14—20
    (The Lord seeks to leave the multitudes to be alone with His disciples.)
    A.  Before Peter's confession—14:1—16:12
    B.  Peter's confession—16:13-28
        (First mention of the cross—16:21)
    C.  After Peter's confession—17:1—20:34
        (Second mention of the cross—17:22)
        (Third mention of the cross—20:17-19)

IV. THE REJECTION OF THE KING—chapters 21—27
("The kingdom of God shall be taken from you. . . ." 21:43)
    A.   His public presentation as King—21:1-16
    B.   His conflict with the rulers—21:17—23:39
    C.   His prophetic message—24—25
    D.   His suffering and death—26—27
V. THE RESURRECTION OF THE KING—chapter 28

One further word about this Gospel. Matthew arranged his material in a topical order, rather than chronological. He grouped 10 miracles together in chapters 8—9 instead of putting them into their historical sequence in the Gospel's narrative. Certain other events are totally omitted. By consulting a good harmony of the Gospels, you will see that, while Matthew does not contradict the other three Gospel writers, he *does* follow his own pattern.

Matthew was not only a bridge-builder who introduced a new book, the New Testament; and a biographer who introduced a new King, Jesus Christ; but he also accomplished a third task when he wrote his book.

**The Believer:** He Introduced a New People
This new people, of course, was the church. Matthew is the only Gospel writer to use the word *church* (16:18; 18:17). The Greek word translated *church* means "a called-out assembly." In the New Testament, for the most part, this word refers to a local assembly of believers. In the Old Testament, Israel was God's called-out people, beginning with the call of Abraham (Gen. 12:1ff; Deut. 7:6-8). In fact, Stephen called the nation of Israel "the church (assembly) in the wilderness" (Acts 7:38), for they were God's called-out people.

But the New Testament church is a different people, for it is composed of *both* Jews and Gentiles. In this church there were no racial distinctions (Gal. 3:28). Even though Matthew wrote primarily for the Jews, he has a "universal" element in his book that includes the Gentiles. For example, Gentile leaders came to worship the infant Jesus (Matt. 2:1-12). Jesus performed miracles for Gentiles and even commended them for their faith (8:5-13, 15:21-28). The Gentile Queen of Sheba was praised for her willingness to make a long journey to hear God's wisdom (12:42). At a crisis hour in Jesus' ministry, He turned to a prophecy about the Gentiles

(12:14-21). Even in the parables, Jesus indicated that the blessings which Israel refused would be shared with the Gentiles (22:8-10, 21:40-46). The Olivet Discourse stated that the message would go "unto all nations" (24:14); and the Lord's commission involves all nations (28:19-20).

There were only believing Jews and believing Jewish proselytes in the church at the beginning (Acts 2—7). When the Gospel went to Samaria (Acts 8), people who were part Jewish and part Gentile came into the church. When Peter went to the household of Cornelius (Acts 10), the Gentiles became fully accepted in the church. The conference at Jerusalem (Acts 15), settled the decision that a Gentile did not have to become a Jew before he could become a Christian.

But Matthew anticipated all of this. And when his book was read by members of the early church, both Jews and Gentiles, it helped to settle differences and create unity. Matthew made it clear that this new people, the church, must not maintain a racial or social exclusiveness. Faith in Jesus Christ makes believers "all one" in the body of Christ, the church.

Matthew's own experience with the Lord is recorded in Matthew 9:9-17; and it is a beautiful example of the grace of God. His old name was Levi, the son of Alphaeus (Mark 2:14). "Matthew" means "the gift of God." Apparently, the name was given to commemorate his conversion and his call to be a disciple.

Remember that tax collectors were among the most hated people in Jewish society. To begin with, they were traitors to their own nation because they "sold themselves" to the Romans to work for the government. Each tax collector purchased from Rome the right to gather taxes, and the more he gathered, the more he could keep. They were considered thieves as well as traitors; and their constant contacts with Gentiles made them religiously suspect, if not unclean. Jesus reflected the popular view of the publicans when He classified them with harlots and other sinners (Matt. 5:46-47, 18:17); but it was obvious that He was the "friend of publicans and sinners" (11:19, 21:31-32).

Matthew opened his heart to Jesus Christ and became a new person. This was not an easy decision for him to make. He was a native of Capernaum, and Capernaum had rejected the Lord (11:23). Matthew was a well-known businessman in the city, and his old friends probably persecuted him. Certainly Matthew lost a great deal of income when he left all to follow Christ.

Matthew not only opened his heart, but he also opened his home. He knew that most, if not all, of his old friends would drop him when he began to follow Jesus Christ; so Matthew took advantage of the situation and invited them to meet Jesus. He gave a great feast and invited all the other tax collectors (some of whom could have been Gentiles), and the Jewish people who were not keeping the Law ("sinners").

Of course, the Pharisees criticized Jesus for daring to eat with such a defiled group of people. They even tried to get the disciples of John the Baptist to create a disagreement (Luke 5:33). The Lord explained why He was fellowshipping with "publicans and sinners": They were spiritually sick and needed a physician. He had not come to call the righteous *because there were no righteous people*. He came to call sinners, and that included the Pharisees. Of course, His critics did not consider themselves "spiritually sick," but they *were* just the same.

Matthew not only opened his heart and home, but he also opened his hands and worked for Christ. Alexander Whyte of Edinburgh once said that, when he left his job to follow Christ, Matthew brought his pen with him! Little did this ex-publican realize that the Holy Spirit would one day use him to write the first of the four Gospels in the New Testament.

According to tradition, Matthew ministered in Palestine for several years after the Lord's return to heaven, and then made missionary journeys to the Jews who were dispersed among the Gentiles. His work is associated with Persia, Ethiopia, and Syria, and some traditions associate him with Greece. The New Testament is silent on his life, but this we do know: Wherever the Scriptures travel in this world, the Gospel written by Matthew continues to minister to hearts.

# 2

# THE KING'S BIRTH

(Matthew 1—2)

If a man suddenly appears and claims to be a king, the public immediately asks for proof. What is his background? Who pays homage to him? What credentials can he present? Anticipating these important questions, Matthew opened his book with a careful account of the birth of Jesus Christ and the events that accompanied it. He presented four facts about the King.

## The Heredity of the King (1:1-25)

Since royalty depends on heredity, it was important for Jesus to establish His rights to David's throne. Matthew gave His human heredity (vv. 1-17) as well as His divine heredity (vv. 18-25).

*His human heredity (1:1-17).* Genealogies were very important to the Jews, for without them they could not prove their tribal memberships or their rights to inheritances. Anyone claiming to be "the Son of David" had to be able to prove it. It is generally concluded that Matthew gave our Lord's family tree through His foster father, Joseph, while Luke gave Mary's lineage (Luke 3:23ff).

Many Bible readers skip over this list of ancient (and, in some cases, unpronounceable) names. But this "list of names" is a vital part of the Gospel record. It shows that Jesus Christ is a part of history; that all of Jewish history prepared the way for His birth. God in His providence ruled and overruled to accomplish His great purpose in bringing His Son into the world.

This genealogy also illustrates God's wonderful grace. It is most unusual to find the names of women in Jewish genealogies, since names and inheritances came through the fathers. But in this list we find references to four women from Old Testament history: Tamar (1:3), Rahab and Ruth (1:5), and Bathsheba "the wife of Uriah" (1:6).

Matthew clearly omitted some names from this genealogy. Probably, he did this to give a systematic summary of 3 periods in Israel's history, each with 14 generations. The numerical value of the Hebrew letters for "David" equals 14. Matthew probably used this approach as a memory aid to help his readers remember this difficult list.

But there were many Jewish men who could trace their family back to King David. It would take more than human pedigree to make Jesus Christ "the Son of David" and heir to David's throne. This is why the divine heredity was so important.

*His divine heredity (1:18-25).* Matthew 1:16 and 18 make it clear that Jesus Christ's birth was different from that of any other Jewish boy named in the genealogy. Matthew pointed out that Joseph did not "beget" Jesus Christ. Rather, Joseph was the "husband of Mary, of whom was born Jesus, who is callled Christ." Jesus was born of an earthly mother without the need of an earthly father. This is known as the doctrine of the virgin birth.

Every child born into the world is a totally new creature. But Jesus Christ, being eternal God (John 1:1, 14), existed before Mary and Joseph or any of His earthly ancestors. If Jesus Christ were conceived and born just as any other baby, then He could not be God. It was necessary for Him to enter this world through an earthly mother, but not to be begotten by an earthly father. By a miracle of the Holy Spirit, Jesus was conceived in the womb of Mary, a virgin (Luke 1:26-38).

Some have raised the question that perhaps Mary was not a virgin. They say that Matthew 1:23 should be translated "young woman." But the world translated *virgin* in this verse always means virgin and cannot be translated "young woman."

Both Mary and Joseph belonged to the house of David. The Old Testament prophecies indicated that the Messiah would be born of a woman (Gen. 3:15), of the seed of Abraham (22:18), through the tribe of

Judah (49:10) and of the family of David (2 Sam. 7:12-13). Matthew's genealogy traced the line through Solomon, while Luke's traced it through Nathan, another one of David's sons. It is worth noting that Jesus Christ is the only Jew alive who can actually prove His claims to the throne of David! All of the other records were destroyed when the Romans took Jerusalem in A.D. 70.

To the Jewish people in that day, betrothal (engagement) was equivalent to marriage—except that the man and woman did not live together. They were called "husband and wife," and, at the end of the engagement period, the marriage was consummated. If a betrothed woman became pregnant, it was considered adultery (see Deut. 22:13-21). But Joseph did not punish or divorce Mary when he discovered she was with child, for the Lord had revealed the truth to him. All of this fulfilled Isaiah 7:14.

Before we leave this important section, we must consider the three names assigned to God's Son. The name Jesus means "Saviour" and comes from the Hebrew name, Joshua ("Jehovah is salvation"). There were many Jewish boys with the name Joshua (or, in the Greek, Jesus); but Mary's boy was called "Jesus the Christ." The word Christ means "anointed"; it is the Greek equivalent of Messiah. He is "Jesus the Messiah." Jesus is His human name, Christ is His official title; and Immanuel describes who He is—"God with us." Jesus Christ is God! We find this name "Immanuel" in Isaiah 7:14 and 8:8.

The King, then, was a Jewish male who was also the divine Son of God. But, did anybody acknowledge His Kingship? Yes, the magi from the East came and worshiped Him.

### The Homage to the King (2:1-12)

We must confess that we know little about these men. The word translated "wise men" (magi) refers to a group of scholars who studied the stars. Their title connects them with magic, but they were probably more like astrologers. However, their presence in the biblical record is not a divine endorsement of astrology.

God gave them a special sign, a miraculous star that announced the birth of the King. This star led them to Jerusalem where God's Word had told them that the King would be born in Bethlehem. They went to Bethlehem, and there they worshiped the Christ Child.

We do not know how many magi there were. From the three gifts listed in Matthew 2:11, some people have assumed there were three kings from the Orient, though this is not certain. But when their caravan arrived in Jerusalem, there were enough of them to trouble the whole city.

Keep in mind that these men were *Gentiles*. From the very beginning, Jesus came to be "the Saviour of the world" (John 4:42). These men were also wealthy, and they were scholars—scientists in their own right. No scholarly person who follows the light God gives him can miss worshiping at the feet of Jesus. In Jesus Christ "are hid all the treasures of wisdom and knowledge" (Col. 2:3). In Him dwells "all the fullness of the Godhead bodily" (2:9).

The magi were seeking the King, but Herod was afraid of the King and wanted to destroy Him. This was Herod the Great, called *king* by the Roman senate because of the influence of Mark Antony. Herod was a cruel and crafty man who permitted no one, not even his own family, to interfere with his rule or prevent the satisfying of his evil desires. A ruthless murderer, he had his own wife and her two brothers slain because he suspected them of treason. He was married at least nine times in order to fulfill his lusts and strengthen his political ties.

It is no surprise that Herod tried to kill Jesus, for Herod alone wanted to bear the title "King of the Jews." But there was another reason. Herod was not a full-blooded Jew; he was actually an Idumaean, a descendant of Esau. This is a picture of the old struggle between Esau and Jacob that began even before the boys were born (Gen. 25:19-34). It is the spiritual versus the carnal, the godly versus the worldly.

The magi were seeking the King; Herod was opposing the King; and the Jewish priests were ignoring the King. These priests knew the Scriptures and pointed others to the Saviour, *but they would not go to worship Him themselves!* They quoted Micah 5:2 but did not obey it. They were *five miles* from the very Son of God, yet they did not go to see Him! The Gentiles sought and found Him, but the Jews did not.

Verse 9 of chapter 2 indicates that the miraculous star was not always visible to the magi. As they started toward Bethlehem, they saw the star again; and it led them to the house where Jesus was. By now, Joseph had moved Mary and the baby from the temporary dwelling where the Lord Jesus had been born (Luke 2:7). The traditional manger scenes that assemble together the shepherds and wise men are not true to Scripture, since the magi arrived much later.

Matthew cites a second fulfilled prophecy to prove that Jesus Christ is the King (Matt. 2:5). *How* He was born was a fulfillment of prophecy, and *where* He was born was a fulfillment of prophecy. Bethlehem means "house of bread," and this was where the "Bread of Life" came to earth (John 6:48ff). Bethlehem in the Old Testament was associated with David who was a type of Jesus Christ in His suffering and glory.

### Hostility Against the King (2:13-18)

A person is identified not only by his friends, but also by his enemies. Herod pretended that he wanted to worship the newborn King (v. 8), when in reality he wanted to destroy Him. God warned Joseph to take the Child and Mary and flee to Egypt. Egypt was close. There were many Jews there, and the treasures received from the magi would more than pay the expenses for traveling and living there. But there was also another prophecy to fulfill, Hosea 11:1: "I called My son out of Egypt."

Herod's anger was evidence of his pride; he could not permit anyone to get the best of him, particularly some Gentile scholars! This led him to kill the boy babies two years of age and under who were still in Bethlehem. We must not envision hundreds of little boys being killed, for there were not that many male children of that age in a small village like Bethlehem. Even today only about 20,000 people live there. It is likely that not more than 20 children were slain. But, of course, *one* is too many!

Matthew introduced here the theme of hostility, which he focused on throughout his book. Satan is a liar and a murderer (John 8:44), as was King Herod. He lied to the magi and he murdered the babies. But even this horrendous crime of murder was the fulfillment of prophecy found in Jeremiah 31:15. In order to understand this fulfillment, we must review Jewish history.

The first mention of Bethlehem in Scripture is in connection with the death of Jacob's favorite wife, Rachel (Gen. 35:16-20). Rachel died giving birth to a son whom she named Benoni, "son of my sorrow." Jacob renamed his son Benjamin, "son of my right hand." Both of these names relate to Jesus Christ, for He was a "man of sorrows, and acquainted with grief" (Isa. 53:3), and He is now the Son of God's right hand (Heb. 1:3; Acts 5:31). Jacob put up a pillar to mark Rachel's grave which is near Bethlehem.

Jeremiah's prophecy was given about 600 years before Christ was born. It grew out of the captivity of Jerusalem. Some of the captives were taken to Ramah in Benjamin, near Jerusalem; and this reminded Jeremiah of Jacob's sorrow when Rachel died. However, now it is *Rachel* who is weeping. She represented the mothers of Israel weeping as they saw their sons going into captivity. It was as though Rachel said, "I gave my life to bear a son, and now his descendants are no more."

Jacob saw Bethlehem as a place of death, but the birth of Jesus made it a place of life! Because of His coming, there would be spiritual deliverance for Israel and, in the future, the establishment of David's throne and kingdom. Israel "the son of my sorrow" would one day become "the son of My right hand." Jeremiah gave a promise to the nation that they would be restored to their land again (Jer. 31:16-17), and this promise was fulfilled. But he gave an even greater promise that the nation would be regathered in the future, and the kingdom established (31:27ff). This promise shall also be fulfilled.

Very few people today think of Bethlehem as a burial place; they think of it as the birthplace of Jesus Christ. And because He died for us and rose again, we have a bright future before us. We shall live forever with Him in that glorious city where death is no more and where tears never fall.

### The Humility of the King (2:19-23)

Herod died in 4 B.C., which means that Jesus was born sometime between 6 and 5 B.C. It is impossible not to notice the parallel between Matthew 2:20 and Exodus 4:19, the call of Moses. As God's Son, Jesus was in Egypt and was called out to go to Israel. Moses was outside Egypt, hiding for his life, and he was called to return to Egypt. But in both cases, God's program of redemption was involved. It took courage for Joseph and his family to leave Egypt, and it took courage for Moses to return to Egypt.

Archelaus was one of Herod's sons, and to him Herod had willed the title of king. However, the Jews discovered that, in spite of his promises of kindness, Archelaus was as wicked as his father. So they sent a delegation to Rome to protest his crowning. Augustus Caesar agreed with the Jews and made Archelaus an ethnarch over half of his father's kingdom. (Jesus may have had this bit of Jewish history in mind when He told the Parable of the Pounds in Luke 19:11-27.)

The whole episode is a good example of how God leads His children. Joseph knew that he and his family were no safer under the rule of

Archelaus than they had been under Herod the Great. It is likely they were heading back to Bethlehem when they discovered that Archelaus was on the throne. Certainly, Joseph and Mary prayed, waited, and sought God's will. Common sense told them to be careful; faith told them to wait. In due time, God spoke to Joseph in a dream, and he took his wife and her Son to Nazareth, which had been their home earlier (Matt. 2:19-20).

But even this fulfilled prophecy! Once again, Matthew points out that every detail in the life of Jesus was foretold in the Scriptures. It is important to note that Matthew did not refer to only one prophet in 2:23, but instead says ". . . that it might be fulfilled which was spoken by the *prophets* . . ." (plural).

We will not find any specific prophecy that called Jesus a "Nazarene." The term *Nazarene* was one of reproach: "Can there any good thing come out of Nazareth?" (John 1:46). In many Old Testament prophecies, the Messiah's lowly life of rejection is mentioned; and this may be what Matthew had in mind. (See Ps. 22; Isa. 53:2-3, 8.) The term "Nazarene" was applied both to Jesus and His followers (Acts 24:5); and He was often called "Jesus of Nazareth" (Matt. 21:11; Mark 14:67; John 18:5, 7).

But perhaps Matthew, led by the Spirit, saw a spiritual connection between the name "Nazarene" and the Hebrew word *netzer*, which means "a branch or shoot." Several prophets apply this title to Jesus. (See Isa. 4:2, 11:1; Jer. 23:5, 33:15; Zech. 3:8, 6:12-13.)

Our Lord grew up in Nazareth and was identified with that city. In fact, His enemies thought He had been born there; for they said that He came from Galilee (John 7:50-52). Had they investigated the temple records, they would have discovered that He had been born in Bethlehem.

Who ever heard of a king being born in a humble village and growing up in a despised city? The humility of the King is certainly something to admire and imitate (Phil. 2:1-13).

# 3

# THE KING'S CREDENTIALS

(Matthew 3—4)

Some 30 years passed between chapters 2 and 3 of Matthew, during which Jesus lived in Nazareth and worked as a carpenter (Matt. 13:55; Mark 6:3). But the time came for Him to begin His public ministry which would culminate at the cross. Was He still qualified to be King? Had anything taken place that would disqualify Him? In chapters two and three, Matthew assembled the testimonies of five witnesses to the person of Jesus Christ, that He is the Son of God and the King.

**John the Baptist** (3:1-15)
For over 400 years, the nation had not heard the voice of a prophet. Then John appeared and a great revival took place. Consider four facts about John.

*His message* (3:1-2, 7-10). John's preaching centered on repentance and the kingdom of heaven. The word *repent* means "to change one's mind and act upon that change." John was not satisfied with regret or remorse; he wanted "fruits meet for repentance" (v. 8). There had to be evidence of a changed mind and a changed life.

All kinds of people came to hear John preach and to watch the great baptismal services he conducted. Many publicans and sinners came in sincere humility (Matt. 21:31-32), but the religious leaders refused to submit. They thought that they were good enough to please God; yet John called them a "generation of vipers." Jesus used the same language when He dealt with this self-righteous crowd (Matt. 12:34, 23:33; John 8:44).

The Pharisees were the traditionalists of their day, while the Sadducees were more liberal (see Acts 23:6-9). The wealthy Sadducees controlled the "temple business" that Jesus cleaned out. These two groups usually fought each other for control of the nation, but when it came to opposing Jesus Christ, the Pharisees and Sadducees united forces.

John's message was one of judgment. Israel had sinned and needed to repent, and the religious leaders ought to lead the way. The ax was lying at the root of the tree; and if the tree (Israel) did not bear good fruit, it would be cut down. (See Luke 13:6-10.) If the nation repented, the way would be prepared for the coming of the Messiah.

*His authority* (3:3-4). John fulfilled the prophecy given in Isaiah 40:3. In a spiritual sense, John was "Elijah who was to come" for he came in the "spirit and power of Elijah" (Luke 1:16-17). He even dressed as Elijah did and preached the same message of judgment (2 Kings 1:8). John was the last of the Old Testament prophets (Luke 16:16) and the greatest of them (Matt. 11:7-15, see 17:9-13).

*His baptism* (3:5-6, 11-12). The Jews baptized Gentile converts, but John was baptizing Jews! His baptism was authorized from heaven (Matt. 21:23-27); it was not something John devised or borrowed. It was a baptism of repentance, *looking forward* to the Messiah's coming (Acts 19:1-7). His baptism fulfilled two purposes: it prepared the nation for Christ and it presented Christ to the nation (John 1:31).

But John mentioned two other baptisms: a baptism of the Spirit and a baptism of fire (Matt. 3:11). The baptism of the Spirit came at Pentecost (Acts 1:5, and note that Jesus said *nothing* about fire). Today, whenever a sinner trusts Christ, he is born again and immediately baptized by the Spirit into the Body of Christ, the church (1 Cor. 12:12-13). In contrast, the baptism of fire refers to the future judgment, as Matthew explains (3:12).

*His obedience* (3:13-15). Jesus was not baptized because He was a repentant sinner. Even John tried to stop Jesus, but the Lord knew it was His Father's will. Why was Jesus baptized? First, His baptism gave approval to John's ministry. Second, He identified Himself with publicans and sinners, the very people He came to save. But mainly, His baptism pictured His future baptism on the cross (Matt. 20:22; Luke

12:50) when all the "waves and billows" of God's judgment would go over Him (Ps. 42:7; Jonah 2:3).

Thus, John the Baptist bore witness to Jesus Christ as the Son of God, and also as the Lamb of God (John 1:29). Because of John's witness, many sinners trusted Jesus Christ (John 10:39-42).

## The Holy Spirit (3:16)

The coming of the Holy Spirit like a dove identified Jesus to John (John 1:31-34), and also assured Jesus as He began His ministry that the Spirit's ministry would always be His (3:34). The dove is a beautiful symbol of the Spirit of God in its purity and in its ministry of peace. The first time we see a dove in Scripture is in Genesis 8:6-11. Noah sent out two birds, a raven and a dove; but only the dove came back. The raven represented the flesh; there was plenty for the raven to eat outside the ark! But the dove would not defile itself on the carcasses, so it came back to the ark. The second time the dove was released, it returned with an olive leaf, a symbol of peace. The third time, the dove did not return.

There may be another picture here. The name Jonah means "dove," and he, too, experienced a baptism! Jesus used Jonah as a type of Himself in death, burial, and resurrection (Matt. 12:38-40). Jonah was sent to the Gentiles, and Jesus would minister to the Gentiles.

## The Father (3:17)

On three special occasions, the Father spoke from heaven: at Christ's baptism, at the Transfiguration (Matt. 17:3), and as Christ approached the cross (John 12:27-30). In the past, God spoke *to* His Son; today He is speaking *through* His Son (Heb. 1:1-2).

The Father's statement from heaven seems to be an echo of Psalm 2:7—"The Lord hath said unto Me, 'Thou art My Son; this day have I begotten Thee.' " Acts 13:22 informs us that this "begetting" refers to His resurrection from the dead, and not to His birth at Bethlehem. This statement ties in perfectly with the Lord's baptismal experience of death, burial, and resurrection.

But the Father's statement also relates Jesus Christ to the "Suffering Servant" prophesied in Isaiah 40—53. In Matthew 12:18, Matthew quoted from Isaiah 42:1-3, where the Messiah-Servant is called "My beloved, in whom My soul is well pleased." The Servant described in

Isaiah is humble, rejected, made to suffer and die, but is also seen to come forth in victory. While the nation of Israel is seen dimly in some of these "Servant Songs," it is the Messiah, Jesus Christ, who is revealed most clearly in them. Again, we see the connection with Christ in death, burial, and resurrection.

Finally, the Father's statement approved all that Jesus had done up to that point. His "hidden years in Nazareth" were years of pleasing the Father. Certainly, the Father's commendation was a great encouragement to the Son as He started His ministry.

## Satan (4:1-11)

From the high and holy experience of blessing at the Jordan, Jesus was led into the wilderness for testing. Jesus was not tempted so that the Father could learn anything about His Son, for the Father had already given Jesus His divine approval. Jesus was tempted so that every creature in heaven, on earth, or under the earth might know that Jesus Christ is the Conqueror. He exposed Satan and his tactics, and He defeated Satan. Because of His victory, we can have victory over the tempter.

Just as the first Adam met Satan, so the Last Adam met the enemy (1 Cor. 15:45). Adam met Satan in a beautiful garden, but Jesus met him in a terrible wilderness. Adam had everything he needed, but Jesus was hungry after 40 days of fasting. Adam lost the battle and plunged humanity into sin and death. But Jesus won the battle and went on to defeat Satan in more battles, culminating in His final victory on the cross (John 12:31; Col. 2:15).

Our Lord's experience of temptation prepared Him to be our sympathetic High Priest (Heb. 2:16-18, 4:15-16). It is important to note that Jesus faced the enemy *as man*, not as the Son of God. His first word was, "Man shall not live by bread alone. . . ." We must not think that Jesus used His divine powers to overcome the enemy, because that is just what the enemy wanted Him to do! Jesus used the spiritual resources that are available to us today: the power of the Holy Spirit of God (Matt. 4:1), and the power of the Word of God ("It is written. . . ."). Jesus had nothing in His nature that would give Satan a foothold (John 14:30), but His temptations were real just the same. Temptation involves *the will*, and Jesus came to do the Father's will (Heb. 10:1-9).

*The first temptation* (4:1-4) involved the love of God and the will of

God. "Since You are God's beloved Son, why doesn't Your Father feed You? Why does He put You into this terrible wilderness?" This temptation sounded like Satan's words to Eve in Genesis 3! It is a subtle suggestion that our Father does not love us.

But there was another suggestion: "Use Your divine powers to meet Your own needs." When we put our physical needs ahead of our spiritual needs, we sin. When we allow circumstances to dictate our actions, instead of following God's will, we sin. Jesus could have turned the stones into bread, but He would have been exercising His powers *independently of the Father*; and He came to obey the Father (John 5:30, 6:38).

The Lord quoted Deuteronomy 8:3 to defeat Satan. Feeding on and obeying God's Word is more important than consuming physical food. In fact, *it is our food* (John 4:32-34).

*The second temptation* (4:5-7) was even more subtle. This time Satan also used the Word of God. "So You intend to live by the Scriptures," he implied. "Then let me quote You a verse of Scripture and see if You will obey it!" Satan took the Lord Jesus to the pinnacle of the temple, probably 500 feet above the Kidron Valley. Satan then quoted from Psalm 91:11-12 where God promised to care for His own. "If You really believe the Scriptures, then jump! Let's see if the Father cares for You!"

Note carefully our Lord's reply: "It is written AGAIN . . ." (Matt. 4:7, emphasis mine). We must never divorce one part of Scripture from another, but we must always "compare spiritual things with spiritual" (1 Cor. 2:13). We can prove almost anything by the Bible *if* we isolate texts from the contexts and turn them into pretexts. Satan had cleverly omitted the phrase "in all Thy ways" when he quoted from Psalm 91. When the child of God is in the will of God, the Father will protect him. He watches over those who are "in His ways."

Jesus replied with Deuteronomy 6:16: "Thou shalt not tempt the Lord thy God." We tempt God when we put ourselves into circumstances that force Him to work miracles on our behalf. The diabetic who refuses to take insulin and argues, "Jesus will take care of me" may be tempting the Lord. We tempt God when we try to force Him to contradict His own Word. It is important for us as believers to read *all* Scripture, and study *all* God has to say, for *all* of it is profitable for daily life (2 Tim. 3:16-17).

*The third temptation* (4:8-11) offered Jesus a shortcut to His kingdom.

Jesus knew that He would suffer and die before He entered into His glory (Luke 24:26; 1 Peter 1:11; 5:1). If He bowed down and worshiped Satan *just once* (this is the force of the Greek verb), He could enjoy all the glory without enduring the suffering. Satan had always wanted worship, because Satan has always wanted to be God (Isa. 14:12-14). Worshiping the creature instead of the Creator is the lie that rules our world today (Rom. 1:24-25).

There are no shortcuts to the will of God. If we want to share in the glory, we must also share in the suffering (1 Peter 5:10). As the prince of this world, Satan could offer these kingdoms to Christ (John 12:31, 14:30). But Jesus did not need Satan's offer. The Father had already promised Jesus the kingdom! "Ask of Me, and I shall give Thee the heathen [nations] for Thine inheritance . . ." (Ps. 2:8). You find the same promise in Psalm 22:22-31, and this is the psalm of the cross.

Our Lord replied with Deuteronomy 6:13: "Thou shalt worship the Lord thy God, and Him only shalt thou serve." Satan had said nothing about service, but Jesus knew that whatever we worship, we will serve. Worship and service must go together.

Satan slunk away, a defeated foe; but he did not cease to tempt Jesus. We could translate Luke 4:13, "And when the devil had ended every possible kind of temptation, he stood off from Him until a suitable season." Through Peter, Satan again tempted Jesus to abandon the cross (Matt. 16:21-23); and through the crowd that had been fed, Satan tempted Jesus to an "easy kingdom" (John 6:15). One victory never guarantees freedom from further temptation. If anything, each victory we experience only makes Satan try harder.

Notice that Luke's account reverses the order of the second and third temptations as recorded in Matthew. The word "then" in Matthew 4:5 seems to indicate sequence. Luke only uses the simple conjunction "and" and does not say he is following a sequence. Our Lord's command at the end of the third temptation ("Get thee hence, Satan!") is proof that Matthew followed the historical order. There is no contradiction since Luke did not claim to follow the actual sequence.

After Jesus Christ had defeated Satan, He was ready to begin His ministry. No man has a right to call others to obey who has not obeyed himself. Our Lord proved Himself to be the perfect King whose sovereignty is worthy of our respect and obedience. But, true to his

purpose, Matthew had one more witness to call to prove the Kingship of
Jesus Christ.

### Christ's Ministry of Power (4:12-15)

Matthew has already shown us that every detail of our Lord's life was
controlled by the Word of God. Remember that between the end of His
temptation and the statement in Matthew 4:12 comes the ministry described in John 1:19 through John 3:36. We must not think that John the
Baptist was thrown into prison immediately after our Lord's temptation.
Matthew wrote his book *topically* rather than chronologically. Consult a
good harmony of the Gospels to study the sequence of events.

In verse 16, Matthew quoted Isaiah (see Isa. 9:1-2). The prophet wrote
about people who "walked" in darkness, but by the time Matthew quoted
the passage, the situation was so discouraging that the people were *sitting*
in darkness! Jesus Christ brought the Light to them. He made His
headquarters in Capernaum in "Galilee of the Gentiles," another reference to the universal outreach of the Gospel's message. In Galilee there
was a mixed population that was somewhat despised by the racially
"pure" citizens of Judea.

How did Jesus bring this Light to Galilee? We are told in verse 23:
through His teaching, preaching, and healing. This emphasis is found
often in the Gospel of Matthew; see 9:35, 11:4-5, 12:15, 14:34-36,
15:30, 19:2. Matthew was quite clear that He healed "all manner of
sickness and all manner of disease" (Matt. 4:23). There was no case too
difficult for Him!

The result of these great miracles was a tremendous *fame* for Jesus, and
a great *following* of people from many areas. "Syria" refers to an area in
northern Galilee. "Decapolis" means "10 cities" and was a district
made up of 10 cities originally built by followers of Alexander the Great.
The Decapolis was in the northeastern part of Galilee. "Beyond Jordan"
means Perea, the area east of the Jordan. News traveled fast, and those
who had afflicted friends or family members brought them to Jesus for
healing.

Matthew listed some of the "cases" in verse 24. "Diseases and
torments" could cover almost any disease. Of course, our Lord often
delivered people from demons. The term "lunatic" did not refer to
people who were insane. Rather, it was used to describe those afflicted

with epilepsy (see Matt. 17:15). "Palsy" meant "paralytic."

Miracles of healing were but a part of Christ's ministry throughout Galilee; for He also taught and preached the Word. The "light" that Isaiah promised was the Light of the Word of God, as well as the Light of His perfect life and compassionate ministry. The word "preach" in verses 17 and 23 means "to announce as a herald." Jesus proclaimed with authority the Good News that the kingdom of heaven was at hand.

The phrase *kingdom of heaven* is found 32 times in Matthew's Gospel. The phrase *kingdom of God* is found only 5 times (Matt. 6:33; 12:28; 19:24; 21:31, 43). Out of reverence for the holy name of the Lord, the Jews would not mention "God" but would substitute the word "heaven." The Prodigal Son confessed that he had sinned "against heaven," meaning, of course, against God. In many places where Matthew uses *kingdom of heaven*, the parallel passages in Mark and Luke use *kingdom of God*.

In the New Testament, the word *kingdom* means "rule, reign, authority" rather than a place or a specific realm. The phrase "kingdom of heaven" refers to the rule of God. The Jewish leaders wanted a political leader who would deliver them from Rome; but Jesus came to bring *spiritual* rule to the hearts of people. This does not deny the reality of a future kingdom as we have already noted.

But Jesus not only proclaimed the Good News and taught the people God's truth, He also called to Himself a few disciples whom He could train for the work of the kingdom. In Matthew 4:17-22 we read of the call of Peter, Andrew, James, and John, men who had already met Jesus and trusted Him (John 1:29-42). They had gone back to their fishing business, but He came and called them to give up their business and follow Him. The details of this call may be found in Mark 1:16-20 and Luke 5:1-11.

The term "fishers of men" was not new. For centuries, Greek and Roman philosophers had used it to describe the work of the man who seeks to "catch" others by teaching and persuasion. "Fishing for men" is but one of many pictures of evangelism in the Bible, and we must not limit ourselves to it. Jesus also talked about the shepherd seeking the lost sheep (Luke 15:1-7), and the workers in the harvest-field (John 4:34-38). Since these four men were involved in the fishing business, it was logical for Jesus to use this approach.

Jesus had four and possibly seven men in the band of disciples who were professional fishermen (see John 21:1-3). Why would Jesus call so many fishermen to His side? For one thing, fishermen were busy people; usually professional fishermen did not sit around doing nothing. They either sorted their catch, prepared for a catch, or mended their equipment. The Lord needs busy people who are not afraid to work.

Fishermen have to be courageous and patient people. It certainly takes patience and courage to win others to Christ. Fishermen must have skill; they must learn from others where to find the fish and how to catch them. Soul-winning demands skill, too. These men must work together, and the work of the Lord demands cooperation. But most of all, fishing demands faith: Fishermen cannot see the fish and are not sure their nets will enclose them. Soul-winning requires faith and alertness, too, or we will fail.

Matthew has presented to us the person of the King. Every witness affirms, "This is the Son of God, this is the King!"

# 4

# THE KING'S PRINCIPLES: TRUE RIGHTEOUSNESS

(Matthew 5)

The Sermon on the Mount is one of the most misunderstood messages that Jesus ever gave. One group says it is God's plan of salvation, that if we ever hope to go to heaven we must obey these rules. Another group calls it a "charter for world peace" and begs the nations of the earth to accept it. Still a third group tells us that the Sermon on the Mount does not apply to today, but that it will apply at some future time, perhaps during the Tribulation or the millennial kingdom.

I have always felt that Matthew 5:20 was the key to this important sermon: "For I say unto you, that except your righteousness shall exceed the righteousness of the scribes and Pharisees, ye shall in no case enter into the kingdom of heaven." The main theme is true righteousness. The religious leaders had an artificial, external righteousness based on law. But the righteousness Jesus described is a true and vital righteousness that begins internally, in the heart. The Pharisees were concerned about the minute details of conduct, but they neglected the major matter of *character*. Conduct flows out of character.

Whatever applications the Sermon on the Mount may have to world problems, or to future events, it is certain that this sermon has definite applications for us today. Jesus gave this message to individual believers, not to the unsaved world at large. What was taught in the Sermon on the Mount is repeated in the New Testament epistles for the church today.

Jesus originally gave these words to His disciples (v. 1), and they have shared them with us.

In this chapter, Jesus gave three explanations about true, spiritual righteousness.

## What True Righteousness Is (5:1-16)

Being a master Teacher, our Lord did not begin this important sermon with a negative criticism of the scribes and Pharisees. He began with a positive emphasis on righteous character and the blessings that it brings to the life of the believer. The Pharisees taught that righteousness was an external thing, a matter of obeying rules and regulations. Righteousness could be measured by praying, giving, fasting, etc. In the Beatitudes and the pictures of the believer, Jesus described Christian character that flowed from within.

Imagine how the crowd's attention was riveted on Jesus when He uttered His first word: "Blessed." (The Latin word for blessed is *beatus*, and from this comes the word *beatitude*.) This was a powerful word to those who heard Jesus that day. To them it meant "divine joy and perfect happiness." The word was not used for humans; it described the kind of joy experienced only by the gods or the dead. "Blessed" implied an inner satisfaction and sufficiency that did not depend on outward circumstances for happiness. This is what the Lord offers those who trust Him!

The Beatitudes describe the attitudes that ought to be in our lives today. Four attitudes are described here.

*Our attitude toward ourselves* (5:3). To be poor in spirit means to be humble, to have a correct estimate of one's self (Rom. 12:3). It does not mean to be "poor spirited" and have no backbone at all! "Poor in spirit" is the opposite of the world's attitudes of self-praise and self-assertion. It is not a false humility that says, "I am not worth anything, I can't do anything!" It is honesty with ourselves: we know ourselves, accept ourselves, and try to be ourselves to the glory of God.

*Our attitude toward our sins* (5:4-6). We mourn over sin and despise it. We see sin the way God sees it and seek to treat it the way God does. Those who cover sin or defend sin certainly have the wrong attitude. We should not only mourn over our sins, but we should also meekly submit to God (see Luke 18:9-14; Phil. 3:1-14).

Meekness is not weakness, for both Moses and Jesus were meek men

(Num. 12:3; Matt. 11:29). This word translated "meek" was used by the Greeks to describe a horse that had been broken. It refers to power under control.

*Our attitude toward the Lord* (5:7-9). We experience God's mercy when we trust Christ (Eph. 2:4-7), and He gives us a clean heart (Acts 15:9) and peace within (Rom. 5:1). But having received His mercy, we then *share* His mercy with others. We seek to keep our hearts pure that we might see God in our lives today. We become peacemakers in a troubled world and channels for God's mercy, purity, and peace.

*Our attitude toward the world* (5:10-16). It is not easy to be a dedicated Christian. Our society is not a friend to God nor to God's people. Whether we like it or not, there is *conflict* between us and the world. Why? Because we are different from the world and we have different attitudes.

As we read the Beatitudes, we find that they represent an outlook radically different from that of the world. The world praises pride, not humility. The world endorses sin, especially if you "get away with it." The world is at war with God, while God is seeking to reconcile His enemies and make them His children. We must expect to be persecuted *if* we are living as God wants us to live. But we must be sure that our suffering is not due to our own foolishness or disobedience.

## How True Righteousness Comes (5:17-20)

Certainly after the crowd heard our Lord's description of the kind of person God blesses, they said to themselves, "But we could *never* attain that kind of character. How can we have this righteousness? Where does it come from?" They wondered how His teaching related to what they had been taught all their lives. What about Moses and the Law?

In the Law of Moses, God certainly revealed His standards for holy living. The Pharisees defended the Law and sought to obey it. But Jesus said that the true righteousness that pleases God must *exceed* that of the scribes and Pharisees—and to the common people, the scribes and Pharisees were the holiest men in the community! If *they* had not attained, what hope was there for anybody else?

Jesus explained His own attitude toward the Law by describing three possible relationships.

*We can seek to destroy the Law* (5:17a). The Pharisees thought Jesus was doing this. To begin with, His *authority* did not come from any of the recognized leaders or schools. Instead of teaching "from authorities" as did the scribes and Pharisees, Jesus taught *with authority*.

Not only in His authority, but also in His *activity*, Jesus seemed to defy the Law. He deliberately healed people on the Sabbath Day and paid no attention to the traditions of the Pharisees. Our Lord's *associations* also seemed contrary to the Law, for He was the friend of publicans and sinners.

Yet, it was the Pharisees who were destroying the Law! By their traditions, they robbed the people of the Word of God; and by their hypocritical lives, they disobeyed the very Law that they claimed to protect. The Pharisees thought they were *conserving* God's Word, when in reality they were *preserving* God's Word: embalming it so that it no longer had life! Their rejection of Christ when He came to earth proved that the inner truth of the Law had not penetrated their hearts.

Jesus made it clear that He had come to honor the Law and help God's people love it, learn it, and live it. He would not accept the artificial righteousness of the religious leaders. Their righteousness was only an external masquerade. Their religion was a dead ritual, not a living relationship. It was artificial; it did not reproduce itself in others in a living way. It made them proud, not humble; it led to bondage, not liberty.

*We can seek to fulfill the Law* (5:17b). Jesus Christ fulfilled God's Law in every area of His life. He fulfilled it in His birth because He was "made under the Law" (Gal. 4:4). Every prescribed ritual for a Jewish boy was performed on Him by His parents. He certainly fulfilled the Law in His life, for nobody was ever able to accuse Him of sin. While He did not submit to the traditions of the scribes and Pharisees, He always did what God commanded in the Law. The Father was "well pleased" with His Son (Matt. 3:17; 17:5).

Jesus also fulfilled the Law in His teaching. It was this that brought Him into conflict with the religious leaders. When He began His ministry, Jesus found the living Word of God encrusted with man-made traditions and interpretations. He broke away this thick crust of "religion" and brought the people back to God's Word. Then, He opened the Word to them in a new and living way—they were accustomed to the "letter" of the Law and not the inner "kernel" of life.

But it was in His death and resurrection that Jesus especially fulfilled the Law. He bore the curse of the Law (Gal. 3:13). He fulfilled the Old Testament types and ceremonies so that they no longer are required of the people of God (see Heb. 9—10). He set aside the Old Covenant and brought in the New Covenant.

Jesus did not destroy the Law by fighting it; He destroyed it by *fulfilling* it! Perhaps an illustration will make this clear. If I have an acorn, I can destroy it in one of two ways. I can put it on a rock and smash it to bits with a hammer. Or, I can plant it in the ground and let it *fulfill itself* by becoming an oak tree.

When Jesus died, He rent the veil of the temple and opened the way into the holiest (Heb. 10:19). He broke down the wall that separated the Jews and Gentiles (Eph. 2:11-13). Because the Law was fulfilled in Christ, we no longer need temples made with hands (Acts 7:48ff), or religious rituals (Col. 2:10-13).

How can we fulfill the Law? By yielding to the Holy Spirit and allowing Him to work in our lives (Rom. 8:1-3). The Holy Spirit enables us to experience the "righteousness of the law" in daily life. This does not mean we live sinlessly perfect lives, but it does mean that Christ lives out His life through us by the power of His Spirit (Gal. 2:20).

When we read the Beatitudes, we see the perfect character of Jesus Christ. While Jesus never had to mourn over His sins, since He was sinless, He was still a "man of sorrows and acquainted with grief" (Isa. 53:3). He never had to hunger and thirst after righteousness since He was the holy Son of God, but He did delight in the Father's will and find His satisfaction in doing it (John 4:34). The only way we can experience the righteousness of the Beatitudes is through the power of Christ.

*We can seek to do and teach the Law* (5:19). This does not mean we major on the Old Testament and ignore the New! Second Corinthians 3 makes it clear that ours is a ministry of the *New* Covenant. But there is a proper ministry of the Law (1 Tim. 1:9ff) that is not contrary to the glorious message of God's grace. Jesus wants us to know more of the righteousness of God, obey it, and share it with others. The moral law of God has not changed. Nine of the Ten Commandments are repeated in the New Testament epistles and commanded to believers. (The exception is the Sabbath commandment, which was given as a sign to Israel, see Neh. 9:14.)

We do not obey an external Law because of fear. No, believers today obey an internal Law *and live* because of love. The Holy Spirit teaches us the Word and enables us to obey. Sin is still sin, and God still punishes sin. In fact, we in this present age are *more* responsible because we have been taught and given more!

## How Righteousness Works in Daily Life (5:21-48)

Jesus took six important Old Testament laws and interpreted them for His people in the light of the new life He came to give. He made a fundamental change without altering God's standards: He dealt with the attitudes and intents of the heart and not simply with the external action. The Pharisees said that righteousness consisted of performing certain actions, but Jesus said it centered in the attitudes of the heart.

Likewise, with sin: The Pharisees had a list of external actions that were sinful, but Jesus explained that sin came from the attitudes of the heart. Anger is murder in the heart; lust is adultery in the heart. The person who says that he "lives by the Sermon on the Mount" may not realize that the Sermon on the Mount is *more difficult* to keep than the original Ten Commandments!

*Murder* (5:21-26; Ex. 20:13). I have read that one out of every 35 deaths in Chicago is a murder, and that most of these murders are "crimes of passion" caused by anger among friends or relatives. Jesus did not say that anger leads to murder; He said that anger *is* murder.

There is a holy anger against sin (Eph. 4:26), but Jesus talked about an unholy anger against people. The word He used in Matthew 5:22 means "a settled anger, malice that is nursed inwardly." Jesus described a sinful experience that involved several stages. First there was *causeless anger*. This anger then exploded into *words:* "Raca—empty-headed person!" These words added fuel to the fire so that the person said, "You fool—rebel!"

Anger is such a foolish thing. It makes us destroyers instead of builders. It robs us of freedom and makes us prisoners. To hate someone is to commit murder in our hearts (1 John 3:15).

This does not mean that we should go ahead and murder someone we hate, since we have already sinned inwardly. Obviously, sinful feelings are not excuses for sinful deeds. Sinful anger robs us of fellowship with God as well as with our brothers, but it does not put us into jail as murderers. However, more than one person has become a murderer because he failed to control sinful anger.

Sinful anger must be faced honestly and must be confessed to God as sin. We must go to our brother and get the matter settled, and we must do it quickly. The longer we wait, the worse the bondage becomes! We put ourselves into a terrible prison when we refuse to be reconciled. (See Matt. 18:15-20 for additional counsel.) It has well been said that the person who refuses to forgive his brother destroys the very bridge over which he himself must walk.

*Adultery* (5:27-30; Ex. 20:14). Jesus affirmed God's law of purity, and then explained that the intent of this law was to reveal the sanctity of sex and the sinfulness of the human heart. God created sex, and God protects sex. He has the authority to regulate it and to punish those who rebel against His laws. He does not regulate sex because He wants to rob us, but rather, because He wants to bless us. Whenever God says, "No" it is that He might say "Yes."

Sexual impurity begins in the desires of the heart. Again, Jesus is not saying that lustful desires are identical to lustful deeds, and therefore a person might just as well go ahead and commit adultery. The desire and the deed are not identical, but, spiritually speaking, they are equivalent. The "look" that Jesus mentioned was not a casual glance, but a constant stare *with the purpose of lusting*. It is possible for a man to glance at a beautiful woman and know that she is beautiful, but not lust after her. The man Jesus described looked at the woman *for the purpose of feeding his inner sensual appetites* as a substitute for the act. It was not accidental; it was planned.

How do we get victory? By purifying the desires of the heart (appetite leads to action) and disciplining the actions of the body. Obviously, our Lord is not talking about literal surgery; for this would not solve the problem in the heart. The eye and the hand are usually the two "culprits" when it comes to sexual sins, so they must be disciplined. Jesus said, "Deal immediately and decisively with sin! Don't taper off—cut off!" Spiritual surgery is more important than physical surgery, for the sins of the body can lead to eternal judgment. We think of passages like Colossians 3:5 and Romans 6:13; 12:1-2; 13:14.

*Divorce* (5:31-32). Our Lord dealt with this in greater detail in 19:1-12, and we shall consider it there.

*Swearing* (5:33-37; Lev. 19:12; Deut. 23:23). This is not the sin of "cursing," but the sin of using oaths to affirm that what is said is true. The Pharisees used all kinds of tricks to sidestep the truth, and oaths were among them. They would avoid using the holy name of God, but they would come close by using the city of Jerusalem, heaven, earth, or some part of the body.

Jesus taught that our conversation should be so honest, and our character so true, that we would not need "crutches" to get people to believe us. Words depend on character, and oaths cannot compensate for a poor character. "In the multitude of words there wanteth not sin; but he that refraineth his lips is wise" (Prov. 10:19). The more words a man uses to convince us, the more suspicious we should be.

*Retaliation* (5:38-42; Lev. 24:19-22). The original law was a fair one; it kept people from forcing the offender to pay a greater price than the offense deserved. It also prevented people from taking personal revenge. Jesus replaced a law with an attitude: be willing to suffer loss yourself rather than cause another to suffer. Of course, He applied this to *personal insults*, not to groups or nations. The person who retaliates only makes himself and the offender feel worse; and the result is a settled war and not peace.

In order to "turn the other cheek," we must stay where we are and not run away. This demands both faith and love. It also means that *we* will hurt, but it is better to be hurt on the outside than to be harmed on the inside. But it further means that *we should try to help the sinner*. We are vulnerable, because he may attack us anew; but we are also victorious, because Jesus is on our side, helping us and building our characters. Psychologists tell us that violence is born of weakness, not strength. It is the strong man who can love and suffer hurt; it is the weak man who thinks only of himself and hurts others to protect himself. He hurts others then runs away to protect himself.

*Love of enemies* (5:43-48; Lev. 19:17-18). Nowhere did the Law teach hatred for one's enemies. Passages like Exodus 23:4-5 indicate just the opposite! Jesus defined our enemies as those who curse us, hate us, and exploit us selfishly. Since Christian love is an act of the will, and not simply an emotion, He has the right to command us to love our enemies. After all, He loved us when we were His enemies (Rom. 5:10). We may show this love by blessing those who curse us, doing good to them, and praying for them. When we pray for our enemies, we find it easier to love them. It takes the "poison" out of our attitudes.

Jesus gave several reasons for this admonition. (1) This love is a mark of maturity, proving that we are *sons* of the Father, and not just little children. (2) It is God-like. The Father shares His good things with those who oppose Him. Verse 45 suggests that our love "creates a climate" of blessings that makes it easy to win our enemies and make them our friends. Love is like the sunshine and rain that the Father sends so graciously. (3) It is a testimony to others. "What do ye more than others?" is a good question. God expects us to live on a much higher plane than the lost people of the world who return good for good and evil for evil. As Christians, we must return good for evil as an investment of love.

The word *perfect* in verse 48 does not imply *sinlessly* perfect, for that is impossible in this life (although it is a good goal to strive for). It suggests completeness, maturity, as the sons of God. The Father loves His enemies and seeks to make them His children, and we should assist Him!

# 5

# THE KING'S PRINCIPLES: TRUE WORSHIP

(Matthew 6)

The true righteousness of the kingdom must be applied in the everyday activities of life. This is the emphasis in the rest of the Sermon on the Mount. Jesus related this principle to our relationship to God in worship (6:1-18), our relationship to material things (6:19-34), and our relationship to other people (7:1-20).

Jesus also warned about the danger of hypocrisy (6:2, 5, 16), the sin of using religion to cover up sin. A hypocrite is not a person who falls short of his high ideals, or who occasionally sins, because all of us experience these failures. A hypocrite *deliberately* uses religion to cover up his sins and promote his own gains. The Greek word translated *hypocrite* originally meant "an actor who wears a mask."

The righteousness of the Pharisees was insincere and dishonest. They practiced their religion for the applause of men, not for the reward of God. But true righteousness must come from within. We should test ourselves to see whether we are sincere and honest in our Christian commitment. In this chapter, Christ applied this test to four different areas of life.

**Our Giving** (6:1-4)
Giving alms to the poor, praying, and fasting were important disciplines in the religion of the Pharisees. Jesus did not condemn these practices, but

He did caution us to make sure that our hearts are right as we practice them. The Pharisees used almsgiving to gain favor with God and attention from men, both of which were wrong motives. No amount of giving can purchase salvation; for salvation is the gift of God (Eph. 2:8-9). And to live for the praise of men is a foolish thing because the glory of man does not last (1 Peter 1:24). It is the glory and praise of God that really counts!

Our sinful nature is so subtle that it can defile even a good thing like sharing with the poor. If our motive is to get the praise of men, then like the Pharisees, we will call attention to what we are doing. But if our motive is to serve God in love and please Him, then we will give our gifts without calling attention to them. As a result, we will grow spiritually; God will be glorified; and others will be helped. But if we give with the wrong motive, we rob ourselves of blessing and reward and rob God of glory, even though the money we share might help a needy person.

Does this mean that it is wrong to give openly? Must all giving be anonymous? Not necessarily, for everyone in the early church knew that Barnabas had given the income from the sale of his land (Acts 4:34-37). When the church members laid their money at the Apostles' feet, it was not done in secret. The difference, of course, was in the *motive* and *manner* in which it was done. A contrast is Ananias and Sapphira (Acts 5:1-11), who tried to use their gift to make people think they were more spiritual than they really were.

### Our Praying (6:5-15)

Jesus gave four instructions to guide us in our praying.

*We must pray in secret before we pray in public* (6:6). It is not wrong to pray in public in the assembly (1 Tim. 2:1ff), or even when blessing food (John 6:11) or seeking God's help (John 11:41-42; Acts 27:35). But it is wrong to pray in public if we are not in the habit of praying in private. Observers may think that we are practicing prayer when we are not, and this is hypocrisy. The word translated *closet* means "a private chamber." It could refer to the store-chamber in a house. Our Lord prayed privately (Mark 1:35); so did Elisha (2 Kings 4:32ff) and Daniel (Dan. 6:10ff).

*We must pray sincerely* (6:7-8). The fact that a request is repeated does not make it a "vain repetition"; for both Jesus and Paul repeated their petitions (Matt. 26:36-46; 2 Cor. 12:7-8). A request becomes a "vain repetition" if it is only a babbling of words without a sincere heart desire to seek and do God's will. The mere reciting of memorized prayers can be vain repetition. The Gentiles had such prayers in their pagan ceremonies (see 1 Kings 18:26).

My friend Dr. Robert A. Cook has often said, "All of us have one routine prayer in our system; and once we get rid of it, then we can really start to pray!" I have noticed this, not only in my own praying, but often when I have conducted prayer meetings. With some people, praying is like putting the needle on a phonograph record *and then forgetting about it*. But God does not answer insincere prayers.

*We must pray in God's will* (6:9-13). This prayer is known familiarly as "The Lord's Prayer," but "The Disciples' Prayer" would be a more accurate title. Jesus did not give this prayer to us to be memorized and recited a given number of times. In fact, He gave this prayer *to keep us* from using vain repetitions. Jesus did not say, "Pray in these words." He said, "Pray after this manner"; that is, "Use this prayer as a pattern, not as a substitute."

The purpose of prayer is to glorify God's name, and to ask for help to accomplish His will on earth. This prayer begins with *God's* interests, not ours: God's name, God's kingdom, and God's will. Robert Law has said, "Prayer is a mighty instrument, not for getting man's will done in heaven, but for getting God's will done in earth." We have no right to ask God for anything that will dishonor His name, delay His kingdom, or disturb His will on earth.

It is worth noting that there are *no singular pronouns* in this prayer; they are all plural. It begins with "OUR Father." When we pray, we must remember that we are part of God's worldwide family of believers. We have no right to ask for ourselves anything that would harm another member of the family. If we are praying in the will of God, the answer will be a blessing to all of God's people in one way or another.

If we put God's concerns first, then we can bring our own needs. God is concerned about our needs and knows them even before we mention them (v. 8). If this is the case, then why pray? Because prayer is the God-appointed way to have these needs met (see James 4:1-3). *Prayer prepares us for the proper use of the answer*. If we know our need, and if we voice it to God, trusting Him for His provision, then we will make better use of the answer than if God forced it on us without our asking.

It is right to pray for daily physical needs, for forgiveness, and for guidance and protection from evil. "Lead us not into temptation" does not mean that God tempts His children (James 1:13-17). In this petition we are asking God to guide us so that we will not get out of His will and get involved in a situation of temptation (1 John 5:18), or even in a situation of tempting God so that He must miraculously rescue us (Matt. 4:5-7).

*We must pray, having a forgiving spirit toward others* (6:14-15). In this "appendix" to the prayer, Jesus expanded the last phrase of verse 12, ". . . as we forgive our debtors." He later repeated this lesson to His disciples (Mark 11:19-26). He was not teaching that believers earned God's forgiveness by forgiving others; for this would be contrary to God's free grace and mercy. However, if we have truly *experienced* God's forgiveness, then we will have a readiness to forgive others (Eph. 4:32; Col. 3:13). Our Lord illustrated this principle in the parable of the unmerciful servant (Matt. 18:21-35).

We have seen that true praying is a "family affair" ("Our Father. . ."). If the members of the family are not getting along with one another, how can they claim to have a right relationship with the Father? The emphasis in 1 John 4 is that we show our love for God by loving our brothers. When we forgive each other, we are not *earning* the right to prayer; for the privilege of prayer is a part of our *sonship* (Rom. 8:15-16). Forgiveness belongs to the matter of *fellowship:* If I am not in fellowship with God, I cannot pray effectively. But fellowship with my brother helps to determine my fellowship with God; hence, forgiveness is important to prayer.

Since prayer involves glorifying God's name, hastening the coming of God's kingdom (2 Peter 3:12), and helping to accomplish God's will on earth, the one praying must not have sin in his heart. If God answered the prayers of a believer who had an unforgiving spirit, He would dishonor His own name. How could God work through such a person to get His will done on earth? If God gave him his requests, He would be encouraging sin! The important thing about prayer is not simply getting an answer, but *being the kind of person whom God can trust with an answer*.

## Our Fasting (6:16-18)
The only fast that God actually required of the Jewish people was on the annual Day of Atonement (Lev. 23:27). The Pharisees fasted each Mon-

day and Thursday (Luke 18:12) and did so in such a way that people knew they were fasting. Their purpose, of course, was to win the praise of men. As a result, the Pharisees lost God's blessing.

It is not wrong to fast, if we do it in the right way and with the right motive. Jesus fasted (Matt. 4:3); so did the members of the early church (Acts 13:2). Fasting helps to discipline the appetites of the body (Luke 21:34) and keep our spiritual priorities straight. But fasting must never become an opportunity for temptation (1 Cor. 7:7). Simply to deprive ourselves of a natural benefit (such as food or sleep) is not *of itself* fasting. We must devote ourselves to God and worship Him. Unless there is the devotion of the heart (see Zech. 7) there is no lasting spiritual benefit.

As with giving and praying, true fasting must be done in secret; it is between the believer and God. To "make unsightly" our faces (by looking glum and asking for pity and praise) would be to destroy the very purpose of the fast. Our Lord here laid down a basic principle of spiritual living: Nothing that is truly spiritual will violate that which God has given us in nature. God usually does not tear down one good thing in order to build up another. If we have to look miserable to be considered spiritual, then there is something wrong with our views of spirituality.

*Remember that hypocrisy robs us of reality in Christian living.* We substitute reputation for character, mere words for true prayer, money for the devotion of the heart. No wonder Jesus compared the Pharisees to tombs that were whitewashed on the outside, but filthy on the inside! (Matt. 23:27-28)

But hypocrisy not only robs us of character, it also *robs us of spiritual rewards.* Instead of the eternal approval of God, we receive the shallow praise of men. We pray, but there are no answers. We fast, but the inner man shows no improvement. The spiritual life becomes hollow and lifeless. We miss the blessing of God here and now, and also lose the reward of God when Christ returns.

Hypocrisy also *robs us of spiritual influence.* The Pharisees were a negative influence; whatever they touched was defiled and destroyed. The people who admired them and obeyed the Pharisees' words thought they themselves were being helped, when in reality, they were being hurt.

The first step toward overcoming hypocrisy is to be honest with God in our secret life. We must never pray anything that we do not mean from the heart; otherwise, our prayers are simply empty words. Our motive must be to please God alone, no matter what men may say or do. We must cultivate the heart in the secret place. It has well been said, "The most important part of a Christian's life is the part that only God sees." When reputation becomes more important than character, we have become hypocrites.

## Our Use of Wealth (6:19-34)

We are accustomed to divide life into the "spiritual" and the "material"; but Jesus made no such division. In many of His parables, He made it clear that a right attitude toward wealth is a mark of true spirituality (see Luke 12:13ff; 16:1-31). The Pharisees were covetous (v. 14) and used religion to make money. If we have the true righteousness of Christ in our lives, then we will have a proper attitude toward material wealth.

Nowhere did Jesus magnify poverty or criticize the legitimate getting of wealth. God made all things, including food, clothing, and precious metals. God has declared that all things He has made are good (Gen. 1:31). God knows that we need certain things in order to live (Matt. 6:32). In fact, He has given us "richly all things to enjoy" (1 Tim. 6:17). It is not wrong to possess things, *but it is wrong for things to possess us*. The sin of idolatry is as dangerous as the sin of hypocrisy! There are many warnings in the Bible against covetousness (Ex. 20:17; Ps. 119:36; Mark 7:22; Luke 12:15ff; Col. 3:5; Eph. 5:5).

Jesus warned against the sin of living for the things of this life. He pointed out the sad consequences of covetousness and idolatry.

*Enslavement* (6:19-24). Materialism will enslave the heart (vv. 19-21), the mind (vv. 22-23), and the will (v. 24). We can become shackled by the material things of life, but we ought to be liberated and controlled by the Spirit of God.

If the heart loves material things, and puts earthly gain above heavenly investments, then the result can only be a tragic loss. The treasures of earth may be used for God. But if we gather material things for ourselves, we will lose them; *and we will lose our hearts with them*. Instead of spiritual enrichment, we will experience impoverishment.

What does it mean to lay up treasures in heaven? It means to use *all that we have* for the glory of God. It means to "hang loose" when it comes to the material things of life. It also means measuring life by the true riches of the kingdom and not by the false riches of this world.

Wealth not only enslaves the heart, but it also enslaves the mind (vv. 22-23). God's Word often uses the eye to represent the attitudes of the mind. If the eye is properly focused on the light, the body can function properly in its movements. But if the eye is out of focus and seeing double, it results in unsteady movements. It is most difficult to make progress while trying to look in two directions at the same time.

If our aim in life is to get material gain, it will mean darkness within. But if our outlook is to serve and glorify God, there will be light within. If what should be light is really darkness, then we are being controlled by darkness; and outlook determines outcome.

Finally, materialism can enslave the will (v. 24). We cannot serve two masters simultaneously. Either Jesus Christ is our Lord, or money is our lord. It is a matter of the will. "But those who want to get rich fall into temptation and a snare . . . " (1 Tim. 6:9). If God grants riches, and we use them for His glory, then riches are a blessing. But if we *will* to get rich, and live with that outlook, we will pay a great price for those riches.

*Devaluation* (6:25-30). Covetousness will not only cheapen our riches, but it will also cheapen *us*! We will start to become worried and anxious, and this anxiety is unnatural and unspiritual. The person who pursues money thinks that riches will solve his problems, when in reality, riches will create more problems! Material wealth gives a dangerous, false sense of security, and that feeling ends in tragedy. The birds and lilies do not fret and worry; yet they have God's wealth in ways that man cannot duplicate. All of nature depends on God, and God never fails. Only mortal man depends on money, and money always fails.

Jesus said that worry is sinful. We may dignify worry by calling it by some other name—concern, burden, a cross to bear—but the results are still the same. Instead of helping us live longer, anxiety only makes life shorter (v. 27). The Greek word translated *take no thought* literally means "to be drawn in different directions." Worry pulls us apart. Until man interferes, everything in nature works together, because all of nature trusts God. Man, however, is pulled apart because he tries to live his own life by depending on material wealth.

God feeds the birds and clothes the lilies. He will feed and clothe us. It is our "little faith" that hinders Him from working as He would. He has great blessings for us if only we will yield to Him and live for the riches that last forever.

*Loss of testimony* (6:31-33). To worry about material things is to live like the heathen! If we put God's will and God's righteousness first in our lives, He will take care of everything else. What a testimony it is to the world when a Christian dares to practice Matthew 6:33! What a tragedy it is when so many of us *fail* to practice it.

*Loss of joy today* (6:34). Worrying about tomorrow does not help either tomorrow or today. If anything, it robs us of our effectiveness today—which means we will be even less effective tomorrow. Someone has said that the average person is crucifying himself between two thieves: the regrets of yesterday and the worries about tomorrow. It is right to plan for the future and even to save for the future (2 Cor. 12:14; 1 Tim. 5:8). But it is a sin to worry about the future and permit tomorrow to rob today of its blessings.

Three words in this section point the way to victory over worry: *faith* (v. 30), trusting God to meet our needs; (2) *Father* (v. 32), knowing He cares for His children; and (3) *first* (v. 33), putting God's will first in our lives so that He might be glorified. If we have faith in our Father and put Him first, He will meet our needs.

Hypocrisy and anxiety are sins. If we practice the true righteousness of the kingdom, we will avoid these sins and live for God's glory.

# 6

# THE KING'S PRINCIPLES: TRUE JUDGMENT

(Matthew 7)

The scribes and Pharisees were guilty of exercising a false judgment about themselves, other people, and even the Lord. Their false righteousness helped to encourage this false judgment. This explains why our Lord closed this important sermon with a discussion of judgment. In it He discussed three different judgments.

## Our Judgment of Ourselves (7:1-5)

The first principle of judgment is that we begin with ourselves. Jesus did not forbid us to judge others; for careful discrimination is essential in the Christian life. Christian love is not blind (Phil. 1:9-10). The person who believes all that he hears, and accepts everyone who claims to be spiritual will experience confusion and great spiritual loss. But before we judge others, we must judge ourselves. There are several reasons for this.

*We shall be judged* (7:1). The tense of the verb *judged* signifies a once-for-all final judgment. If we first judge ourselves, then we are preparing for that final judgment when we face God. The Pharisees "played God" as they condemned other people; but they never considered that God would one day judge them.

*We are being judged* (7:2). The parallel passage in Luke 6:37-38 is helpful here. Not only will God judge us at the end, but people are also judging us right now; and we receive from people exactly what we give.

The kind of judgment, and the measure of judgment, comes right back to us. We reap what we have sown.

*We must see clearly to help others* (7:3-5). The purpose of self-judgment is to prepare us to serve others. Christians are obligated to help each other grow in grace. When we do not judge ourselves, we not only hurt ourselves, but we also hurt those to whom we could minister. The Pharisees judged and criticized *others* to make themselves look good (Luke 18:9-14). But Christians should judge *themselves* so that they can help others look good. There is a difference!

Let's look at our Lord's illustration of this point. Jesus chose the symbol of the eye because this is one of the most sensitive areas of the human body. The picture of a man with a two-by-four stuck in his eye, trying to remove a speck of dust from another man's eye, is ridiculous indeed! If we do not honestly face up to our own sins, and confess them, we blind ourselves to ourselves; and then we cannot see clearly enough to help others. The Pharisees saw the sins of other people, but they would not look at their own sins.

In Matthew 6:22-23, Jesus used the illustration of the eye to teach us how to have a spiritual outlook on life. *We must not pass judgment on others' motives.* We should examine their actions and attitudes, but we cannot judge their motives—for only God can see their hearts. It is possible for a person to do a good work with a bad motive. It is also possible to fail in a task and yet be very sincerely motivated. When we stand before Christ at the last judgment, He will examine the secrets of the heart and reward us accordingly (Col. 3:22-25; Rom. 2:16).

The image of the eye teaches us another truth: We must exercise love and tenderness when we seek to help others (Eph. 4:15). I have had extensive eye examinations, and once had surgery to remove an imbedded speck of steel; and I appreciated the tenderness of the physicians. Like eye doctors, we should minister to people we want to help with tender loving care. We can do more damage than a speck of dirt in the eye if we approach others with impatience and insensitivity.

Two extremes must be avoided in this matter of spiritual self-examination. The first is the deception of a shallow examination. Sometimes we are so sure of ourselves that we fail to examine our hearts honestly and thoroughly. A quick glance into the mirror of the Word will never reveal the true situation (James 1:22-25).

The second extreme is what I call a "perpetual autopsy." Sometimes we get so wrapped up in self-examination that we become unbalanced. But we should not look only at ourselves, or we will become discouraged and defeated. We should look by faith to Jesus Christ and let Him forgive and restore us. Satan is the accuser (Rev. 12:10), and he enjoys it when we accuse and condemn ourselves!

After we have judged ourselves honestly before God, and have removed those things that blind us, then we can help others and properly judge their works. But if we know there are sins in our lives, and we try to help others, we are hypocrites. In fact, it is possible for ministry to be a device to cover up sin! The Pharisees were guilty of this, and Jesus denounced them for it.

## Our Judgment of Others (7:6-20)

Christians must exercise discernment; for not everyone is a sheep. Some people are dogs or hogs, and some are wolves in sheep's clothing! We are the Lord's sheep, but this does not mean we should let people pull the wool over our eyes!

*The reason we must judge* (7:6). As God's people, we are privileged to handle the "holy things" of the Lord. He has entrusted to us the precious truths of the Word of God (2 Cor. 4:7), and we must regard them carefully. No dedicated priest would throw meat from the altar to a filthy dog, and only a fool would give pearls to a pig. While it is true that we must carry the Gospel "to every creature" (Mark 16:15), it is also true that we must not cheapen the Gospel by a ministry that lacks discernment. Even Jesus refused to talk to Herod (Luke 23:9), and Paul refused to argue with people who resisted the Word (Acts 13:44-49).

The reason for judgment, then, is not that we might condemn others, but that we might be able to minister to them. Notice that Jesus always dealt with individuals according to their needs and their spiritual condition. He did not have a memorized speech that He used with everybody. He discussed the new birth with Nicodemus, but He spoke of living water to the Samaritan woman. When the religious leaders tried to trap Him, He refused to answer their question (Matt. 21:23-27). It is a wise Christian who first assesses the condition of a person's heart before sharing the precious pearls.

*The resources God gives us* (7:7-11). Why did our Lord discuss prayer at this point in His message? These verses seem to be an interruption, but they are not. You and I are human and fallible; we make mistakes. Only God can judge perfectly. Therefore, we must pray and seek His wisdom and direction. "If any of you lack wisdom, let him ask of God . . . " (James 1:5).

Young King Solomon knew that he lacked the needed wisdom to judge Israel, so he prayed to God; and the Lord graciously answered (1 Kings 3:3ff). If we are to have spiritual discernment, we must keep on asking God, keep on seeking His will, keep on knocking at the door that leads to greater ministry. God meets the needs of His children.

*The guiding principle* (7:12). This is the so-called "Golden Rule," one of the most misunderstood statements in the Bible. This statement is not the sum total of Christian truth, nor is it God's plan of redemption. We should no more build our theology on the Golden Rule than we should build our astronomy on "Twinkle, Twinkle Little Star."

This great truth is a principle that ought to govern our attitudes toward others. It only applies to believers, and it must be practiced in every area of life. *The person who practices the Golden Rule refuses to say or do anything that would harm himself or others.* If our judging of others is not governed by this principle, we will become proud and critical, and our own spiritual character will degenerate.

Practicing the Golden Rule releases the love of God in our lives and enables us to help others, even those who want to hurt us.

But remember that practicing the Golden Rule means paying a price. If we want God's best for ourselves and others, but others resist God's will, then they will oppose us. We are salt, and salt stings the open wound. We are light, and light exposes dirt.

*The basis for judging* (7:13-20). Since there are false prophets in the world, we must be careful of deception. But the greatest danger is *self-deception.* The scribes and Pharisees had fooled themselves into believing that they were righteous and others were sinful. It is possible for people to know the right language, believe intellectually the right doctrines, obey the right rules, and still not be saved. Jesus used two pictures to help us judge ourselves and others.

*The two ways* (vv. 13-14) are, of course, the way to heaven and the way to hell. The broad way is the easy way; it is the popular way. But we must not judge spiritual profession by statistics; the majority is not always right. The fact that "everybody does it" is no proof that what they are doing is right.

Quite the contrary is true: God's people have always been a remnant, a small minority in this world. The reason is not difficult to discover: The way of life is narrow, lonely, and costly. We can walk on the broad way and keep our "baggage" of sin and worldliness. But if we enter the narrow way, we must give up those things.

Here, then, is the first test: *Did your profession of faith in Christ cost you anything?* If not, then it was not a true profession. Many people who "trust" Jesus Christ never leave the broad road with its appetites and associations. They have an easy Christianity that makes no demands on them. Yet Jesus said that the narrow way was *hard*. We cannot walk on two roads, in two different directions, at the same time.

*The two trees* (vv. 15-20) show that true faith in Christ changes the life and produces fruit for God's glory. Everything in nature reproduces after its kind, and this is also true in the spiritual realm. Good fruit comes from a good tree, but bad fruit comes from a bad tree. The tree that produces rotten fruit is cut down and thrown into the fire. "Wherefore, by their fruits you shall know them" (v. 20).

The second test is this: *Did my decision for Christ change my life?* False prophets who teach false doctrine can produce only a false righteousness. (See Acts 20:29.) Their fruit (the results of their ministry) is false and cannot last. The prophets themselves are false; the closer we get to them, the more we see the falsity of their lives and doctrines. They magnify themselves, not Jesus Christ; and their purpose is to exploit people, not to edify them. The person who believes false doctrine, or who follows a false prophet, will never experience a changed life. Unfortunately, some people do not realize this until it is too late.

### God's Judgment of Us (7:21-29)

From picturing two ways and two trees, our Lord closed His message by picturing two builders and their houses. The two ways illustrate the *start* of the life of faith; the two trees illustrate the *growth* and results of the life of faith here and now; and the two houses illustrate the *end* of this life of faith, when God shall call everything to judgment. There are false prophets at the gate that leads to the broad way, making it easy for people to enter. But at the end of the way, there is destruction. The final test is not what we think of ourselves, or what others may think. The final test is: *What will God say?*

How can we prepare for this judgment? *By doing God's will.* Obedience to His will is the test of true faith in Christ. The test is not words, not saying "Lord, Lord," and not obeying His commands. How easy it is to learn a religious vocabulary, and even memorize Bible verses and religious songs, and yet not obey God's will. When a person is truly born again, he has the Spirit of God living within (Rom. 8:9); and the Spirit enables him to know and do the Father's will. God's love in his heart (Rom. 5:5) motivates him to obey God and serve others.

Words are not a substitute for obedience, and neither are religious works. Preaching, casting out demons, and performing miracles can be divinely inspired, but they give no assurance of salvation. It is likely that even Judas participated in some or all of these activities, and yet he was not a true believer. In the last days, Satan will use "lying wonders" to deceive people (2 Thes. 2:7-12).

We are to *hear* God's words and *do* them (see James 1:22-25). We must not stop with only hearing (or studying) His words. Our hearing must result in doing. This is what it means to build on the rock foundation. We should not confuse this symbol with the "rock" in 1 Corinthians 3:9ff. Paul founded the local church in Corinth on Jesus Christ when he preached the Gospel and won people to Christ. This is the only foundation for a local church.

The foundation in this parable is *obedience to God's Word* —obedience that is an evidence of true faith (James 2:14ff). The two men in this story had much in common. Both had desires to build a house. Both built houses that looked good and sturdy. But when the judgment came (the storm), one of the houses collapsed. What was the difference? Not the mere external looks, to be sure. The difference was in the foundation: The successful builder "dug deep" (Luke 6:48) and set his house on a solid foundation.

A false profession will last until judgment comes. Sometimes this judgment is in the form of the trials of life. Like the person who received the seed of God's Word into a shallow heart (Matt. 13:4-9), the commitment fails when the testing comes. Many people have professed faith in Christ, only to deny their faith when life becomes spiritually costly and difficult.

But the judgment illustrated here probably refers to the final judgment before God. We must not read into this parable all the doctrine that we are taught in the Epistles; for the Lord was illustrating one main point: *profession will ultimately be tested before God.* Those who have trusted Christ, and have proved their faith by their obedience will have nothing to fear. Their house is founded on the Rock, and it will stand. But those who have professed to trust Christ, yet who have not obeyed God's will, will be condemned.

How shall we test our profession of faith? By popularity? No, for there are many on the broad road to destruction. And there are many who are depending on words, saying "Lord, Lord"—but this is no assurance of salvation. Even religious activities in a church organization are no assurance. How then shall we judge ourselves and others who profess Christ as Saviour?

*The two ways* tell us to examine the cost of our profession. Have we paid a price to profess faith in Christ? *The two trees* tell us to investigate whether our lives have really changed. Are there godly fruits from our lives? And *the two houses* remind us that true faith in Christ will last, not only in the storms of life, but also in the final judgment.

The congregation was astonished at this sermon. Why? Because Jesus spoke with divine authority. The scribes and Pharisees spoke "from authorities," always quoting the various rabbis and experts of the law. Jesus needed no human teacher to add authority to His words; for He spoke as the Son of God. We cannot lightly dismiss this sermon, for it is God who gave it to us! We must either bow before Him and submit to His authority, or we will be condemned.

# 7

# THE KING'S POWER

(Matthew 8—9)

We have been introduced to the Person of the King (chapters 1—4) and the principles of the King (chapters 5—7); and now we are ready for the power of the King. After all, if a king does not have the power to accomplish anything, what good are his credentials or his principles? In chapters 8 and 9, Matthew reported 10 miracles. They are not given in chronological order, except for the last four, since Matthew followed his own approach of grouping messages or events.

Before we survey these miracles, however, we must pause to answer the obvious question: Why did our Lord perform miracles? Certainly He wanted to meet human needs. God is concerned about the temporal well-being of His creatures as well as their eternal happiness. It is wrong to separate ministry to the body and ministry to the soul, since we must minister to the whole person. (See Matt. 4:23-25.)

Certainly our Lord's miracles were additional credentials to prove His claim as the Messiah of Israel. "The Jews require a sign" (1 Cor. 1:22). While miracles of themselves are not proof that a man has been sent by God (even Satan can perform miracles [2 Thes. 2:9]), they do add weight to his claim, especially if his character and conduct are godly. In the case of Jesus Christ, His miracles also fulfilled Old Testament prophecies (see Isa. 29:18-19; 35:4-6). Matthew 8:17 refers us to Isaiah 53:4; and Jesus Himself in Matthew 11:1-5 referred John the Baptist to the Old Testament promises. These same "signs and wonders" would be the credentials of His followers in their ministries (Matt. 10:8; Heb. 2:1-4).

Along with His compassion and credentials, there was a third reason for miracles: His concern to reveal saving truth to people. The miracles were "sermons in action." Even Nicodemus was impressed with them (John 3:1-2). It is worth noting that five of these miracles were performed at Capernaum, and yet the city rejected Him (Matt. 11:21-23). Even the rejection by the nation of Israel fulfilled Old Testament prophecy (see John 12:37-41). Like the judgments against Egypt in Moses' day, the miracles of the Lord were judgments in Israel; for the people had to face facts and make decisions. The religious leaders decided that Jesus was working for Satan (Matt. 9:31-34, 12:24).

One thing is certain: Jesus did not perform miracles to "get a crowd." He always avoided the crowd. Time after time, Jesus instructed those whom He had healed not to talk too much (Matt. 8:4, 18; 9:30; Luke 8:56). He did not want people trusting Him simply on the basis of spectacular deeds (see John 4:46-54). Faith must be based on His Word (Rom. 10:17).

The miracles in these chapters are recorded in three groups, with an event relating to discipleship separating the groups. Matthew did not tell his readers why he used this arrangement, but we will follow it. To help us grasp some of the spiritual lessons, I have characterized each section with a special emphasis.

### Grace to the Outcasts (8:1-22)

Lepers, Gentiles, and women were considered outcasts by many Jewish people, especially the Pharisees. Many Pharisees would pray each morning, "I give thanks that I am a man and not a woman, a Jew and not a Gentile, a free-man and not a slave."

*Cleansing the leper* (8:1-4). There were a number of afflictions that our Bible categorizes as leprosy. This dreaded infection forced the victim to live apart from others and to cry, "Unclean! Unclean!" when others approached, so they would not be defiled. That the leper ran up to Jesus and violated the code is evidence of his great faith that Jesus would heal him.

Leprosy is an illustration of sin (Isa. 1:5-6). The instructions given to the priests in Leviticus 13 help us understand the nature of sin: Sin is deeper than the skin (v. 3); it spreads (v. 7); it defiles and isolates (vv. 45-46); and it is fit only for the fire (vv. 52, 57).

When Jesus touched the leper, He contracted the leper's defilement; *but He also conveyed His health!* Is this not what He did for us on the cross when He was made sin for us? (2 Cor. 5:21) The leper did not question His *ability* to heal; he only wondered if He were willing. Certainly God is willing to save! He is "God our Saviour, who will have all men to be saved . . . " (1 Tim. 2:3-4). God is "not willing that any should perish" (2 Peter 3:9).

Jesus commanded the man not to tell others but to go to the priests and have them declare him restored and fit for society. This ceremony is described in Leviticus 14 and is another beautiful picture of Christ's work for sinners. The bird slain pictures the death of Christ; the bird released pictures His resurrection. Putting the bird into the jar pictures the incarnation, when Christ took a human body that He might die for us. The application of the blood to the ear, thumb, and toe illustrates the need for personal faith in His death. The oil on the blood reminds us of the Spirit of God, who enters the person when he trusts the Saviour.

The man did not obey Christ; he told everybody what the Lord had done! (Christ tells us to tell everybody, *and we keep quiet!*) Mark 1:45 tells us that the healed leper's witness forced Jesus to avoid the city; and yet the crowds came to Him.

*The centurion's servant healed* (8:5-13). A centurion was an officer over 100 men in the Roman army. Every centurion mentioned in the Gospels and Acts was a gentleman of high character and sense of duty, and this man was no exception. The fact that he was concerned about a lowly servant-boy indicates this. The word "palsy" indicates a kind of paralysis.

It would seem that everything about this man would prevent him from coming to Jesus. He was a professional soldier, and Jesus was a man of peace. He was a Gentile, and Jesus was a Jew. But this soldier had one thing working for him: he was a man of great faith. This centurion understood that Jesus, like himself, was under authority. All Christ had to do was speak the word and the disease would obey Him the way a soldier obeyed his officer. It is worth noting that only those who are *under* authority have the right to *exercise* authority.

Twice in the Gospels it is recorded that Jesus marvelled: here, at the *great faith* of the Gentile centurion; and in Mark 6:6, at the *great unbelief* of the Jews. Matthew recorded two "Gentile" miracles: this one, and the healing of the daughter of the Syrophenecian woman (Matt. 15:21-28). In both cases, the Lord was impressed with their great faith. This is an early indication that the Jews would not believe, but the Gentiles would. Also, in both of these miracles, our Lord healed *from a distance*. This was a reminder of the spiritual position of the Gentiles "afar off" (Eph. 2:12).

*Peter's mother-in-law healed* (8:14-17). She was in bed with a fever and Peter and Andrew told Jesus about her need when they all arrived home after the synagogue service (Mark 1:21). Women did not hold a high position in Israel, and it is doubtful that a Pharisee would have paid much attention to the need in Peter's home. Jesus healed her with a touch, and she responded by serving Him and the other men.

This seems like a "minor miracle," but the results were major; for after sundown (when the Sabbath ended), *the whole city* gathered at the door that the Lord might meet their needs (Mark 1:32-34). Blessing in the home ought to lead to blessing in the community. The change in one woman's life led to miracles in the lives of many people.

Matthew saw this as a fulfillment of Isaiah 53:4. Please note that Jesus fulfilled this prophecy *in His life* and not on the cross. He bore man's sicknesses and infirmities *during His ministry on earth*. To say that there is "healing in the atonement," and that every believer has the "right" to claim it, is to misinterpret Scripture. First Peter 2:24 applies this same truth to the forgiving of our sins which He bore on the cross. Sin and sickness do go together (see Ps. 103:3), since sickness is a consequence of Adam's sin and also an illustration of sin. But God is not obligated to heal all sicknesses. He is obligated to save all sinners who call upon Him.

*First "discipleship" interlude* (8:18-22). Because great crowds followed Jesus, and opposition had not yet begun, many would-be disciples wanted to follow Him. However, they would not pay the price. This is the first use of "Son of man" in Matthew as a name for Jesus. It comes from Daniel 7:13 and is definitely a messianic title and a claim to kingship. Verse 22 might be expressed, "Let the spiritually dead bury the physically dead." Jesus was not asking the man to be disrespectful to his father (who was not yet dead), but to have the right priorities in life. It is better to preach the Gospel and give life to the spiritually dead, than to wait for your father to die and bury him.

## Peace to the Disturbed (8:23—9:17)

The persons involved in these three miracles all had a need for peace, and Jesus provided that peace.

*Peace in the storm* (8:23-27). The Sea of Galilee is about 13 miles long and 8 miles wide. It was not unusual for violent storms suddenly to sweep across the water. Jesus undoubtedly knew the storm was coming, and certainly could have prevented it. But He permitted it that He might teach His disciples some lessons.

The storm came because they *obeyed* the Lord, and not because (like Jonah) they disobeyed Him. Jesus was asleep because He rested confidently in the will of His Father; and this is what the disciples should have done. Instead, they became frightened and accused Jesus of not caring! Matthew wanted his readers to contrast the "little faith" of the disciples with the "great faith" of the Gentile centurion.

*Peace in a community* (8:28-34). This dramatic incident is most revealing. It shows what *Satan* does for a man: robs him of sanity and self-control; fills him with fears; robs him of the joys of home and friends; and (if possible) condemns him to an eternity of judgment. It also reveals what *society* does for a man in need: restrains him, isolates him, threatens him, but society is unable to change him. See, then, what Jesus Christ can do for a man whose whole life—within and without—is bondage and battle. What Jesus did for these two demoniacs, He will do for anyone else who needs Him.

*Christ came to them*, and even braved a storm to do it. This is the grace of God! *He delivered them* by the power of His Word. *He restored them* to sanity, society, and service. The account in Mark 5:1-21 shows that one of the men asked to become a disciple of the Lord. But, instead of granting his request, Jesus sent him home to be a witness. Christian service must begin at home.

There are three prayers in this event: (1) the demons besought Jesus to send them into the swine; (2) the citizens besought Him to leave; and (3) the one man besought Him to let him follow (see Mark 5:18-20). Jesus answered the prayers of the demons and the citizens, but not the prayer of the healed man!

We can construct a "statement of faith" from the words of the demons. (Demons do have faith; see James 2:19.) They believed in the existence of God and the deity of Christ, as well as the reality of future judgment.

They also believed in prayer. They knew Christ had the power to send them into the swine.

The fact that the demons destroyed 2000 pigs is nothing compared with the fact that Jesus delivered two men from the powers of Satan. God owns everything (Ps. 50:10-11) and can do with it as He pleases. Jesus values men more than pigs or sheep (Matt. 12:12). He brought peace to these men's lives and to the community where, for a long time, they had been causing trouble.

*Peace in the conscience* (9:1-8). The Lord had shown Himself powerful over sickness and storms, but what could He do about *sin*? Palsy was a gradual paralysis. This man was unable to help himself, but fortunately he had four friends with love, faith, and hope. They brought him to Jesus and permitted nothing to stand in their way. Was the man's physical condition the result of his sin? We do not know. But we do know that Jesus dealt with the sin problem first, for this is always the greatest need.

We must not conclude from this miracle that all sickness is caused by sin, or that forgiveness automatically means physical healing. A pastor of mine often says, "God can heal every sickness *except the last one*." More important than the healing of this man's body was the cleansing of his heart. He went home with both a sound body and a heart at peace with God. "There is no peace, saith my God, to the wicked" (Isa. 57:21).

*Second "discipleship" interlude* (9:9-17). We have covered the call of Matthew in the first chapter of this study. We need only to comment on the four pictures of His ministry that Jesus gave in this message. As the *Physician*, He came to bring spiritual health to sick sinners. As the *Bridegroom*, He came to give spiritual joy. The Christian life is a feast, not a funeral. The illustration of the *cloth* reminds us that He came to bring spiritual wholeness; He did not come to "patch us up" and then let us fall apart. The image of the *wineskins* teaches that He gives spiritual fullness. Jewish religion was a worn-out wineskin that would burst if filled with the new wine of the Gospel. Jesus did not come to renovate Moses or even mix law and grace. He came with new life!

## Restoration to the Broken (9:18-38)

In this section Matthew recorded four miracles involving five persons.

*A broken home* (9:18-19, 23-26). It must have been difficult for Jairus to come to Jesus, since he was a devout Jew and the leader in the synagogue. But Jairus' love for his dying daughter compelled him to seek Jesus' help, even if the religious leaders were opposing Him. When Jairus first came to Jesus, his daughter was close to death. The delay caused by the healing of the woman gave "the last enemy" opportunity to do its work. The ruler's friends came and told him that his daughter had died.

Jesus quickly reassured the man and went with him. In fact, the delay should have helped to strengthen Jairus' faith; for he saw what the woman's meager faith had accomplished in her own life. We must learn to trust Christ and His promises no matter how we feel, no matter what others say, and no matter how the circumstances may look. The scene at home must have frightened Jairus, yet Jesus took command and raised the girl from the dead.

*A broken hope* (9:20-22). Mark 5:26 informs us that this woman had tried many physicians, but none could help her. Imagine the despair and discouragement she felt. Her hopes were shattered. Because of this hemorrhage, the woman was ceremonially unclean (Lev. 15:25ff), which only added to her hopelessness. The "hem" refers to the special tassles that the Jews wore on their garments to remind them they were God's people (Num. 15:37-41; Deut. 22:12).

It is interesting that Jairus and this woman—two opposite people—met at the feet of Jesus. Jairus was a leading Jewish man; she was an anonymous woman with no prestige or resources. He was a synagogue leader, while her affliction kept her from worship. Jairus came pleading for his daughter; the woman came with a need of her own. The girl had been healthy for 12 years, and then died; the woman had been ill for 12 years and was now made whole. Jairus' need was public—all knew it; but the woman's need was private—only Jesus understood. Both Jairus and the woman trusted Christ, and He met their needs.

Jairus may have resented the woman, because she kept Jesus from getting to his daughter before the girl died. But his real problem was not the woman, *but himself*: He needed faith in Christ. Jesus forced the woman to give her testimony (see Mark's account) both for her sake and for the sake of Jairus. The fact that God has helped others ought to encourage us to trust Him more. We ought not to be so selfish in our praying that we cannot wait on the Lord, knowing He is never late.

This woman's faith was almost superstitious; and yet Jesus honored it and healed her. People must "touch Christ" where they are able, even if they must start at the hem of His garment. The Pharisees enlarged their hems and tassels in order to appear more spiritual, but they lacked the power to heal (Matt. 23:5). Others touched the hem of Christ's garment and were also healed (14:34-36).

When Sir James Simpson, the inventor of chloroform, was dying, a friend said to him, "You will soon be resting on His bosom." The scientist replied: "I don't know as I can do that, but I think I have hold of the hem of His garment." It is not the strength of our faith that saves us, but faith in a strong Saviour.

*Broken bodies* (9:27-34). We are not told why these men were blind. Blindness was a serious problem in the East in that day. The records state that Jesus healed at least six blind men, and each case was different. These two blind men acknowledged Christ as the Son of David (see Matt. 1:1) and persisted in following Him right into the house. (No doubt they had friends who helped guide them.) It was their faith that Christ honored. Their "Yes, Lord" was the confession that released the power for their healing and their sight was restored.

Blindness is a picture of spiritual ignorance and unbelief (Matt. 15:14; Isa. 6:10; Rom. 11:25). The sinner must be born again before he can see the things of God (John 3:3). And the believer must be careful to grow spiritually or he will damage his spiritual vision (2 Peter 1:5-9).

The final miracle in this series involved a demon (9:32-34). While there is a difference between sicknesses and demonic workings (Matt. 10:8), the demons do have the power to cause physical afflictions. In this case, the demon made the man mute. Think of what a handicap this would be! Jesus delivered him, and the people admitted that this was a new thing in Israel.

But the religious leaders would not admit that Jesus was the Messiah. How, then, could they explain His miracles? Only by saying that His miracles were wrought in the power of the wicked one. They would repeat this charge later, and Jesus would refute it (Matt. 12:22ff). In their unbelief, the Pharisees were playing right into Satan's hands!

*Third "discipleship" interlude* (9:35-38). Not only did Jesus heal; He also taught and preached. But He could not do the work alone—He needed others to help Him. He requested that His disciples pray that God would provide the needed workers. It was not long before the disciples themselves were involved in the ministry of preaching, teaching, and healing (see Chapter 10). In the same way, when we pray as He commanded, we will see what He saw, feel what He felt, and do what He did. God will multiply our lives as we share in the great harvest that is already ripe (John 4:34-38).

# 8

# THE
# KING'S
# AMBASSADORS

(Matthew 10)

The work of salvation could be accomplished only by Jesus Christ, and He did it alone. But the *witness* of this salvation could only be accomplished by His people, those who have trusted Him and been saved. The King needed ambassadors to the message—and He *still* needs them. "Whom shall I send, and who will go for us?" (Isa. 6:8) It is not enough that we *pray* for laborers (Matt. 9:36-38). We must also make ourselves available to serve Him.

Before Jesus sent His ambassadors out to minister, He preached an "ordination sermon" to encourage and prepare them. In this sermon, the King had something to say to *all* of His servants—past, present, and future. Unless we recognize this fact, the message of this chapter will seem hopelessly confused.

### Instructions for Past Apostles (10:1-15)
A "disciple" is a learner, one who follows a teacher and learns his wisdom. Jesus had many disciples, some of whom were merely "hangers-on," and some who were truly converted (John 6:66). From this large group of followers, Jesus selected a smaller group of 12 men; and these He called "apostles." This word comes from the Greek word *apostello*, which means "to send forth with a commission." It was used by the Greeks for the personal representatives of the king, ambassadors who

functioned with the king's authority. To make light of the king's envoys was to be in danger of insubordination.

A man had to meet certain qualifications to be an apostle of Jesus Christ. He must have seen the risen Christ (1 Cor. 9:1) and fellowshipped with Him (Acts 1:21-22). He had to be chosen by the Lord (Eph. 4:11). The apostles laid the foundation of the church (Eph. 2:20) and then passed from the scene. While all believers are sent forth to represent the King (John 20:21; 17:18), no believer today can honestly claim to be an apostle; for none of us has seen the risen Christ (1 Peter 1:8).

These apostles were given special power and authority from Christ to perform miracles. These miracles were a part of their "official credentials" (Acts 2:43; 5:12; 2 Cor. 12:12; Heb. 2:1-4). They healed the sick (and note that this included *all* kinds of diseases), cleansed the lepers, cast out demons, and even raised the dead. These four ministries paralleled the miracles that Jesus performed in chapters 8 and 9. In a definite way, the apostles represented the King and extended His work.

Christ's commission to these 12 men is not our commission today. He sent them only to the people of Israel. "To the Jew first" is the historic pattern, for "Salvation is of the Jews" (John 4:22). These 12 ambassadors announced the coming of the kingdom just as John the Baptist had done (Matt. 3:2) and Jesus Himself (Matt. 4:17). Sad to say, the nation rejected both Christ and His ambassadors, and the kingdom was taken from them (Matt. 21:43).

The apostles depended on the hospitality of others as they ministered from town to town. In those days, for a town to refuse a guest was a breach of etiquette. However, the ambassadors were to remain only with those who were "worthy," those who trusted Christ and received His message of peace and forgiveness. The apostles were not to compromise. If a town rejected their words, they were to warn the people and depart. To shake off the dust was an act of judgment (Acts 13:51).

We do not know how long this "evangelistic campaign" lasted. Jesus Himself went out to preach (see Matt. 11:1), and later the apostles returned to Him and reported what had happened (Luke 9:10). Mark 6:7 tells us that Jesus had sent the men out in pairs, which explains why their names are listed in pairs in verses 2-4. Revelation 21:14 tells us that the names of the apostles will be on the foundations of the heavenly walls. The name of Judas will, of course, be replaced by Matthias (Acts 1:26).

While we may learn from the spiritual principles in this paragraph, we should not apply these instructions to our lives. The Lord's commission to us includes "all the world" (Matt. 28:19-20), not just the nation of Israel. We preach the gospel of the grace of God (Acts 20:24). Our message is "Christ died for our sins" and not "The kingdom of heaven is at hand." The King has come; He has already suffered, died, and risen from the dead. Now He offers His salvation to all who will believe.

### Instructions for Future Disciples (10:16-23)

The "atmosphere" of this section is different from that in the previous section. Here the Lord spoke of persecution, but we have no record that the 12 suffered during their tour. Jesus also spoke of a ministry to the Gentiles (v. 18). The Holy Spirit had not been given, yet Jesus talked about the Spirit speaking in them (v. 20). Verse 22 seems to indicate a worldwide persecution; yet the apostles were ministering only in their own land. Finally, verse 23 speaks about the return of the Lord, which certainly moves these events into the future. It is difficult to escape the conclusion that these instructions apply to witnesses at some future time.

But, *what* time? To some degree, some of these events took place in the Book of Acts; yet Jesus Christ did not return at that time. And the ministry in Acts was not limited to "the cities of Israel" (v. 23). It seems that the period described in this section closely parallels the time of tribulation that Jesus described in His "Olivet Discourse" (Matt. 24—25). In fact, the statement "He that shall endure unto the end, the same shall be saved" (v. 13) is definitely a part of our Lord's prophetic discourse (Mark 13:13; Matt. 24:13). It does not refer to a person keeping himself saved, but rather enduring persecution and being faithful.

If, then, these instructions apply to that future time of tribulation, we can easily understand why Jesus said so much about hatred and persecution. The Tribulation period will be a time of *opposition*. God's servants will be like sheep in the midst of wolves. They will need to be "tough-minded but tender-hearted." This opposition will come from organized religion (Matt. 10:17), government (v. 18), and even the family (v. 21).

While believers in scattered parts of the world are experiencing some of this persecution today, the indication is that this opposition will be worldwide. "Religion" has always persecuted true believers. Even the Apostle Paul persecuted the church when he was the unconverted Saul of

Tarsus. Church history reveals that "organized religion" that has no Gospel has opposed men and women who have dared to witness boldly for Christ.

Matthew 10:18 states that *government* will also share in this program of persecution. The prophetic Scriptures teach that, in the last days, government and religion will work together to control the world. Revelation 13 describes a time during the Tribulation period when a world ruler (the Antichrist) will force the world to worship him and his image. He will control world religion, economics, and government; and he will use all three to persecute those who stand true to Christ.

There will also be a decay of *family* love and loyalty. "Without natural affection" is one of the marks of the end times (2 Tim. 3:3). Jesus quoted Micah 7:6 to prove this point (Matt. 10:21). The three institutions which God established in this world are the home, human government, and the church. In the last days, all three of these institutions will oppose the truth instead of promote it.

But the tribulation period will also be a time of *opportunity*. The believers will be able to witness to governors and kings (v. 18). Their enemies will try to trip them up, but the Spirit of God will teach the witnesses what to say. Believers today must not use Matthew 10:19-20 as an excuse not to study the Word in preparation for witnessing, teaching, or preaching. These verses describe an emergency situation; they are not God's regular pattern for ministry today. Even during the days of the apostles, the Spirit gave them their messages when they faced their enemies (Acts 4:8). This unusual ministry of the Spirit will be evident during the tribulation period.

The Tribulation will be a time of opposition and opportunity; but it will also be a time of *obligation*. The ambassadors of the King must "endure to the end" and faithfully perform their ministry, even if it costs them their lives. In spite of scourging, rejection by their families, persecution from city to city, and trials before leaders, the servants must remain true to their Lord. Their witness will be used by God to win others. Revelation 7:1-8 indicates that 144,000 Jewish witnesses will carry God's Word throughout the world during the Tribulation; and as a result, great multitudes will come to Christ (Rev. 7:9ff).

No doubt these words in Matthew 10 will become very precious and meaningful to witnesses during that time. We, today, can learn from these words, even though their primary interpretation and application are for God's servants at a future time. No matter how difficult our circumstances may be, we can turn opposition into opportunities for witness. We can trust the Spirit of God to help us remember what the Lord has taught us (John 14:26). Instead of fleeing and looking for an easier place, we can "endure to the end," knowing that God will help us and see us through.

## Instructions for Present Disciples (10:24-42)

While the truths in this section would apply to God's servants during any period of Bible history, they seem to have a special significance for the church today. The emphasis is, "Fear not!" (vv. 26, 28, 31). The particular fear Christ discussed is explained in verses 32-33: the fear of confessing Christ openly before men. God has no "secret service." The public confession of faith in Christ is one evidence of true salvation (Rom. 10:9-10). Several reasons show why we must not be afraid to openly confess Christ. Let's examine these reasons that are found in Matthew 10.

*Suffering is to be expected* (10:24-25). Men persecuted Jesus Christ when He was ministering on earth, so why should we expect anything different? We are His disciples, and the disciple does not "out-rank" the Master. They said that Jesus was in league with Satan (Beelzebub: lord of the dung; lord of the house); so they will say the same thing about His followers. However, we should count it a privilege to suffer *for* Him and *with* Him (Acts 5:41; Phil. 3:10).

*God will bring everything to light* (10:26-27). The enemies of Christ use secret and deceptive means to oppose the Gospel. But true believers are open and courageous in their lives and witness. We have nothing to hide. "In secret have I said nothing," said Jesus (John 18:20). False witnesses lied about Jesus during His trial, but God saw to it that the truth came out. We have nothing to fear because the Lord will one day reveal the secrets of men's hearts (Rom. 2:16) and expose them and judge them. Our task is not to please men, but to proclaim God's message. The present judgment of men does not frighten us, because we are living in the light of the future judgment of God.

*We fear God alone* (10:28). All that men can do is kill the body; and, if they do, the believer's soul goes home to be with the Lord. But God is able to destroy *both* body and soul in hell! Of course, God will never condemn one of His own children (Rom. 8:1; John 5:24). Martin Luther caught this truth when he wrote:

> Let goods and kindred go,
> This mortal life also;
> The body they may kill:
> God's truth abideth still;
> His kingdom is forever.

The person who fears God alone need never fear any man or group of men. The fear of God is the fear that cancels fear.

*God cares for His own* (10:29-31). It did not cost much to purchase sparrows in the market. If we compare these verses with Luke 12:6, we discover that sparrows were so cheap that the dealer threw in an extra one! Yet the Father knows when a sparrow falls to the ground; *and the Father is there.* If God cares for sparrows in such a marvelous way, will He not also care for His own who are serving Him? He certainly will! To God, we are of greater value than many sparrows.

God is concerned about all of the details of our lives. Even the hairs of our head are numbered—not "counted" in a total, but numbered individually! God sees the sparrow fall to the ground, and God sees when a hair falls from the head of one of His children. When He protects His own, He protects them down to the individual hairs (Luke 21:18). There is no need for us to fear when God is exercising such wonderful care over us.

*Christ honors those who confess Him* (10:32-33). To confess Him means much more than to make a statement with the lips. It also means to back up that statement with the life. It is one thing to say "Jesus Christ is Lord" and quite another thing to surrender to Him and obey His will. The walk and the talk must go together.

In heaven, Jesus has two special ministries. As our High Priest, He gives us grace to keep us from sinning. As our Advocate, He forgives and restores us when we do sin (1 John 2:1-2). The *merits* of His heavenly intercessory work do not depend on our faithfulness, for He is faithful even if we are not (2 Tim. 2:12-13). But the *benefits* of His heavenly ministry are for those who are faithful to Him. When Christ confesses us before the Father, He is securing for us the benefits of His sacrificial work on the cross. When He denies us before the Father, He is unable to share these graces with us. The fault is ours, not His.

But something else is involved. One day we shall stand before His judgment seat where the rewards will be distributed (2 Cor. 5:10; Rom. 14:10). If we have denied Him, we will lose rewards and the joy of hearing His "Well done." To be sure, anyone who denies Him on earth may be forgiven. Peter denied the Lord three times, was forgiven, and was restored.

*We cannot escape conflict* (10:34-39). Once we have identified with Jesus Christ and confessed Him, we are part of a war. We did not start the war; God declared war on Satan (Gen. 3:15). On the night our Lord was born, the angels declared "on earth peace" (Luke 2:14). But Jesus seemed to deny this truth. "I came not to send peace, but a sword" (Matt. 10:34). Had Israel accepted Him, He would have given them peace. But the people refused Him, and the result was "a sword." Instead of there being "peace on earth," there is "peace in heaven" (Luke 19:38). He has made peace through the blood of His cross (Col. 1:20) so that men can be reconciled to God and to each other.

The only way a believer can escape conflict is to deny Christ and compromise his witness, and this would be sin. Then the believer would be at war with God and with himself. We will be misunderstood and persecuted even by those who are the closest to us; yet we must not allow this to affect our witness. It is important that we suffer for Jesus' sake, and for righteousness' sake, and not because we ourselves are difficult to live with. There is a difference between the "offense of the cross" (Gal. 5:11) and offensive Christians.

Each believer must make the decision once and for all to love Christ supremely and take up his cross and follow Christ. The love in verse 37 is the motive for the cross in verse 38. To "carry the cross" does not mean to wear a pin on our lapel or put a sticker on our automobile. It means to confess Christ and obey Him in spite of shame and suffering. It means to die to self daily. If the Lord went to a cross for us, the least we can do is carry a cross for Him.

Verse 39 presents us with only two alternatives: spare your life or sacrifice your life. There is no middle ground. If we protect our own interests, we will be losers; if we die to self and live for His interests, we will be winners. Since spiritual conflict is inevitable in this world, why not die to self and let Christ win the battle *for* us and *in* us? After all, the real war is *inside*—selfishness versus sacrifice.

*We can be a blessing to others* (10:40-42). Not everyone will reject our witness. There are those who will welcome us and receive a blessing. After all, we are the ambassadors of the King! Our King will see to it that they are rewarded for what they do. When people receive us, they welcome the King; for we are His representatives. Read 2 Samuel 10 for an example of what happens when people mistreat the envoys of the King.

The blessing, however, is not automatic. It all depends on the attitude of the host. If he receives the ambassador as a prophet (a spokesman for God), then he gets one reward; if he receives him only as a righteous man, there is another reward. But even a cup of cold water, given with the right spirit, brings its own reward.

Keep in mind that the theme of this last section is discipleship, not sonship. We become the children of God through faith in Christ; we are disciples as we faithfully follow Him and obey His will. Sonship does not change, but discipleship does change as we walk with Christ. There is a great need today for faithful disciples, believers who will learn from Christ and live for Him.

This brings us to the close of the first major division of Matthew, *The Revelation of the King*. We have seen His Person (chaps. 1—4), His principles (chaps. 5—7), and His power (chaps. 8—10). How will the nation respond to this revelation?

# 9

# THE KING'S CONFLICTS

(Matthew 11—12)

All of the evidence had been presented. John the Baptist had introduced the King to the nation. Jesus had revealed His person, principles, and power. It was now up to the leaders of the nation to make their decision. Instead of receiving their King, they began to rebel against Him. In these two chapters four areas of rebellion are presented.

### Rebellion against His Prophet (11:1-30)

*Explanation* (vv. 1-15). John the Baptist was in prison in the fortress of Machaerus because he had courageously denounced the adulterous marriage of Herod Antipas and Herodias (Luke 3:19-20). It seems that the Jewish leaders would have opposed Herod and sought to free John, but they did nothing. Their attitude toward John reflected their feeling toward Jesus, for John had pointed to Jesus and honored Him.

It is not difficult to sympathize with John as he suffered in prison. He was a man of the desert, and he was confined indoors. He was an active man, with a divine mandate to preach; and he was silenced. He had announced judgment, and yet that judgment was slow in coming (Matt. 3:7-12). He received only partial reports of Jesus' ministry and could not see the total picture.

Our Lord's reply to John revealed both tact and tenderness. He reminded John of the Old Testament prophecies about the works of Messiah

(Isa. 29:18-19; 35:4-6). John's disciples had already told him what Jesus was doing (Luke 7:18), but Jesus asked them to "show John again." John had come in the spirit and power of Elijah (Luke 1:17), and even Elijah had his days of discouragement! Jesus assured John that He was fulfilling the Father's will.

After answering John, Jesus then praised him. John was not a "popular preacher" who catered to the crowd, nor was he a reed in the wind who vacillated with every change. He was a man of conviction and courage, the greatest of the prophets. The fact that John was privileged to announce the Messiah gave him this high position. His ministry marked the climax of the law and the prophets.

In what sense was John "Elijah who was to come"? (v. 14) He came in the spirit and power of Elijah (Luke 1:17), and even dressed and ministered like Elijah (Matt. 3:4; 2 Kings 1:7-8). Like Elijah, John had a message of judgment for the apostate nation of Israel. His ministry was prophesied (Isa. 40:3) and he fulfilled it. But Malachi 4:5 prophesied the coming of Elijah "before the coming of the great and dreadful day of the Lord." This "day of the Lord" is the time of tribulation that will come on all the earth (see Matt. 24:15). But no such judgments followed the ministry of John the Baptist. Why?

John's ministry was to prepare the nation for Jesus and to present Jesus to the nation (Luke 1:15-17; John 1:29-34). Had the people received John's witness and accepted their Messiah, John would have fulfilled the prophecies literally. Instead, they were fulfilled in a spiritual sense in the lives of those who trusted Christ. Jesus made this clear in Matthew 17:10-13. Many Bible students believe that Malachi 4:5 will be fulfilled literally when Elijah comes as one of the "two witnesses" spoken of in Revelation 11.

The common people held John in high regard (Matt. 21:26), and many of them had repented and been baptized by John. But the leaders refused to honor John, and this proved their unbelief and hardness of heart. Instead of being *childlike* and humbling themselves, the leaders were *childish* and stubborn, like children pouting because they could not have their way. The parable in Matthew 11:16-19 revealed the spiritual condition of the leaders, and unfortunately it also reveals the hearts of unbelievers today.

*Condemnation* (vv. 16-24). How unusual to find the word *woe* on the lips of Jesus! This word means judgment, but it also includes pity and sorrow. How tragic that these cities should treat lightly their opportunities to see and hear the Christ of God, and be saved! The Gentile cities of Tyre and Sidon, and the godless cities of Sodom and Gomorrah, would have repented had they seen the miracles that Jesus and His disciples performed. Capernaum had been "exalted to heaven" by being privileged to have the Messiah live there. Yet her greater privileges only brought greater responsibilities and greater judgment. Five of the ten miracles recorded in Matthew 8—9 were performed in Capernaum.

*Invitation* (vv. 25-30). Why did the religious leaders rebel against John and Jesus? Because they (the leaders) were intellectually and spiritually proud and would not become little babes in humility and honesty. There is a vast difference between the spoiled children of the parable (vv. 16-19) and the submissive children of this statement of praise. The Father reveals Himself to the Son, and the Son reveals Himself and the Father to those who are willing to come to the Son in faith. These verses indicate both the sovereignty of the Father and the responsibility of the sinner. Three commands summarize this invitation.

*"Come."* The Pharisees all said "Do!" and tried to make the people follow Moses and the traditions. But true salvation is found only in a person, Jesus Christ. To come to Him means to trust Him. This invitation is open to those who are exhausted and burdened down. That is exactly how the people felt under the yoke of Pharisaical legalism (Matt. 23:4; Acts 15:10).

*"Take."* This is a deeper experience. When we come to Christ by faith, *He gives* us rest. When we take His yoke and learn, *we find* rest, that deeper rest of surrender and obedience. The first is "peace with God" (Rom. 5:1); the second is "the peace of God" (Phil. 4:6-8). To "take a yoke" in that day meant to become a disciple. When we submit to Christ, we are yoked to Him. The word "easy" means "well-fitting"; He has just the yoke that is tailor-made for our lives and needs. The burden of doing His will is not a heavy one (1 John 5:3).

*"Learn."* The first two commands represent a crisis as we come and yield to Christ; but this step is into a *process*. As we learn more about Him, we find a deeper peace, because we trust Him more. Life is simplified and unified around the person of Christ. This invitation is for "all"—not just the people of Israel (Matt. 10:5-6).

### Rebellion against His Principles (12:1-21)

Jesus deliberately violated the Sabbath traditions on several occasions. He had taught the people that mere external laws could never save them or make them holy; true righteousness had to come from the heart. The Hebrew word *sabboth* means "repose or rest," which explains why Matthew introduced these Sabbath conflicts at this point. Jesus offers rest to all who will come to Him; there is no rest in mere religious observances.

It was lawful to satisfy your hunger from your neighbor's field (Deut. 23:24-25). But to do it on the Sabbath was a breach of the law according to the traditions of the scribes and Pharisees; for it meant doing work. Jesus gave a threefold reply to their accusation.

*He appealed to a king* (12:3-4). The consecrated bread was to be eaten only by the priests, yet David and his soldiers ate it. Certainly the Son of David had a right to eat His Father's grain from the field! And if David broke the law and was not condemned, surely Jesus could break man's traditions and be guiltless. See 1 Samuel 21:1ff.

*He appealed to the priests* (12:5-6). The priests had to offer a given number of sacrifices on the Sabbath (Num. 28:9-10) and yet were not condemned. In fact, their service was in obedience to the law given by God. This suggests that man's traditions about the Sabbath were wrong, for they contradicted God's own law.

*He appealed to a prophet* (12:7). The quotation is from Hosea 6:6, one that Jesus had already quoted (Matt. 9:13). The Sabbath law was given to Israel as a mark of her relationship to God (Neh. 9:12-15; Ex. 20:9-11; 31:13-17). But it was also an act of mercy for both man and beast, to give them needed rest each week. Any religious law that is contrary to mercy and the care of nature should be looked upon with suspicion. God wants mercy, not religious sacrifice. He wants love, not legalism. The Pharisees who sacrificed to obey their Sabbath laws thought they were serving God. When they accused Christ and His disciples, they thought they were defending God. How like religious legalists today!

Note that Jesus appealed to prophet, priest, and king; for He is Prophet, Priest, and King. Note, too, the three "greater" statements that He made: as the *Priest*, He is "greater than the temple" (v. 6); as *Prophet*, He is "greater than Jonah" (v. 41); and as *King*, He is "greater than Solomon" (v. 42).

In declaring Himself "Lord of the Sabbath," Jesus was actually affirming equality with God; for God had established the Sabbath (Gen. 2:1-3). He then proved this claim by healing the man with the paralyzed hand. It is sad that the religious leaders used this man and his handicap as a weapon to fight against Jesus. But the Lord was not afraid of their threats. Not doing good on the Sabbath Day (or any other day) is the same as doing evil. Jesus argued that if a farmer could care for his animals on the Sabbath, shouldn't we care for man, made in the image of God?

They responded to this deliberate challenge by plotting to kill Him. They had accused Him of blasphemy when He healed the paralytic (Matt. 9:1-8), and of lack of separation when He ate with Matthew's friends (Matt. 9:11-13). But this deed was even worse. He had deliberately violated the law of God! He had *worked* on the Sabbath by harvesting grain and healing a man.

Our Lord's response to their hatred was withdrawal. He did not openly fight His enemies, but fulfilled the prophecy in Isaiah 42:1-4. His enemies were but broken reeds and smoking flax. Note the double mention of the Gentiles, another hint from Matthew that Israel would reject her King and the kingdom would go to the Gentiles.

The Lord's withdrawal at this point is an anticipation of His "retirement" described in Matthew 14—20. During that time, Jesus avoided direct conflict with His enemies that He might stay on the "divine timetable" and be crucified. Also, during that time, He taught His disciples and prepared them for the crucifixion.

### Rebellion against His Power (12:22-37)

*The accusation* (12:22-24). The man that was brought to Jesus was certainly in a sad state, for he was blind, unable to speak, and possessed with a demon. Jesus delivered the man, something the Pharisees could not do. Their accusation was that He worked by the power of Satan and not by the power of God. They did not agree with Nicodemus' evaluation of His miracles (John 3:2).

*The answer* (12:25-30). Jesus pointed out that their statement was illogical and impractical. Why would Satan fight against himself? Jesus affirmed that Satan had a kingdom, for he is the god of this age (Matt. 4:8-9; John 12:31). He also stated that Satan had a "house," which seems to refer to the body of the man who was possessed (see 12:43-44). If Satan casts out his own demonic helpers, then he is opposing himself, dividing his kingdom, and destroying his house.

Their accusation was also illogical from their own point of view, although they did not see it. There were Jewish exorcists (see Acts 19:13-16) who apparently were successful. By whose power did *they* cast out demons? If it was by Satan's power, they were in league with the devil! Of course, no Pharisee was about to draw that conclusion.

Jesus was able to cast out demons because He had first defeated Satan, the prince of the demons. Jesus entered Satan's kingdom, overcame his power, and claimed his spoils. His victory was through the Spirit of God ("the finger of God," Luke 11:20) and not in the power of the evil one. This means that God is victor over Satan, and that men must decide on whose side they will stand. There can be no compromise. We are either with God or against God.

*The admonition* (12:31-37). Jesus warned them that their words gave evidence of the evil in their hearts. The sin against the Holy Spirit is not a matter of speech; the words spoken are only "fruit" from the sinful heart. If the heart is a treasury of good, that good will overflow through the lips and do good to others. But if the heart is a treasury of evil, that evil will spill over through the lips and do harm to the person speaking and those listening.

But what is this terrible "sin against the Holy Spirit"? Can it be committed today, and, if so, how? Our Lord said that God will forgive evil words spoken against the Son, but not against the Spirit. Does this mean that the Holy Spirit is more important than Jesus Christ, God's Son? Surely not. We often hear the name of God or Jesus Christ used in blasphemy, but rarely if ever the name of the Holy Spirit. How can God forgive words spoken against His Son, and yet not forgive words spoken against the Spirit?

It appears that this situation existed *only while Christ was ministering on earth*. Jesus did not appear to be different from any other Jewish man (Isa. 53:2). To speak against Christ could be forgiven *while He was on earth*. But when the Spirit of God came at Pentecost as proof that Jesus was the Christ, and was alive, to reject the witness of the Spirit was final. The only consequence would be judgment.

When the leaders rejected John the Baptist, they were rejecting *the Father* who sent him. When they rejected Jesus, they were rejecting *the*

*Son*. But when they rejected the ministry of the apostles, they rejected *the Holy Spirit*—and that is the end. There is no more witness. Such rejection cannot be forgiven.

The phrase "idle word" in verse 36 means "words that accomplish nothing." If God is going to judge our "small talk," how much more will He judge our deliberate words? It is by our conversation *at unguarded moments* that we reveal our true character.

Is there an "unpardonable sin" today? Yes, the final rejection of Jesus Christ. Jesus made it clear that *all* sins can be forgiven (v. 31). Adultery, murder, blasphemy, and other sins can all be forgiven; they are not unpardonable. But God cannot forgive the rejection of His Son. It is the Spirit who bears witness to Christ (John 15:26) and who convicts the lost sinner (John 16:7-11).

### Rebellion against His Person (12:38-50)

"The Jews require a sign" (1 Cor. 1:22). To ask for a sign was evidence of unbelief: They wanted Him to *prove* that He was the Messiah. We wonder what further proof could have been given! Had they searched their own Scriptures, and sincerely examined His life, they would have concluded, "This is the Son of God!" But for Jesus to have given them a sign would have been wrong. He would have catered to their unbelief and allowed them to set the standards for faith. No matter what miracle He performed, it would not have pleased them.

Jesus gave three responses to their challenge.

*He reviewed their history* (12:39-42). The prophet Jonah was a Jew sent to the Gentiles, and the Queen of Sheba was a gentile who came to visit Solomon, a Jew (2 Chron. 9:1-12). Because of the bitterness between the Jews and the Gentiles, this reference to the Gentiles must have irritated the Pharisees. But we have noted other occasions when either Jesus or Matthew mentioned the Gentiles.

Jonah was a sign to the people of Nineveh because he had experienced (in the great fish) death, burial, and resurrection. The only sign Jesus would give to His nation was death, burial, and resurrection. The messages in the first seven chapters of Acts center on the resurrection of Christ, not on His death on the cross. The Jews of that day believed that He had died, for this was the chief topic of conversation (Luke 24:18). *But they did not believe that He was alive* (Matt. 28:11-15). In Acts 2—7, the Holy Spirit gave to the nation of Israel abundant witness that Jesus was alive. This was the only sign they needed.

Jesus is greater than Jonah in many ways. He is greater in His person, for Jonah was a mere man. He was greater in His obedience, for Jonah disobeyed God and was chastened. Jesus actually died, while Jonah's "grave" was in the belly of the great fish. Jesus arose from the dead under His own power. Jonah ministered only to one city, while Jesus gave His life for the whole world. Certainly Jesus was greater in His love, for Jonah did not love the people of Nineveh—he wanted them to die. Jonah's message saved Nineveh from judgment; he was a messenger of the wrath of God. Jesus' message was that of grace and salvation. When we trust Christ, we are not only saved from judgment, but we receive eternal, abundant life.

Jesus is also greater than Solomon in His wisdom, wealth, and works. The Queen of Sheba was amazed at what she saw in Solomon's kingdom; but what we have in the kingdom of God through Christ far surpasses Solomon's glories. To sit at Christ's table and hear His words, and to share His blessings, is much more satisfying than to visit and admire the most spectacular kingdom, even that of Solomon.

The main lesson behind this history lesson is this: The citizens of Nineveh will witness against the rulers of Israel, for they repented at Jonah's preaching. The Queen of Sheba will also witness against them. She traveled a long distance to hear Solomon's wisdom, yet the Jewish leaders rejected the wisdom of Christ *who was in their very midst!* The greater the opportunity, the greater the judgment. It is a tragic feature in the history of Israel that the nation rejected their deliverers the first time, but accepted them the second time. This was true with Joseph, Moses, David, the prophets (Matt. 23:29), and Jesus Christ.

*He revealed their hearts* (12:43-45). We must connect these verses with Matthew 12:24-29. Satan's "house" is the body of the person who is possessed by the demon. It appears that the demons are restless and seek bodies in which to reside (8:28-31). When the demon left, this man's life was changed for the better; *but his life was still empty.* When the demon returned, he brought others with him; and the man's life ended in tragedy.

The primary application is to the nation of Israel, especially that generation present when Jesus ministered on earth. The nation had been purged of the demon of idolatry which had plagued them in the Old Testament. But reformation was not enough. Reformation could cleanse, but it could not fill. The nation should have received the Saviour and been filled with spiritual life. Instead, the people rejected Him and the end was destruction.

There is a personal application. It is not enough to clean house; we must also invite in the right tenant. The Pharisees were proud of their "clean houses," *but their hearts were empty!* Mere religion, or reformation, will not save. There must be regeneration, the receiving of Christ into the heart (see Rev. 3:20).

*He rejected their honor* (12:46-50). Even our Lord's earthly family did not fully understand Him or His ministry (John 7:1-5). Some of His friends thought He was mad (Mark 3:21). But Jesus did not want the honor that comes from people. While He was not disrespectful toward His physical family, He did emphasize the family of God.

Note His use of the word "whosoever" (v. 50). This paralleled His beautiful invitation in Matthew 11:28-30 where He encouraged all to trust Him. If the nation would not receive Him, at least individuals within the nation—and among the Gentiles—could trust Him. But what will happen to the promised kingdom?

# 10

# THE KING'S SECRETS

(Matthew 13)

This chapter records the events of a crisis day in the ministry of Jesus Christ. He knew that the growing opposition of the religious leaders would lead to His crucifixion. This fact He had to explain to His disciples. But their logical question would be, "What will happen to the kingdom about which we have been preaching?" That question is answered in this series of parables. So, He first explained the truth concerning the kingdom, and then later explained to them the facts about the cross.

Our Lord's use of parables puzzled the disciples. He had used some parables in His teaching already, but on that day He gave a series of seven interrelated parables, then added an eighth. The word *parable* means "to cast along side." It is a story, or comparison, that is put along side something else to help make the lesson clear. But these are not ordinary parables; Jesus called them "the mysteries of the kingdom of heaven" (13:11). In the New Testament, a "mystery" is a spiritual truth understood only by divine revelation. It is a "sacred secret" known only to those "on the inside" who learn from the Lord and obey Him.

In this series of parables, Jesus explained the course of the Gospel in the world. If Israel had received Him as King, the blessings would have flowed out from Jerusalem to the ends of the earth. But the nation rejected Him, and God had to institute a new program on earth. During this present age, "the kingdom of heaven" is a mixture of true and false, good and bad, as pictured in these parables. It is "Christendom," professing allegiance to the King, and yet containing much that is contrary to the principles of the King.

Why did Jesus teach in parables? Two reasons were given: because of the sluggishness of the people (13:10-17); and because it was prophesied in Psalm 78:2 (13:34-35). Jesus did not teach in parables to confuse or condemn the people. Rather, He sought to excite their interest and arouse their curiosity. These parables would give light to those with trusting, searching hearts. But they would bring darkness to the unconcerned and unrepentant.

The seven parables describe for us the spiritual course of "the kingdom of heaven" in this present age. In them we see three stages of spiritual development.

## The Beginning of the Kingdom (13:1-9, 18-23)

The parable of the sower does not begin with "The kingdom of heaven is like . . ." because it describes how the kingdom begins. It begins with the preaching of the Word, the planting of the seed in the hearts of people. When we say, "Let me plant this thought in your mind" we express the idea of this parable. The seed is God's Word; the various soils represent different kinds of hearts; and the varied results show the different responses to the Word of God. Jesus explained this parable so there is no doubt of its meaning.

Why compare God's Word to seed? Because the Word is "living and powerful" (Heb. 4:12, sco). Unlike the words of men, the Word of God has life in it; and that life can be imparted to those who will believe. The truth of God must take root in the heart, be cultivated, and permitted to bear fruit. It is shocking to realize that three-fourths of the seed did not bear fruit. Jesus did not describe an age of great harvest, but one in which the Word would be rejected. He was not impressed with the "great multitudes" that followed Him, for He knew that most of the people would not receive His Word within and bear fruit.

Fruit is the test of true salvation (Matt. 7:16). This would include holiness (Rom. 6:22), Christian character (Gal. 5:22-23), good works (Col. 1:10), winning others to Christ (Rom. 1:13), sharing what we have (Rom. 15:25-28), and praising God (Heb. 13:15). If a plant is to bear fruit, it must be rooted in soil and exposed to sunshine.

In the parable, the sun represents persecution that comes because of the Word. *Persecution helps believers grow.* But the sunshine will kill a plant with no roots. This explains why some "believers" do not last: Their faith was weak, their understanding was meager, and their decision was not sincere. It is possible to "believe" and yet not be saved (John 2:23-25). Unless there is fruit in the life, there is not saving faith in the heart.

Nineteen times in Matthew 13 we find the word "hear." The Parable of the Sower is found in the first three Gospels, and in each one, the closing admonition is different. It is important that we hear God's Word, because "Faith cometh by hearing, and hearing by the Word of God" (Rom. 10:17). Jesus said, "who hath ears to hear" (Matt. 13:9), "Take heed *what* you hear!" (Mark 4:24), and "Take heed *how* you hear!" (Luke 8:18).

## Opposition to the Kingdom (13:24-43)

Satan opposes the kingdom by trying to snatch the Word from hearts (13:4, 19). But when that fails, he has other ways of attacking God's work. These three parables reveal that Satan is primarily an *imitator*: He plants false Christians, he encourages a false growth, and he introduces false doctrine.

*The tares—false Christians* (13:24-30, 36-43). Satan cannot uproot the plants (true Christians), so he plants counterfeit Christians in their midst. In this parable, the good seed is not the Word of God. It represents people converted through trusting the Word. The field is not human hearts; the field is the world. Christ is sowing true believers in various places that they might bear fruit (John 12:23-26). But, wherever Christ sows a true Christian, Satan comes and sows a counterfeit.

We must beware of Satan's counterfeits. He has counterfeit Christians (2 Cor. 11:26) who believe a counterfeit Gospel (Gal. 1:6-9). He encourages a counterfeit righteousness (Rom. 10:1-3), and even has a counterfeit church (Rev. 2:9). At the end of the age, he will produce a counterfeit Christ (2 Thes. 2:1-12).

We must also stay awake to make sure that Satan's ministers do not get into the true fellowship and do damage (2 Peter 2; 1 John 4:1-6). It is when God's people go to sleep that Satan works. Our task is not to pull up the false, but to plant the true. (This does not refer to discipline within the local church.) We are not detectives but evangelists! We must oppose Satan and expose his lies. But we must also sow the Word of God and bear fruit in the place where He has planted us.

What will happen to the tares? God will gather them together and burn them. It is interesting to see that some of this "bundling" is already going on as various religious groups merge and strive for union. Spiritual unity among true Christians is one thing, but religious uniformity among mere professing Christians is quite another. It is difficult to tell the false from the true today; but at the end of the age, the angels will separate them.

*The mustard seed—false growth* (13:31-32). In the East, the mustard seed symbolizes something small and insignificant. It produces a large plant, but not a "tree" in the strictest sense. However, the plant is large enough for birds to sit in the branches.

Since Jesus did not explain this parable, we must use what He did explain in the other parables to find its meaning. The birds in the parable of the sower represented Satan (13:19). Passages like Daniel 4:12 and Ezekiel 17:23 indicate that a tree is a symbol of a world power. These facts suggest that the parable teaches an abnormal growth of the kingdom of heaven, one that makes it possible for Satan to work in it. Certainly "Christendom" has become a worldwide power with a complex organization of many branches. What started in a humble manner today boasts of material possessions and political influences.

Some make this parable teach the worldwide success of the Gospel. But that would contradict what Jesus taught in the first parable. If anything, the New Testament teaches a growing decline in the ministry of the Gospel as the end of the age draws near.

*The leaven—false doctrine* (13:33). The mustard seed illustrates the false *outward* expansion of the kingdom, while the leaven illustrates the *inward* development of false doctrine and false living. Throughout the Bible, leaven is a symbol of evil. It had to be removed from the Jewish homes during Passover (Ex. 12:15-19; 13:7). It was excluded from the sacrifices (Ex. 34:35), with the exception of the loaves used at the Feast of Pentecost (Lev. 23:15-21). But there the loaves symbolized Jews and Gentiles in the church, and there is sin in the church.

Jesus used leaven to picture hypocrisy (Luke 12:1), false teaching (Matt. 16:6-12), and worldly compromise (Matt. 22:16-21). Paul used leaven to picture carnality in the church (1 Cor. 5:6-8) as well as false doctrine (Gal. 5:9). Sin is like leaven (yeast): It quietly grows, it corrupts, and it "puffs up" (1 Cor. 5:2; 4:18-19; 8:1). It would seem that making the growth of the leaven a picture of the spread of the Gospel throughout the world would violate the meaning of this important symbol. It would also contradict the other parables.

Satan has worked hard to introduce false doctrine and false living into the ministry of the Word of God. From the very early days of the church, true believers have battled false doctrine and hypocrisy. How sad it is that some churches and schools that were once true to the Word have turned from the truth to fables. "Prove all things; hold fast that which is good" is sound counsel (1 Thes. 5:21).

The kingdom of heaven began with the sowing of the Word of God in the hearts of men. Much of the seed did not bear fruit; but some was fruitful. Satan opposed the work of God by sowing counterfeit Christians, by encouraging a false growth, and by introducing false doctrine. It would seem that Satan is winning! But the test is at *the end* of the age, not *during* the age.

### The Outcome of the Kingdom (13:44-50)

At the close of this age, God will have three peoples: the Jews (the hidden treasure), the church (the pearl), and the saved Gentile nations who will enter into the kingdom (the dragnet).

*The hidden treasure* (13:44). The common interpretation of this parable is that the sinner finds Christ and gives up all that he possesses to gain Him and be saved. But this interpretation presents several problems. To begin with, Jesus Christ is not a hidden treasure. He is perhaps the best-known person of history. In the second place, the sinner cannot "find Christ" for he is blind and stubborn (Rom. 3:10ff). It is the Saviour who finds the lost sinner (Luke 19:10). And no sinner could ever *purchase* salvation! Please note that the man in the parable did not purchase the treasure; he purchased *the whole field*. "The field is the world" (Matt. 13:38). Must the lost sinner purchase the world to gain Christ? Does he hide Him again?

Once again, Old Testament symbolism assists us in our interpretation. The treasure is the nation of Israel (Ex. 19:5; Ps. 135:4). That nation was placed in the world to bring glory to God, but it failed. It became a nation hidden, a treasure not being invested to produce dividends for God. Jesus

Christ gave His all to purchase the whole world in order to save the nation (John 11:51). On the cross, Jesus died for the whole world; but in a special way, He died for Israel (Isa. 53:8). The nation suffered judgment and seeming destruction, but in God's sight it is "hidden" and will be revealed again in glory.

There is, then, a future for Israel. Politically, the nation was reborn on May 14, 1948. But the nation is far from what it ought to be spiritually. God sees Israel as His treasure, and one day He will establish her in her glorious kingdom.

*The pearl of great price* (13:45-46). A well-known Gospel song perpetuates the interpretation that this pearl is Jesus Christ and His salvation. But the same objections apply to this interpretation as applied to the previous parable. The sinner does not find Christ; Christ finds the sinner. No sinner is able to pay for salvation, even though he sells all that he has.

The pearl represents the church. The Bible makes a distinction between Jews, Gentiles, and the church (1 Cor. 10:32). Today, the church, the body of Christ, is composed of believing Jews and Gentiles (Eph. 2:11ff). Unlike most other gems, the pearl is a *unity*—it cannot be carved like a diamond or emerald. The church is a unity (Eph. 4:4-6), even though the professing church on earth is divided. Like a pearl, the church is the product of suffering. Christ died for the church (Eph. 5:25) and His suffering on the cross made possible her birth.

A pearl grows gradually, and the church grows gradually as the Spirit convicts and converts sinners. No one can see the making of the pearl, for it is hidden in the shell of the oyster under the waters. No one can see the growth of His church in the world. The church is among the nations today (waters in the Bible represent nations, Dan. 7:1-3; Rev. 13:1; 17:15) and one day will be revealed in its beauty.

So, in spite of Satan's subtle working in this world, Christ is forming His church. He sold all that He had to purchase His church, and nothing Satan can do will cause Him to fail. There is but one church, a pearl of great price, though there are many local churches. Not everyone who is a member of a local church belongs to the one church, the body of Christ. It is only through repentance and faith in Christ that we become a part of His church. Of course, all true believers ought to identify with a local assembly where they can worship and serve.

*The net* (13:47-50). The preaching of the Gospel in the world does not convert the world. It is like a huge dragnet that gathers all kinds of fish, some good and some bad. The professing church today has in it both true and false believers (the parable of the tares) and good and bad. At the end of the age, God will separate the true believers from the false and the good from the bad. When Jesus Christ returns to earth, to fight the battle of Armageddon (Rev. 19:llff), He will separate believers and unbelievers *already on the earth*. These are living people who are not a part of the church (which was already in heaven) or Israel. These Gentiles will be dealt with in righteousness: The saved will enter into the kingdom, but the unsaved will be cast into the furnace of fire. The same idea is found in the "sheep and goats" parable (Matt. 25:31ff).

Twice in this series of parables Jesus used the phrase "the end of the world" (13:39, 49). He was not referring to the end of this "church age," because the truth about the church was not shared with the disciples until later (Matt. 16:18). The "age" He referred to is the Jewish age at the close of the great Tribulation described in Matthew 24:1-31 and Revelation 6—19. We must be careful not to "read into" these passages in Matthew the truths later given through Paul and the other apostles.

When Jesus had completed this series of parables, He asked His disciples if they understood them, and they confidently replied, "Yes, Lord." Understanding involves responsibility. To explain this, the Lord added a final parable (13:51-52) to remind them of their responsibilities.

*They must be scribes who discover the truth.* The scribes began as a noble group under the leadership of Ezra. Their purpose was to preserve the Law, study it, and apply its truths to daily life. Over the years, their noble cause degenerated into a routine task of preserving traditions and man-made interpretations, and adding burdens to the lives of the people (Luke 11:46-52). They were so wrapped up in the past that they ignored the present! Instead of sharing living truth from God's Word, they merchandised dead doctrines and "embalmed" traditions that could not help the people.

As believers, we do not search *after* truth, because we have truth in God's Son (John 14:6) and God's Word (John 17:17). We are taught by the Spirit of truth (John 16:13) who is truth (1 John 5:6). We search *into* truth that we might discover more truth. We are scribes—students—who sit at the feet of Jesus and listen to His words. One joy of the Christian life is the privilege of learning God's truth from God's Word. But we must not stop there.

*They must be disciples who do the truth.* "Therefore every scribe who becomes a disciple of the kingdom of heaven . . ." is a more accurate translation of verse 52. The scribe emphasizes *learning,* but the disciple emphasizes *living.* Disciples are doers of the Word (James 1:22ff), and they learn by doing.

It is difficult to keep our lives balanced. We often emphasize learning at the expense of living. Or, we may get so busy serving God that we do not take time to listen to His Word. Every scribe must be a disciple, and every disciple must be a scribe.

*They must be stewards who dispense the truth.* The scribes preserved the Law but did not invest it in the lives of the people. The treasure of the law was encrusted by man's traditions. The seed was not planted so it could bear fruit. The "spiritual gold and silver" was not put to work so it could produce dividends. As Christians we should be *con*servative but not *pre*servative.

The steward guards the treasure, but he also dispenses it as it is needed. He dispenses both the old and the new. New principles and insights are based on old truths. The new cannot contradict the old because the old comes out of the new (Lev. 26:10). The new without the old is mere novelty and will not last. But the old does no good unless it is given new applications in life today. We need both.

When Jesus finished these parables, He went across the sea in a storm and delivered the demoniacs in the country of the Gadarenes. Matthew recorded this in 8:28-34. It was then that Jesus went to His hometown of Nazareth, and this event Matthew recorded in 13:53-58.

Two things amazed the people of Nazareth: the Lord's words and His works. However, they did not trust in Him, and this limited His ministry. What caused the people to doubt Him? They were too familiar with Him in a human way, for He had grown up in their midst. It was a case of knowing Him after the flesh (see 2 Cor. 5:16) and not having the spiritual discernment that God gives to those who will yield to Him (Matt. 11:25-30). These people walked by sight and not by faith.

But, if His own friends and family did not trust Him, what hope was there that the nation would believe on Him? Early in His ministry, Jesus had preached at Nazareth (Luke 4:16-31) and had been rejected; and now

He was rejected again. This was His final visit to Nazareth; those villagers had no more opportunities. Jesus would be known as "Jesus of Nazareth," and His followers would be called "Nazarenes," but Nazareth would not receive Him. Matthew chose this event as a fitting close to the section "Rebellion against the King."

# 11

# THE KING'S WITHDRAWAL

(Matthew 14)

Chapters 14—20 I have called "The Retirement of the King." During the period of time recorded by Matthew in these chapters, Jesus often withdrew from the crowds and spent time alone with His disciples. (See 14:13; 15:21, 29; 16:13; 17:1-8.) There were several reasons for these withdrawals: the growing hostility of His enemies, the need for physical rest, and the need to prepare His disciples for His future death on the cross. Unfortunately, the disciples were often caught up in the excitement generated by the crowds that wanted to make Jesus their king. (See John 6:15.)

However, we must not think that these withdrawals, or periods of retirement from the crowds, were periods of inactivity. Often the crowds followed Jesus and He was unable to remain alone. He would unselfishly minister to their needs in spite of His own need for rest and solitude. In chapters 14—20, we will see these three groups of people: Christ's enemies, the needy multitudes, and the disciples. As the story reaches its climax, it appears that the enemies have won; but this is not true. In the closing chapter, Matthew describes the risen King commissioning His disciples to go into all the world and share the good news with the multitudes!

We see these same three groups of people in this chapter and our Lord's responses to them.

**His Enemies: Caution** (14:1-13)

The Herod family looms large in the four Gospels and the Book of Acts, and it is easy to confuse the various rulers.

*Herod the Great* founded the dynasty and ruled from 37 B.C. to A.D. 4. He was not a true Jew by birth, but was an Edomite, a descendant of Esau. "He was . . . a heathen in practice, and a monster in character" (*Unger's Bible Dictionary*). He had 9 wives (some say 10), and he thought nothing of slaying his own sons or wives if they got in the way of his plans. It was he who had the infants slain in Bethlehem (Matt. 2:13-18).

*Herod Antipas,* the Herod of this chapter, was a son of Herod the Great. His title was "tetrarch," which means "ruler over the fourth part of the kingdom." He ruled from 4 B.C. to A.D. 39, and his rule was deceptive and selfish. He loved luxury and was very ambitious to become a great ruler.

*Herod Agrippa* is the Herod who imprisoned Peter and killed James (Acts 12). He was a grandson of Herod the Great.

*Herod Agrippa II* was the Herod who tried Paul (Acts 25:13ff). He was a son of Agrippa I.

All of the Herods had Edomite blood in them, and, like their ancestor Esau, they were hostile to the Jews (Gen. 25:19ff). They practiced the Jewish religion when it helped fulfill their plans for gaining more power and wealth.

Herod Antipas was guilty of gross sin: He had eloped with Herodias, the wife of his half-brother Philip I, divorcing his own wife and sending her back to her father, the king of Petra (Lev. 18:16; 20:21). Herod listened to the voice of temptation and plunged himself into terrible sin.

But there were other voices that God sent to warn Herod.

*The voice of the prophet* (14:3-5). Boldly, John the Baptist warned Herod and called him to repent. John knew that the sin of a ruler would only pollute the land and make it easier for others to sin, and that God would judge the sinners (Mal. 3:5). We must commend John for his courage in naming sin and denouncing it. Israel was God's convenant nation, and the sins of the rulers (even though they were unbelievers) would bring the chastening of God.

Instead of listening to God's servant and obeying God's Word, Herod arrested John and imprisoned him. John was put in the fortress of

Machaerus, located about four miles east of the Dead Sea. It stood 3,500 feet above sea level on a rocky ridge that was accessible from only one side.

It was Herodias, Herod's wife, who held the grudge against John (see Mark 6:19, NASB); and she influenced her husband. She plotted to have her teenage daughter perform a lascivious dance at Herod's birthday feast. Herodias knew that her husband would succumb to her daughter's charms and make some rash promise to her. She also knew that Herod would want to "save face" before his friends and officials. The plot worked, and John the Baptist was slain.

*The voice of conscience* (14:1-2). When Herod heard of the marvelous works of Jesus, he was sure that John had been raised from the dead. His conscience was troubling him, and neither his wife nor his friends could console him. The voice of conscience is a powerful voice, and it can be the voice of God to those who will listen.

Instead of heeding his conscience, Herod determined to kill Jesus just as he had killed John. Some Pharisees (probably in on the plot) warned Jesus that Herod wanted to kill Him (Luke 13:31-32). But Jesus was not disturbed by the report. The word "fox" in Luke 13:32 is feminine. Jesus said, "Go, tell that vixen . . ." Was He perhaps referring to Herodias, the real power behind the throne?

*The voice of Jesus* (Luke 23:6-11). When he finally did meet Jesus, Herod found that the Son of God was *silent to him!* Herod had silenced the voice of God! "Today, if you will hear His voice, harden not your hearts . . ." (Heb. 3:7-8).

*The voice of history.* Herod should have known that he could not get away with his sin. History records that Herod lost prestige and power. His armies were defeated by the Arabs, and his appeals to be made a king (urged by his wife) were refused by Emperor Caligula. Herod was banished to Gaul (France) and then Spain, where he died.

Herod is remembered as a weak ruler whose only concern was his own pleasure and position. He did not serve the people, he served himself. He has the dubious honor of being the man who killed the greatest prophet ever sent to proclaim God's Word.

What was our Lord's response to the news of John's murder? *Caution*: He quietly withdrew from that area and went to a "lonely place." He lived according to a divine timetable (see John 2:4; 7:6; 7:30; 8:20;

12:23; 12:27; 13:1; 17:1), and He did not want to deliberately provoke trouble with Herod. Because Herod's agents were all around the Lord had to exercise wisdom and caution.

Certainly Jesus was deeply moved when He heard that John had been killed. The Jewish nation *permitted* John to be slain because they did nothing to assist him. But these same leaders would *ask* for Jesus to be slain! Jesus would never permit the Jewish rulers to forget the witness of John (Matt. 21:23ff). Because they rejected John's witness, they rejected their own Messiah and King.

### The Multitudes: Compassion (14:14-21)

Jesus and His disciples desperately needed rest (Mark 6:31); yet the needs of the multitudes touched His heart. The word translated "moved with compassion" literally means "to have one's inner being (viscera) stirred." It is stronger than sympathy. The word is used 12 times in the Gospels, and 8 of these references are to Jesus Christ.

Jesus was "moved with compassion" when He saw the needy multitudes (Matt. 9:36). They were like sheep that had been lacerated from brutal fleecing—torn, exhausted, and wandering. Twice He was "moved with compassion" when He beheld the hungry multitudes without food (Matt. 14:14; 15:32). The two blind men (Matt. 20:34) and the leper (Mark 1:41) also stirred His compassion, as did the sorrow of the widow at Nain (Luke 7:13).

Jesus used this word in three of His parables. The king had compassion on his bankrupt servant and forgave him his debt; and we ought to forgive one another (Matt. 18:21-35). The Samaritan had compassion on the Jewish victim and cared for him in love (Luke 10:25-37). The father had compassion on his wayward son and ran and greeted him when he came home (Luke 15:20). If our heavenly Father has such compassion toward us, should we not have compassion toward others?

The miracle of the feeding of the 5,000 is recorded in all four Gospels (Mark 6:35-44; Luke 9:12-17; John 6:4-13). It was definitely a miracle. Those who teach that Jesus only encouraged the people to bring out their own hidden lunches have ignored the clear statements of God's Word. John 6:14 definitely calls the event a "sign" or "miracle." Would the crowd have wanted to crown Jesus king simply because He tricked them into sharing their lunches? (John 6:14-15) Not likely!

It takes little imagination to picture the embarrassing plight of the disciples. Here were more than 5,000 hungry people and they had nothing to feed them! Certainly the disciples knew that Jesus was powerful enough to meet the need, yet they did not turn to Him for help. Instead, they took inventory of their own food supply (a lad had five barley loaves and two fish) and their limited treasury. When they considered the time (evening) and the place (a desolate place), they came to the conclusion that nothing could be done to solve the problem. Their counsel to the Lord was: "Send them away!"

How like many of God's people today. For some reason, it is never the right time or place for God to work. Jesus watched His frustrated disciples as they tried to solve the problem, but "He Himself knew what He was intending to do" (John 6:6, NASB). He wanted to teach them a lesson in faith and surrender. Note the steps we must take in solving life's problems.

*Start with what you have.* Andrew found a lad who had a small lunch, and he brought the lad to Jesus. Was the boy willing to give up his lunch? Yes, he was! God begins where we are and uses what we have.

*Give what you have to Jesus.* Jesus took the simple lunch, blessed it, and shared it. The miracle of multiplication was in His hands! "Little is much if God is in it." Jesus broke the bread and gave the pieces to the disciples, and they, in turn, fed the multitudes.

*Obey what He commands.* The disciples had the people sit down as Jesus ordered. They took the broken pieces and distributed them, and discovered that there was plenty for everybody. As His servants, we are "distributors," not "manufacturers." If we give what we have to Him, He will bless it and give it back to us to use in feeding others.

*Conserve the results.* There were 12 baskets filled with pieces of bread and fish after the people had eaten all they wanted. But these pieces were carefully collected so that nothing was wasted (Mark 6:43; John 6:12). I wonder how many of the pieces the lad took back home with him? Imagine his mother's amazement when the boy told her the story!

The Apostle John recorded a sermon on "the Bread of life" that Jesus gave the next day in the synagogue in Capernaum (John 6:22ff). The people were willing to receive the physical bread, but they would not receive the living Bread—the Son of God come down from heaven. The miracle of the feeding of the 5,000 was actually a sermon in action. Jesus is the Bread of Life, and only He can satisfy the spiritual hunger in man's heart. The tragedy is, men waste their time and money on "that which is not bread" (Isa. 55:1-7). People today are making the same mistake.

Jesus still has compassion on the hungry multitudes, and He still says to His church: "Give them something to eat." How easy it is for us to send people away, to make excuses, to plead a lack of resources. Jesus asks that we give Him all that we have and let Him use it as He sees fit. A hungry world is feeding on empty substitutes while we deprive them of the Bread of life. When we give Christ what we have, we never lose. We always end up with more blessing than when we started.

### The Disciples: Care and Concern (14:22-36)

John recorded the reason why Jesus was in such a hurry to dismiss the crowd and send the disciples back in the boat: The crowd wanted to make Jesus king (John 6:14-15). The Lord knew that their motives were not spiritual and that their purposes were out of God's will. If the disciples had stayed, they would certainly have fallen in with the plans of the crowd; for as yet, the disciples did not fully understand Christ's plans. They were guilty of arguing over "who was the greatest," and a popular uprising would have suited them perfectly.

This experience of the disciples in the storm can be an encouragement to us when we go through the storms of life. When we find ourselves in the storm, we can rest upon several assurances.

*"He brought me here."* The storm came because they were *in* the will of God and not (like Jonah) out of the will of God. Did Jesus know that the storm was coming? Certainly! Did He deliberately direct them into the storm? Yes! They were safer in the storm in God's will than on land with the crowds out of God's will. We must never judge our security on the basis of circumstances alone.

As we read our Bibles, we discover that there are two kinds of storms: storms of *correction*, when God disciplines us; and storms of *perfection*, when God helps us to grow. Jonah was in a storm because he disobeyed God and had to be corrected. The disciples were in a storm because they obeyed Christ and had to be perfected. Jesus had tested them in a storm before, when He was in the boat with them (Matt. 8:23-27). But now He tested them by being *out of the boat*.

Many Christians have the mistaken idea that obedience to God's will produces "smooth sailing." But this is not true. "In the world you shall have tribulation," Jesus promised (John 16:33). When we find ourselves in the storm because we have obeyed the Lord, we must remember that He brought us here and He can care for us.

*"He is praying for me."* This entire scene is a dramatic picture of the church and the Lord today. God's people are on the sea, in the midst of a storm. Yet Jesus Christ is in heaven "making intercession for us" (Rom. 8:34). He saw the disciples and knew their plight (Mark 6:48), just as He sees us and knows our needs. He feels the burdens that we feel and knows what we are going through (Heb. 4:14-16). Jesus was praying for His disciples, that their faith would not fail.

If you knew that Jesus Christ was in the next room, praying for you, would it not give you new courage to endure the storm and do His will? Of course it would. He is not in the next room, but He *is* in heaven interceding for you. He sees your need, He knows your fears, and He is in control of the situation.

*"He will come to me."* Often we feel like Jesus has deserted us when we are going through the hard times of life. In the Psalms, David complained that God seemed far away and unconcerned. Yet he knew that God would ultimately rescue him. Even the great Apostle Paul got into a situation that was so difficult he felt " . . . burdened excessively, beyond our strength, so that we despaired even of life" (2 Cor. 1:8, NASB).

Jesus always comes to us in the storms of life. "When you pass through the waters, I will be with you . . ." (Isa. 43:2a, NASB). He may not come at the time we think He should come, because He knows when we need Him the most. He waited until the ship was as far from land as possible, so that all human hope was gone. He was testing the disciples' faith, and this meant removing every human prop.

Why did Jesus walk on the water? To show His disciples that the very thing they feared (the sea) was only a staircase for Him to come to them. Often we fear the difficult experiences of life (such as surgery or bereavement), only to discover that these experiences bring Jesus Christ closer to us.

Why did they not recognize Jesus? Because they were not looking for Him. Had they been waiting by faith, they would have known Him immediately. Instead, they jumped to the false conclusion that the appearance was that of a ghost. Fear and faith cannot live in the same heart, for fear always blinds the eyes to the presence of the Lord.

*"He will help me grow."* This was the whole purpose of the storm, to help the disciples grow in their faith. After all, Jesus would one day leave them, and they would face many storms in their ministries. They had to learn to trust Him even though He was not present with them, and even though it looked as though He did not care.

Now our center of interest shifts to Peter. Before we criticize Peter for sinking, let's honor him for his magnificent demonstration of faith. He dared to be different. Anybody can sit in the boat and watch. But it takes a person of real faith to leave the boat and walk on the water.

What caused Peter to sink? His faith began to waver because he took his eyes off the Lord and began to look at the circumstances around him. "Why did you doubt?" Jesus asked him (v. 31). This word translated *doubt* carries the meaning of "standing uncertainly at two ways." Peter started out with great faith but ended up with little faith because he saw *two* ways instead of *one*.

We must give Peter credit for *knowing* that he was sinking and for crying out to the Lord for help. He cried out when he was "beginning to sink" and not when he was drowning. Perhaps this incident came to Peter's mind years later when he wrote in his first epistle: "For the eyes of the Lord are over the righteous, and His ears are open unto their prayers" (1 Peter 3:12).

This experience was difficult for Peter, but it helped him to grow in his knowledge of himself and of the Lord. The storms of life are not easy, but they *are* necessary. They teach us to trust Jesus Christ alone and to obey His Word no matter what the circumstances may be. It has well been said, "Faith is not believing in spite of evidence, but obeying in spite of consequence."

*"He will see me through."* If Jesus says "Come" then that word is going to accomplish its intended purpose. Since He is the "author and finisher of our faith" (Heb. 12:2), whatever He starts, He completes. We may fail along the way, but in the end, God will succeed. Jesus and Peter walked on the water *together* and went to the ship.

Peter's experience turned out to be a blessing to the other disciples as well as to himself. When they saw the power of Jesus Christ, in conquering and calming the storm, they could only fall down and worship Him.

When Jesus calmed the first storm (Matt. 8:23-27), the disciples said, "What manner of man is this?" But now their clear testimony was, "Thou art the Son of God!"

The disciples had helped to feed 5,000 people, and then God permitted them to go through a storm. In the Book of Acts, they won 5,000 people (Acts 4:4), and then *the storm of persecution began*. No doubt Peter and the disciples recalled their storm experience with the Lord and took courage.

This miracle magnifies the kingship of Jesus Christ. In fact, when Matthew wrote Peter's request "Bid me to come . . . ," he used a Greek word that means "the command of a king." Peter knew that Jesus Christ was King over all nature, including the wind and the waves. His word is law and the elements must obey.

The ship landed at Gennesaret, near Capernaum and Bethsaida; and there Jesus healed many people. Did these people know that He had come through a storm to meet their needs? Do *we* remember that He endured the storm of judgment to save our souls? (Ps. 42:7) He endured the storm for us that we might never face the judgment of God. We ought to imitate the disciples, bow at His feet, and acknowledge that He is King of kings and Lord of lords!

# 12

# THE
# KING'S
# CONCERN

(Matthew 15)

As in the previous chapter, we see the Lord in conflict with His enemies (15:1-11), teaching His own disciples (15:12-20), and ministering to the needy multitudes (15:21-31). This is the pattern during this period of withdrawal.

Our Lord's great concerns are *truth* and *love*. He taught the Jewish leaders the *truth* and exposed their hypocrisy, and He showed the Gentile crowds *love* as He met their needs. By studying these two concerns, we can understand the message of this chapter.

**Truth: He Rejected Jewish Tradition** (15:1-20)
This dramatic event involved three requests and three replies.

*The Scribes and Pharisees* (vv. 1-11). The fact that the scribes and Pharisees united in this attack, and came all the way from Jerusalem to speak to Jesus, indicates the seriousness of their purpose. It is likely that this committee represented the leaders of the Sanhedrin in Jerusalem.

Their accusation about "washing hands" had nothing to do with cleanliness. They were referring to the ceremonial washings of the rigidly orthodox Jews (see Mark 7:1-4). It was bad enough that Jesus and His disciples mingled with outcasts, but they did not even seek to be purified! Of course, in making this accusation, these religious leaders were forcing Jesus to deal with the very *foundation* of their religious faith. If Jesus rejected the sacred traditions of the nation, then He was a heretic!

Where did these traditions come from? They were handed down from the teachers of previous generations. These traditions were originally the "oral law" which (said the rabbis) Moses gave to the elders, and they passed down to the nation. This oral law was finally written down and became the *Mishnah*. Unfortunately, the *Mishnah* became more important and more authoritative than the original Law of Moses.

Our Lord's reply to their charge began with *an accusation* (v. 3). It was *they* who were breaking God's Law by practicing their traditions! He then proceeded with an illustration (vv. 4-6), their practice of "Corban" (see Mark 7:11). The Hebrew word *Corban* means "a gift." If a Jew wanted to escape some financial responsibilities, he would declare his goods to be "Corban—a gift to God." This meant he was free from other obligations, such as caring for his parents. But in so doing, the person was losing the power of God's Word in his life, and thus hurting his character and missing God's blessing.

Jesus concluded His reply with an *application* (vv. 7-11), quoting Isaiah 29:13. Jesus made it clear that obedience to tradition made a person disobedient to the Word of God; and this proved the tradition to be false. Exodus 20:12 taught a man to "honor" father and mother. But the "Corban" rule would make a person dishonor his parents, and, at the same time, disobey God.

Tradition is something *external*, while God's truth is *internal*, in the heart. People obey tradition to please men and gain status (Gal. 1:14), but we obey the Word to please God. Tradition deals with *ritual*, while God's truth deals with *reality*. Tradition brings empty words to the lips, but truth penetrates the heart and changes the life. Actually, tradition robs a person of the power of the Word of God.

Unfortunately, there are many "evangelical traditions" in churches today, man-made teachings that are often considered as authoritative as the Word of God—*even though they contradict His Word*. By obeying these traditions, Christians rob themselves of the power of God's Word.

God wants us to give Him our hearts, and not just our lip service. We *believe* in the heart (Rom. 10:9-10), *love* from the heart (Matt. 22:37), *sing* from the heart (Col. 3:16), *obey* from the heart (Eph. 6:6; Rom. 6:17), and *give* from the heart (2 Cor. 9:7). No wonder David prayed, "Create in me a clean heart, O God!" (Ps. 51:10)

Jesus declared boldly to the multitudes that sin comes from the heart, not from the diet. It is what comes out of the mouth that defiles us, not what goes in.

*The disciples* (vv. 12-14). The disciples were astounded by what Jesus taught about foods. After all, they had been raised good Jews (see Acts 10:14 for Peter's testimony). They knew the difference between the "clean" and "unclean" foods (Lev. 11).

But the disciples had another concern: This teaching had offended the Pharisees and was certain to create serious problems. But Jesus was not worried about the Pharisees. Neither they nor their teachings had been planted by God, and therefore would not last. While there are isolated groups that seek to maintain the traditions, for the most part, Phariseeism is gone. However, the *spirit* of Phariseeism (tradition, legalism, hypocrisy, externals) is still with us, what Jesus called "the leaven of the Pharisees" (16:6).

Jesus also pointed out that the Pharisees were blind and could only lead their converts into the ditch. In Matthew 23:16, He called them "blind guides"—quite a graphic description. Why be afraid of rootless plants that are dying, or blind guides who cannot see where they are going?

*Peter* (vv. 15-20). Peter was not content until he had an explanation of the saying about foods. Patiently our Lord explained the lesson again. The meaning seems obvious to us, but it was astonishingly new to orthodox Jews. Whatever enters the mouth eventually goes into the stomach and comes out in human waste. Food never touches the heart. But what comes out of the mouth *begins* in the heart, and these things defile a person. Of course, *actions* are included with *words*; often actions speak louder than words.

The Lord had to repeat this lesson on foods to Peter a few years later when He was going to call him to preach to the Gentiles (Acts 10). Paul repeated it in 1 Timothy 4:3-6. He also dealt with it in Romans 14—15.

## Compassion: He Responded to Gentile Needs (15:21-39)

Not only did Jesus *teach* that no foods were unclean, but He practiced His teaching by going into Gentile territory. He left Israel and withdrew again, this time into the area of Tyre and Sidon. The Gentiles were "unclean" as far as the Jews were concerned. In fact, Jews referred to the Gentiles as "dogs." That Jesus would minister to Gentiles was no surprise (Matt. 12:17-21), although at that time, the emphasis was on ministering to Israel (10:5-6).

*The demonized* (vv. 21-28). Jesus was trying to remain hidden (Mark 7:24), but somehow this Canaanite woman heard where He was and came to Him with her need. Keep in mind that our Lord responded to this woman as He did, not to destroy her faith, but to develop it. Her own replies showed that she was growing in faith and unwilling to let Him go without getting an answer. Godly Samuel Rutherford stated this principle perfectly: "It is faith's work to claim and challenge lovingkindness out of all the roughest strokes of God."

When she approached Him as "Son of David," she was definitely putting herself on Jewish ground; and this she could not do, because she was a Gentile. Of course, this title did reveal her faith in Him as the Messiah of God, for "Son of David" was a name for the Messiah (Matt. 22:42). Since she came to Him on Jewish terms, He was silent. Of course, He knew her heart, and even His silence encouraged her to continue asking.

Impatient with her persistent following and crying out, the disciples said, "Send her away!" We are not sure whether they meant, "Give her what she wants and get rid of her" or just "Get rid of her!" In either case, they were not showing much compassion for either her or her demonized daughter. Our Lord's reply in verse 24 indicates that they probably wanted Him to answer her request.

We cannot but admire the patience and persistence of this Gentile mother. "Lord, help me!" was her next plea; and this time she avoided any messianic titles. She came as a sinner needing help, and she offered no argument. In His reply, Jesus did not call her a "dog" the way the Pharisees would have addressed a Gentile. The Greek word means "a little pet dog" and not the filthy curs that ran the streets and ate the garbage. "The children" referred, of course, to the people of Israel.

Jesus was not playing games with the woman, nor was He trying to make the situation more difficult. He was drawing out of her a growing response of faith. She immediately seized upon His illustration about the children's bread, *which was exactly what He wanted her to do*. We may paraphrase her reply: "It is true that we Gentiles do not sit at the table as children and eat the bread. But even the pet dogs under the table can eat some of the crumbs!" What a tremendous testimony of faith!

It was this faith that Jesus acknowledged, and immediately He healed her daughter. It is worth noting that both of the persons in the Gospel of Matthew who had "great faith" were Gentiles: this Canaanite woman and the Roman centurion (Matt. 8:5-13). In both cases, Jesus healed the one in need *from a distance*. Spiritually speaking, the Gentiles were "afar off" until Calvary, when Jesus Christ died for both Jews and Gentiles and made reconciliation possible (Eph. 2:11ff).

This woman's faith was great because she persisted in asking and trusting when everything seemed against her. Certainly her race was against her: She was a Gentile. Her sex was against her, for most Jewish rabbis paid little attention to women. It seemed that the disciples were against her, and Christ's words might have led her to believe that even *He* was against her. All of these obstacles only made her persist in asking.

*The sick and handicapped* (vv. 29-31). Jesus departed from the borders of Tyre and Sidon and went to the region of the Decapolis. The Decapolis included 10 cities that were in a league and were authorized by the Romans to mint their own coins, run their own courts, and have their own army. This was predominantly Gentile territory.

Jesus healed there a man who was deaf and dumb (Mark 7:31-37). Even though the Lord cautioned the man to be silent, he and his friends spread the account of the miracle abroad. This apparently caused a great crowd to gather—including people who were lame, blind, dumb, and crippled (maimed). Jesus healed these people, and the Gentiles "glorified the God of Israel."

We cannot help but marvel at the contrast between these Gentiles and the Jewish leaders who knew the Old Testament Scriptures. The Gentiles glorified Israel's God, but the Jewish leaders said that Jesus was in league with Satan (Matt. 12:22-24). Our Lord's miracles did not cause the Jewish cities to repent (Matt. 11:20ff), yet the Gentiles believed in Him. The very miracles that He performed should have convinced the Jews that He was the Messiah (Matt. 11:1-6; Isa. 29:18-19, 35:4-6). Jesus marvelled at the faith of a Gentile soldier and a Gentile mother. Yet He was amazed at the unbelief of His own people (Mark 6:6).

*The hungry* (vv. 32-39). Critics have accused the Gospel writers of deliberately falsifying the records in order to prove that Jesus performed more miracles. They claim that the feeding of the 4,000 was merely an adaptation of the previous miracle of feeding 5,000. A careful examination of the records shows that this accusation is false and that the critics are wrong. This chart shows the differences between the two events.

| *Feeding 5,000* | *Feeding 4,000* |
| --- | --- |
| Primarily Jews | Primarily Gentiles |
| Galilee, near Bethsaida | The Decapolis |
| 5 loaves, 2 fish | 7 loaves, "a few fish" |
| 12 baskets over | 7 baskets over |
| Crowd with Him 1 day | Crowd with Him 3 days |
| Spring of year (green grass) | Summer season |
| Tried to make Him king | No popular response |

Since the crowd of 4,000 had been with Him three days, they had used up their own supplies of food. Our Lord's compassionate heart would not permit Him to send them on their way hungry, lest they faint along the way. The first motive for this miracle was simply the meeting of human needs. The people had already seen His miracles and glorified God, so the miracle was not for the purpose of preaching a sermon or authenticating His ministry.

However, this miracle did have a special purpose for His disciples. We are amazed that they had forgotten the miracle of the feeding of the 5,000. (Read carefully Matt. 16:6-12.) The 12 were perplexed when they should have been saying, "Jesus is able to multiply loaves and fish, so we have no need to worry!" Of course, it may be that they thought He would not perform that kind of a miracle in Gentile territory. Or, perhaps the fact that the previous crowd had tried to make Him king would cause Jesus to avoid repeating the miracle.

As in the feeding of the 5,000, this miracle took place in His hands. As Jesus broke the bread and gave it to His disciples, the bread multiplied. Everybody ate and everybody was satisfied. Again, Jesus ordered the fragments to be collected so that nothing be wasted. The ability to perform miracles does not grant the authority to waste God's gifts.

The word translated *baskets* in verse 37 means "a large hamper." It is the same kind of basket that was used to lower Paul over the Damascus wall (Acts 9:25). The word for *basket* in Matthew 14:20 means "a wicker basket,'' the kind a person carried with food or other goods in it. The fact that these two different words are used is further proof that the two miracles are different.

Jesus did not preach a sermon to this crowd on "the bread of life" as He did to the Jews in Capernaum, following the feeding of the 5,000 (John 6:22ff). The facts about the Old Testament manna and the "bread of God" would have been foreign to these Gentiles. Jesus always adapted His teaching to the needs and the understanding of the people to whom He ministered.

Before leaving Matthew 15, let's review several spiritual lessons that it contains for us.

(1)   The enemies of truth are often religious people who live according to man's traditions. Satan often uses "religion" to blind the minds of sinners to the simple truths of God's Word.

(2)   We must beware of any religious system that gives us an excuse to sin and disobey God's Word.

(3)   We must also beware of worship that comes from the lips only, and not from the heart.

(4)   If we major on the inner man, the outer man will be what God wants it to be. True holiness comes from within.

(5)   It is difficult to break free from tradition. There is something in us that wants to hold to the past and make no changes. Even Peter had to learn his lesson twice!

(6)   ¯We dare not limit Christ to any one nation or people. The Gospel came "to the Jew first" (Rom. 1:16), but today is for all men in all nations. "Whosoever shall call upon the name of the Lord shall be saved" (Rom. 10:13).

# 13

# THE KING'S SURPRISE

(Matthew 16)

The events recorded in Matthew 16 form a dramatic turning point in our Lord's ministry. For the first time, He mentioned the church (v. 18) and openly spoke about His death on the cross (v. 21). He began to prepare the disciples for His arrest, crucifixion, and resurrection. But, as we shall see, they were slow to learn their lessons.

The theme of *faith* runs through the events in this chapter. In these events, we see four different levels of faith and how they relate to Christ.

## No Faith—Tempting Christ (16:1-4)

Their desire to silence Jesus had caused the two opposing religious parties to unite in one common effort. They were waiting for Him when He returned to Galilee. The Pharisees, of course, were the traditionalists of their day, while the Sadducees were quite liberal (see Acts 23:6-10). They united to issue a challenge to Jesus: "Show us a sign from heaven and we will believe you are the Christ."

The word translated *sign* means much more than simply a miracle or a demonstration of power. It means "a wonder by which one may recognize a person or confirm who he is."

This was the fourth time the religious leaders had asked for a sign (John 2:18; Matt. 12:38ff; John 6:30). Later, they did it again (Luke 11:14ff).

But miracles do not convince people of sin or give a desire for salvation (Luke 16:27-31; John 12:10-11; Acts 14:8-20). Miracles will give confirmation where there is faith, but not where there is willful unbelief.

Why did our Lord talk about the weather? To reveal to His enemies their own dishonesty and stubborn blindness. They could examine the evidence in God's world and draw valid conclusions, but they would not examine the evidence He had presented. His enemies *would not* believe, and therefore they *could not* believe (John 12:37ff). The Pharisees and Sadducees did not lack evidence; they lacked honesty and humility.

Their demand for a sign revealed the sad condition of their hearts: they were evil and adulterous. He did not accuse them of being guilty of physical adultery, but of spiritual adultery (Isa. 57; James 4:4). These men were worshiping a false God of their own manufacture, and this was spiritual adultery. Had they been worshiping the true God, they would have recognized His Son when He came.

Jesus had mentioned the sign of Jonah before (see 12:38-45). This was the sign of death, burial, and resurrection. Our Lord's crucifixion, burial, and resurrection were actually a sign to Israel that He was their Messiah. It was this sign that Peter preached about at Pentecost (Acts 2:22ff).

Verse 4 records the Lord's third departure from Galilee. He departed before to avoid Herod (Matt. 14:13) and to avoid the Pharisees (15:21). It was certainly an act of judgment.

## Little Faith—Misunderstanding Christ (16:5-12)
The disciples had but one loaf of bread with them (Mark 8:14). We are not told what happened to the many baskets of leftover food that resulted from His feeding the 4,000 just a short time before. Perhaps they gave it away. Jesus used this embarrassing event as an occasion to teach an important spiritual truth: Beware of the false teachings of the Pharisees and Sadducees.

The disciples misunderstood Him; they thought He was talking about material bread. Often in the ministry of Jesus, people misinterpreted His words by interpreting them literally rather than spiritually. Nicodemus thought that Jesus was talking about an actual physical birth (John 3:4), and the Samaritan woman thought He was referring to material water from the well (John 4:11). The Jewish crowd in the synagogue thought Jesus was speaking about eating actual flesh and blood (John 6:52ff) when He was describing a spiritual experience (John 6:63).

As we noted in our study of Matthew 13, leaven was to the Jews a symbol of evil. Both the Pharisees and the Sadducees had infected the religious beliefs of Israel with false doctrine. The Pharisees were legalists who taught that only obedience to the Law and the traditions would please God and usher in His kingdom for Israel. The Sadducees were liberal in their thinking and denied that there would be such a kingdom on earth. They even denied the truth of the resurrection and the existence of angels.

Why would the Lord's mention of leaven cause the disciples to discuss their lack of bread? Possibly they were planning to purchase bread on the other side of the sea, and they thought Jesus was cautioning them not to buy unclean bread which Jews could not eat. If they had remembered how Jesus had multiplied bread on two occasions, they certainly would not have worried. Their "little faith" kept them from understanding His teaching and depending on His power to meet their needs.

"Little faith" was one of our Lord's favorite names for His disciples (Matt. 6:30, 8:26, 14:31). Of course, "little faith" is better than *no* faith. The disciples had many lessons to learn before they would graduate to "great faith."

### Saving Faith—Confessing Christ (16:13-20)

Jesus took His disciples to Gentile territory, in the region of Caesarea Philippi. They were about 120 miles from Jerusalem in the northern part of Palestine. The region was strongly identified with various religions: It had been a center for Baal worship; the Greek god Pan had shrines there; and Herod the Great had built a temple there to honor Augustus Caesar. It was in the midst of this pagan superstition that Peter confessed Jesus as the Son of God. And it was probably within sight of Caesar's temple that Jesus announced a surprise: He would not yet establish His kingdom, but He would build His church.

If anyone else asked, "Whom do men say that I am?" we would think him either mad or arrogant. But in the case of Jesus, a right confession of who He is is basic to salvation (Rom. 10:9-10; 1 John 2:18-23; 4:1-3). His Person and His work go together and must never be separated. It is amazing to see how confused the public was about Jesus (John 10:19-21). Perhaps, like Herod, the people thought Jesus was John raised from the dead.

It had been prophesied that Elijah would come again (Mal. 4:5), and some thought that this prediction was fulfilled in Christ. However, Jesus did not minister as did Elijah; it was John the Baptist who came "in the spirit and power of Elias" (Luke 1:13-17). Jeremiah was the weeping prophet whose tender heart was broken at the sight of the decay of the nation. Certainly this attitude was seen in Jesus, the Man of sorrows.

One thing is clear: We can never make a true decision about Jesus Christ by taking a poll of the people. (But some people *do* get their "spiritual knowledge" this way.) The important thing is not what others say, but what do you and I personally say? The decisions of the crowd (wrong or right) can never substitute for personal decisions.

Peter had the correct response: "Thou art the Christ (the Messiah), the Son of the living God!" This confession was Peter's response to the revelation God the Father had given him. Jesus Himself explained this experience in Matthew 11:25-27. This revelation was not the result of Peter's own investigation. It came as the gracious act of God. God had hidden these things from the proud Pharisees and Sadducees and revealed them to "babes," the humble disciples.

It should be noted that there had been other confessions of faith prior to this one. Nathanael had confessed Christ as the Son of God (John 1:49), and the disciples had declared Him God's Son after He stilled the storm (Matt. 14:33). Peter had given a confession of faith when the crowds left Jesus after His sermon on the bread of life (John 6:68-69). In fact, when Andrew had brought his brother Simon to Jesus, it was on the basis of this belief (John 1:41).

How, then, did *this* confession differ from those that preceded it? To begin with, *Jesus explicitly asked for this confession.* It was not an emotional response from people who had seen a miracle, but the studied and sincere statement of a man who had been taught by God.

Also, Jesus *accepted this confession* and built upon it to teach them new truth. It must have rejoiced His heart to hear Peter's words. The Lord knew that Peter could now be led into new steps of deeper truth and service. All of our Lord's ministry to His disciples had prepared the way for this experience. Let's look at these great words and concepts individually.

*Rock*—These Jewish men, steeped in Old Testament Scripture, recognized the rock as a symbol of God. "He is the Rock, His work is perfect . . ." (Deut. 32:4). "The Lord is my rock, any my fortress . . ." (Ps. 18:2). "For who is God save the Lord? Or who is a rock save our God?" (Ps. 18:31)

But let's investigate the Greek words that the Holy Spirit led Matthew to use. "Thou art *petros* [a stone], and upon this rock [*petra*—a large rock] I will build My church." Jesus had given Simon the new name of *Peter* (John 1:42) which means "a stone." The Aramaic form is *Cephas*, which also means "a stone." Everyone who believes in Jesus Christ and confesses Him as the Son and God and Saviour, is a "living stone" (1 Peter 2:5, NASB).

Jesus Christ is the foundation rock on which the church is built. The Old Testament prophets said so (Isa. 28:16; Ps. 118:22). Jesus Himself said this (Matt. 21:42), and so did Peter and the other apostles (Acts 4:10-12). Paul also stated that the foundation for the church is Jesus Christ (1 Cor. 3:11). This foundation was laid by the apostles and prophets as they preached Christ to the lost (Eph. 2:20; 1 Cor. 2:1-2; 3:11).

In other words, when the evidence is examined, the total teaching of Scripture is that the church, God's temple (Eph. 2:19-22), is built on Jesus Christ—not on Peter. How could God build His church on a fallible man like Peter? Later, the same Peter who confessed Christ became an adversary and entertained Satan's thoughts (16:22ff). "But that was before Peter was filled with the Spirit," some argue. Then consider Peter's doctrinal blunders recorded in Galatians 2, blunders that had to be dealt with by Paul. This event occurred *after* Peter was filled with the Spirit.

*Church*—This is the first occurrence of this important word in the New Testament. It is the Greek word *ekklesia* (ek-klay-SEE-uh) from which we get our English word "ecclesiastical," referring to things that pertain to the church. The literal meaning is "a called-out assembly." The word is used 114 times in the New Testament and in 90 of these references, a local church (assembly) is in view. However, in this first use of *ekklesia*, it seems likely that Jesus had the whole church in mind. He was not just building a local assembly, but a universal church composed of all who make the same confession of faith that Peter made.

The word *ekklesia* was not new to the disciples. This word was applied to the popular assembly of Greek citizens that helped to govern a city or district (Acts 19:32, 39, 41). Also, the Greek translation of the Old Testament (the Septuagint) used *ekklesia* to describe the congregation of Israel when it was gathered for religious activity (Deut. 31:30; Jud. 20:2). However, this does not mean that the Old Testament congregation of Israel was a "church" in the same sense as the churches of the New Testament. Rather, Jesus was introducing something new to His disciples.

Jesus spoke about "My church" in contrast to these other assemblies. This was to be something new and different, for in His church, Jesus Christ would unite believing Jews and Gentiles and form a new temple, a new body (Eph. 2:11—3:12). In His church, natural distinctions would be unimportant (Gal. 3:28). Jesus Christ would be the Builder of this church, the Head of this church (Eph. 1:22; Col. 1:18).

Each believer in this church is a "living stone" (1 Peter 2:5). Believers would meet in local congregations, or assemblies, to worship Christ and to serve Him; but they would also belong to a universal church, a temple being built by Christ. There is a oneness to the people of God (Eph. 4:1-6) that ought to be revealed to the world by love and unity (John 17:20-26).

*Gates of hell*—A better translation would be "gates of hades." Hell is the final destiny of all unsaved people after the judgment of the great white throne (Rev. 20:11-15). *Hades* is simply "the realm of the dead." It holds the spirits of the unsaved dead and releases them at the resurrection (Rev. 20:13; where "hell" ought to read "hades"). According to Jesus, hades is down (Matt. 11:23), and it is a prison to which He holds the keys (Rev. 1:18).

On the basis of Luke 16:19-31, some people believe that *all* the dead went to hades prior to the death and resurrection of Christ—believers to a paradise portion and unbelievers to a punishment portion. We are certain that believers today, when they die, go immediately into the presence of Christ (Phil. 1:23; 2 Cor. 5:6-8).

"Gates" represent, in the Bible, authority and power. The city gate was to a Jew what city hall is to people in the Western world. Important business was transacted at the city gate (Deut. 16:18; 17:8; Ruth 4:11). "The gates of hades" then would symbolize the organized power of death and Satan. By His death and resurrection, Jesus Christ would conquer death, so that death would not be able to hold any of His people. Christ would "storm the gates" and deliver the captives! This declaration certainly is verified by Hebrews 2:14-15; 1 Corinthians 15:50ff; and other Scriptures.

*Keys of the kingdom*—A key is a badge of authority (Isa. 22:15, 22; Luke 11:52). "The kingdom of heaven" is *not* heaven, for no man on earth carries the keys to heaven! (All of the jokes about "St. Peter at the gate" stem from this misunderstanding. They are both unbiblical and in bad taste.) We use keys to open doors. Peter was given the privilege of opening "the door of faith" to the Jews at Pentecost (Acts 2), to the Samaritans (Acts 8:14ff), and to the Gentiles (Acts 10). But the other apostles shared this authority (Matt. 18:18), and Paul had the privilege of "opening the door of faith" to the Gentiles outside of Palestine (Acts 14:27).

Nowhere in this passage, or in the rest of the New Testament, are we told that Peter or his successors had any special position or privilege in the church. Certainly Peter in his two epistles claimed to be nothing more than an apostle (1 Peter 1:1), an elder (5:1), and a servant of Jesus Christ (2 Peter 1:1).

*Binding and loosing*—This was a very familiar phrase to the Jews, for their rabbis often spoke of "binding and loosing," that is, forbidding or permitting. Our Lord's statement in 16:19 referred to Peter. But His statement later in 18:18 included all of the apostles. As the representatives of their Lord, they would exercise authority according to His Word.

The Greek verbs in verse 19 are most important. The *Expanded Translation* by Dr. Kenneth S. Wuest reads: " . . . and whatever you bind on earth [forbid to be done], shall have been already bound. . .in heaven; and whatever you loose on earth [permit to be done], shall have already been loosed in heaven. . . ." Jesus did not say that God would obey what they did on earth, but that they should do on earth whatever God had already willed. The church does not get man's will done in heaven; it obeys God's will on earth.

The apostles were not to share this truth about Jesus being the Son of God with other people until after His resurrection and ascension. Then the "sign of Jonah" would be completed, the Spirit would be given, and the message could be proclaimed. The nation in general, and certainly the religious leaders in particular, were not yet ready for this message. Read Peter's sermon at Pentecost and see how he proclaimed Jesus as the Christ (Acts 2).

**Serving Faith—Following Christ** (16:21-28)

Having declared His person, Jesus now declared His work; for the two must go together. He would go to Jerusalem, suffer and die, and be raised from the dead. This was His first clear statement of His death, although He had hinted at this before (John 2:19; 3:14; 6:51; Matt. 12:39-40, 16:4). "And He was stating the matter plainly" (Mark 8:32, NASB).

Peter's response to this shocking statement certainly represented the feelings of the rest of the disciples: "Pity Thyself, Lord! This shall never happen to Thee!" Jesus turned His back on Peter and said, "Get behind Me, adversary! You are a stumbling block to Me!" (literal translation) Peter the "stone" who had just been blessed (v. 18) became Peter the stumbling block who was not a blessing to Jesus!

What was Peter's mistake? He was thinking like a man, for most men want to escape suffering and death. He did not have God's mind in the matter. Where do we find the mind of God? In the Word of God. Until Peter was filled with the Spirit, he had a tendency to argue with God's Word. Peter had enough faith to confess that Jesus was the Son of God, but he did not have the faith to believe it was right for Jesus to suffer and die. Of course, Satan agreed with Peter's words, for he used the same approach to tempt Jesus in the wilderness (Matt. 4:8-10).

Today the cross is an accepted symbol of love and sacrifice. But in that day the cross was a horrible means of capital punishment. The Romans would not mention the cross in polite society. In fact, no Roman citizen could be crucified; this terrible death was reserved for their enemies. Jesus had not yet specifically stated that He would be crucified (He did this in Matt. 20:17-19). But His words that follow emphasize the cross.

He presented to the disciples two approaches to life:

| | |
|---|---|
| deny yourself | live for yourself |
| take up your cross | ignore the cross |
| follow Christ | follow the world |
| lose your life for His sake | save your life for your own sake |
| forsake the world | gain the world |
| keep your soul | lose your soul |
| share His reward and glory | lose His reward and glory |

To deny self does not mean to deny things. It means to give yourself wholly to Christ and share in His shame and death. Paul described this in Romans 12:1-2 and Philippians 3:7-10, as well as in Galatians 2:20. To take up a cross does not mean to carry burdens or have problems. (I once met a lady who told me her asthma was the cross she had to bear!) To take up the cross means to identify with Christ in His rejection, shame, suffering, and death.

But suffering always leads to glory. This is why Jesus ended this short sermon with a reference to His glorious kingdom (v. 28). This statement would be fulfilled within a week on the Mount of Transfiguration, described in the next chapter.

# 14

# THE KING'S GLORY

(Matthew 17)

The chapter begins with a glorious scene on a mountaintop, and ends with Peter catching a fish in order to pay his taxes. What a contrast! Yet, Jesus Christ the King is the theme of the entire chapter. The three events in this chapter give us three pictures of the King.

**The King in His Glory** (17:1-13)
Matthew and Mark state that the transfiguration took place "six days later," while Luke says "some eight days after" (Luke 9:28). There is no contradiction; Luke's statement is the Jewish equivalent of "about a week later." During that week, the disciples must have pondered and discussed what Jesus meant by His death and resurrection. No doubt they were also wondering what would happen to the Old Testament promises about the kingdom. If Jesus were going to build a church, what would happen to the promised kingdom?

The text does not name the place where this miracle took place. It was probably on Mount Hermon, which is close to Caesarea Philippi.

The Transfiguration revealed four aspects of the glory of Jesus Christ the King.

*The glory of His person.* As far as the record is concerned, this is the only time Jesus revealed His glory in this way while He was on the earth. The word translated *transfigured* gives us our English word "metamor-

116

phosis." A metamorphosis is a change on the outside that comes from the inside. When a caterpillar builds a cocoon and later emerges as a butterfly, it is due to the process of metamorphosis. Our Lord's glory was not *reflected* but *radiated* from within. There was a change on the outside that came from within as He allowed His essential glory to shine forth (Heb. 1:3).

Certainly this event would strengthen the faith of the disciples, particularly Peter who had so recently confessed Jesus to be the Son of God. Had Peter made his confession *after* the Transfiguration, it would not have been so meaningful. Peter believed, confessed his faith, and then received assurance. (See John 11:40; Heb. 11:6.)

Many years later, John recalled this event as the Spirit guided him to write: " . . . and we beheld His glory, the glory as of the only begotten of the Father, full of grace and truth" (John 1:14). In his Gospel, John emphasized the deity of Christ and the glory of His person (John 20:31; 2:11; 7:39; 11:4; 12:23; 13:31-32).

Jesus Christ laid aside His glory when He came to earth (John 17:5). Because of His finished work on the cross, He has received back His glory and now shares it with us (John 17:22, 24). However, we do not have to wait for heaven to share in this "transfiguration glory." When we surrender ourselves to God, He will "transfigure" our minds (Rom. 12:1-2). As we yield to the Spirit of God, He changes (transfigures) us "from glory to glory" (2 Cor. 3:18). As we look into the Word of God, we see the Son of God and are transfigured by the Spirit of God into the glory of God.

*The glory of His kingdom.* At the close of His sermon about cross-bearing, Jesus promised that some of the disciples would see "the Son of man coming in His kingdom" (Matt. 16:28). He selected Peter, James, and John as witnesses to this event. These three friends and business partners (Luke 5:10) had been with Jesus in the home of Jairus (Luke 8:51), and they would go with Him into the Garden of Gethsemane before His crucifixion (see Matt. 26:37).

Dr. G. Campbell Morgan has pointed out that these three occasions all had to do with *death*. Jesus was teaching these three men that He was victor over death (He raised Jairus' daughter) and surrendered to death (in the Garden). The Transfiguration taught them that He was glorified in death.

The presence of Moses and Elijah was significant. Moses represented the Law and Elijah the prophets. All of the Law and prophets point to Christ and are fulfilled in Christ (Heb. 1:1; Luke 24:27). Not one word of the Old Testament Scriptures will be unfulfilled. The promised kingdom would be established (Luke 1:32-33, 68-77). Just as the three disciples saw Jesus glorified *on earth*, so God's people would see Him in His glorious kingdom on earth (Rev. 19:11—20:6).

Peter caught this message and never forgot it. " . . . we were eyewitnesses of His majesty . . . And so we have the prophetic word made more sure . . . " (see 2 Peter 1:12ff). The experience Peter had on the mount only fortified his faith in the Old Testament prophecies. The important thing is not seeing wonderful sights, but hearing God's Word. "This is My beloved Son, in whom I am well pleased; hear ye Him" (Matt. 17:5).

All who are born again belong to the kingdom of God (John 3:3-5). This is a spiritual kingdom that is separate from the material things of this world (Rom. 14:17). But one day, when Jesus returns to this earth, there will be a glorious kingdom for 1,000 years (Rev. 20:1-7) with Jesus Christ reigning as King. Those who have trusted Him shall reign on the earth with Him (Rev. 5:10).

*The glory of His cross.* The disciples had to learn that suffering and glory go together. Peter had opposed His going to Jerusalem to die, so Jesus had to teach him that, apart from His suffering and death, there could be no glory. Peter certainly learned the lesson, for in his first epistle he repeatedly emphasized "suffering and glory" (1 Peter 1:6-8, 11; 4:12—5:11).

Moses and Elijah talked with Jesus about His "exodus" that He would accomplish at Jerusalem (Luke 9:31). His suffering and death would not be an accident, but an accomplishment. Peter used the word *exodus* in describing his own impending death (2 Peter 1:15). For the believer, death is not a one-way street into oblivion. It is an exodus—a release—from the bondage of this life into the glorious liberty of the life in heaven.

Because Jesus died and paid the price, we have been redeemed—purchased and set free. The two Emmaus disciples had hoped that Jesus would set the nation free from Roman bondage (Luke 24:21). What He died to accomplish was not *political* freedom, but *spiritual* freedom: freedom from the world system (Gal. 1:4); freedom from a vain and empty life (1 Peter 1:18); and freedom from iniquity (Titus 2:14). Our redemption in Christ is final and permanent.

*The glory of His submission.* Peter could not understand why the Son of God would submit to evil men and willingly suffer. The Transfiguration was God's way of teaching Peter that Jesus is glorified when we deny ourselves, take up our cross, and follow Him. The world's philosophy is "Save yourself!" but the Christian's philosophy is "Yield yourself to God!" As He stood there in glory, Jesus proved to the three disciples that surrender always leads to glory. First the suffering, then the glory; first the cross, then the crown.

Each of the three disciples would have a need for this important truth. James would be the first of the disciples to die (Acts 12:1-2). John would be the last of the disciples to die, but he would go through severe persecution on the Isle of Patmos (Rev. 1:9). Peter would experience many occasions of suffering and would, in the end, give his life for Christ (John 21:15-19; 2 Peter 1:12).

Peter opposed the cross when Jesus first mentioned His death (Matt. 16:22ff). In the garden, he used his sword to defend Jesus (John 18:10). In fact, even on the Mount of Transfiguration Peter tried to tell Jesus what to do. He wanted to build three booths for Jesus, Moses, and Elijah—so that all of them could remain there and enjoy the glory! But the Father interrupted Peter and gave other directions: "Hear Him!" The Father will not permit His beloved Son to be put on the same level as Moses and Elijah. "Jesus only" (v. 8) is God's pattern.

As Jesus and His three disciples came down from the mountaintop, He cautioned them not to reveal what they had seen, not even to the other nine disciples. But the three men were still perplexed. They had been taught that Elijah would come first to prepare for the establishing of the kingdom. Was the presence of Elijah on the mountain the fulfillment of this prophecy? (Mal. 4:5-6)

Jesus gave a two-fold answer to their question. Yes, Elijah would come as Malachi 4:5-6 promised. But spiritually speaking, Elijah already came in the person of John the Baptist (see Luke 1:17; Matt. 11:10-15). The nation permitted John to be killed, and would ask for Jesus to be slain. Yet God's program would be fulfilled in spite of the deeds of sinful leaders.

When will Elijah come to restore all things? Some people believe that Elijah will be one of the "two witnesses" whose ministry is described in

Revelation 11. Others believe that the prophecy was fulfilled in the ministry of John the Baptist so that there will be no future coming of Elijah.

## The King in His Power (17:14-21)

We move from the mountain of glory to the valley of need. The sudden appearance of Jesus and the three disciples startled the multitudes (Mark 9:15). The distraught father had brought his demonized son to the nine disciples, begging them to deliver him; but they could not. The scribes had noticed their failure and were using it as a reason for argument. And while the disciples were defending themselves, and the scribes were accusing them, the demon was all but killing the helpless boy.

When we compare the Gospel accounts of this dramatic scene, we discover that this only son was indeed in great trouble and danger. Matthew recorded that the boy was an epileptic (lunatic), very ill, and suicidal, falling into the fire and the water. Mark described him as a mute, who often fell to the ground foaming at the mouth and grinding his teeth. After this display, the boy would go into a kind of *rigor mortis*. Dr. Luke said that the boy was an only son and that he would scream as he went into these convulsions. While some of these symptoms can have natural causes, this boy was at the mercy of a demon. The disciples had been helpless to do anything. No wonder the father rushed to Jesus' feet.

Our Lord's first response was one of sorrow. As He beheld the embarrassed disciples, the arguing scribes, and the needy father and son, He groaned inwardly and said, "How long shall I be with you, and put up with you?" (Luke 9:41, NASB) Their unbelief and spiritual perversity were a burden to Him. What must our Lord feel as He looks at powerless believers today?

Jesus delivered the boy and commanded the spirit never to return to him (Mark 9:25). The demon tried "one last throw" (as Spurgeon put it) so that the crowd thought the boy was dead (v. 26). But Jesus raised the lad up and gave him to his father, while the crowds marvelled and gave glory to God (Luke 9:43).

The nine disciples should have been able to cast out the demon. Jesus had given them this power and authority (Matt. 10:1, 8). But somehow, they had lost their power! When they asked Jesus the cause of their shameful failure, He told them: their lack of faith (Matt. 17:20), their lack of prayer (Mark 9:29), and their lack of discipline (Matt. 17:21, although this verse is not found in many manuscripts).

The nine were perhaps jealous because they had not been called to go to the mountaintop with Jesus. During the Lord's absence, they began to grow self-indulgent. They neglected prayer; their faith weakened. Then, when the crisis came, they were unprepared. Like Samson, they went out to battle without realizing that their power was gone (Jud. 16:20). From their example, we see the importance of staying spiritually healthy.

"Faith as a grain of mustard seed" suggests not only *size* (God will honor even a little faith), but also *life* and *growth*. Faith like a mustard seed is *living* faith that is nurtured and caused to grow. Faith must be cultivated so that it grows and does even greater exploits for God (1 Thes. 3:10; 2 Thes. 1:3). Had the nine disciples been praying, disciplining themselves, and meditating on the Word, they would have been able to cast out the demon and rescue the boy.

This entire scene illustrates what Jesus will do when He leaves the glory of heaven to come to this earth. He will defeat Satan and bind him for 1,000 years (Rev. 20:1-6).

### The King in His Humility (17:22-27)

For a second time, Jesus mentioned His death and resurrection. The disciples were deeply grieved and were afraid to ask Him about it. In fact, His disciples did not believe the reports of His resurrection because they had forgotten His promises (Mark 16:14). But the enemy remembered what He said (John 2:19) and acted accordingly (Matt. 27:62-66).

What a paradox: a King too poverty-stricken to pay the annual temple tax of only a half-shekel! The unique characteristics of this miracle are worth noting.

*It is recorded only by Matthew.* Matthew, a former tax collector, wrote the Gospel of the King, and this miracle affirms our Lord's kingship. The kings of the earth do not take tribute from their own sons. Jesus affirmed Himself to be free from this tribute because He was the Son of the King, the Son of God. Yet, as the Son of God, He was too poor to pay even a half-shekel; and His disciples were as poor as He was. He exercised His kingship over nature to provide what was needed.

God gave Adam and Eve dominion over nature, and this included the fish in the sea (Gen. 1:26; Ps. 8:6-8). Man lost this dominion because of sin, so Peter was not able to command the fish and find the money. Jesus Christ exercised dominion over not only the fish, but also over the animals (Matt. 21:1-7) and the birds (Matt. 26:34, 74-75). What Adam lost because of his disobedience, Jesus Christ regained through His obedience (Heb. 2:6).

While today believers do not have complete dominion over nature, one day we shall reign with Christ and exercise dominion with Him. Meanwhile, God cares for His own and makes sure that all of nature is working for those who trust and obey.

*It is the only miracle He performed to meet His own needs.* Satan had tempted Christ to use His divine powers for Himself (Matt. 4:3-4), but He had refused. However, in this case, He did not use His power selfishly, for others were involved in this miracle. "Lest we cause them to stumble," was our Lord's explanation for the miracle. He did not want the people to be offended because He, being a Jew, did not support the temple ministry. While Jesus did not hesitate to break the man-made traditions of the Pharisees, He was careful to obey the Law of God.

As Christians, we must never use our freedom in Christ to hurt or destroy others. Technically, Jesus did not have to pay the tax; but for practical reasons, He paid it. He also included Peter so that their testimony would not be hurt.

*It is the only miracle using money.* Since Matthew had been a tax collector, we would expect him to be interested in this miracle. This tax had its origin in the days of Moses (Ex. 30:11ff). The original tax money was used to make the silver sockets on which the tabernacle poles were erected (Ex. 38:25-27). Subsequent taxes were used to support the ministry of the tabernacle and then the temple. The money was to be a reminder to the Jews that they had been redeemed from Egyptian slavery. We have been redeemed by the precious blood of Christ (1 Peter 1:18-19).

*It is the only miracle using one fish.* Jesus had multiplied the fish for Peter (Luke 5:1-11), and He would repeat that miracle (John 21:1ff). But in this case, He used only one fish. When we consider the complexity of this miracle, it amazes us. First, someone had to lose a coin in the water. Then, a fish had to take that coin in its mouth and retain it. That same fish then had to bite on Peter's hook—with an impediment in its mouth—and be caught. You cannot explain all of this in a natural way. It is too complex for an accident, and too difficult for human management.

*It was performed for Peter.* How the other disciples paid their taxes, we are not told. This was one of many miracles that Jesus performed for Peter. He healed Peter's mother-in-law (Mark 1:29-34), helped Peter to catch fish (Luke 5:1-11), enabled him to walk on the water (Matt. 14:22-33), healed Malchus' ear (26:47-56), and delivered Peter from prison (Acts 12:1ff). No wonder Peter wrote, "Casting all your care upon Him, for He cares for you" (1 Peter 5:7).

Jesus knew Peter's need and was able to meet that need. Peter thought he had the problem solved when he entered the house. But before he could tell Jesus what to do, Jesus told *him* what to do! God the Father had interrupted Peter on the mountain (17:5), and now God the Son interrupted him in the house. If only we would let Jesus give the directions, we would see Him meet our needs for His glory.

*It is the only miracle which does not have the results recorded.* We would expect another verse that would read: "And Peter went to the sea, cast in a hook, and drew up a fish; and when he had opened its mouth, he found there a coin, and used it to pay the temple tax for himself and for Jesus." But verse 28 is not there. Then, how do we know that the miracle took place? *Because Jesus said it would!* "There hath not failed one word of all His good promise" (1 Kings 8:56).

We must commend Peter for his faith. The people at the seashore were accustomed to seeing Peter with a net in his hand, not a hook and line. But Peter had faith in God's Word, and God honored that faith. If we trust the King, He will meet our needs as we obey His Word.

# 15

# THE
# KING'S
# REBUKE

(Matthew 18)

Why do some of God's children have such a difficult time getting along with each other? A poem I heard states the problem perfectly:

To live above, with saints we love

Will certainly be glory.

To live below, with saints we know—

Well, that's another story!

With so much division and dissension among professing Christians these days, we desperately need what Matthew 18 has to teach. Jesus rebuked His disciples for their pride and desire for worldly greatness, and He taught them the three essentials for unity and harmony among God's people.

## Humility (18:1-14)

Someone has accurately defined humility as "that grace that, when you know you have it, you've lost it!" It has well been said, "True humility is not thinking meanly of one's self; it is simply not thinking of one's self at all."

*The need for humility* (18:1). "Which one of us is the greatest?" was a repeated topic of discussion among the disciples, for we find it mentioned often in the Gospel records. Recent events would have aggravated the problem, particularly with reference to Peter. After all, Peter had walked on the water, had been on the mountaintop with the Lord, and had even had his taxes paid by means of a miracle.

The fact that Jesus had been sharing with the disciples the truth about His coming suffering and death did not affect them. They were thinking only of themselves and what position they would have in His kingdom. So absorbed were the disciples in this matter that they actually *argued* with each other! (Luke 9:46)

The selfishness and disunity of God's people is a scandal to the Christian faith. What causes these problems? Pride—thinking ourselves more important than we really are. It was pride that led man into sin at the beginning (Gen. 3:5). When Christians are living for themselves and not for others, then there is bound to be conflict and division (Phil. 2:1ff).

*The example of humility* (18:2-6, 10-14). The disciples waited breathlessly for Jesus to name the greatest man among them. But He bypassed them completely and called a little child into their midst. This child was the example of true greatness.

True humility means knowing yourself, accepting yourself, and being your self—your *best* self—to the glory of God. It means avoiding two extremes: thinking *less* of yourself than you ought to (as did Moses when God called him, Ex. 3:11ff), or thinking *more* of yourself than you ought to (Rom. 12:3). The truly humble person does not deny the gifts God has given him, but uses them to the glory of God.

An unspoiled child has the characteristics that make for humility: trust (v. 6), dependence, the desire to make others happy, an absence of boasting or selfish desire to be greater than others. By nature, all of us are rebels who want to be celebrities instead of servants. It takes a great deal of teaching for us to learn the lessons of humility.

The disciples wanted to know who was greatest *in* the kingdom. But Jesus warned them that, apart from humility, they could not even *enter* the kingdom! They had to be converted—turned around in their thinking—or they would never make it.

It seems that Jesus is, in these verses, blending two concepts: the human child as an example of humility, and the child of God no matter what his age might be. As Christians, we must not only accept the little children for Jesus' sake; but we must also receive *all* of God's children and seek to minister to them (Rom. 14:1ff). It is a serious matter to cause a child to sin or to lead him astray. It is equally as serious to cause another believer to stumble because of our poor example (Rom. 14:13ff; 1 Cor. 8:9ff). True humility thinks of others, not of self.

Jesus explained that we can have four different attitudes toward the children and, consequently, toward true humility. We can seek to *become like the children* (vv. 3-4) in true humility, as to the Lord. Or, we can only *receive them* (v. 5) because Jesus told us to. If we are not careful, we will *cause them to stumble* (v. 6), and even end up *despising them* (v. 10).

It is a dangerous thing to look down upon the children, because God values them highly. When we welcome a child (or a Christian believer), we welcome Christ (v. 5). The Father cares for them and the angels watch over them (v. 10). Like the good shepherd, God seeks the lost and saves them; and we must not cause them to perish. If the shepherd goes after an adult sheep, how much more important is it that he protect the lambs!

In these days of child neglect and child abuse, we need to take Christ's warning seriously. It is better to drown with a heavy millstone around one's neck, than to abuse a child and face the judgment of God (v. 6).

*The cost of humility* (18:7-9). The truly humble person helps to build up others, not to tear them down. He is a stepping-stone, not a stumbling block. Therefore, anything that makes me stumble must be removed from my life, for if it is not, I cause others to stumble. Jesus had uttered similar words in the Sermon on the Mount (Matt. 5:29-30). Paul used the eye, hand, and foot to illustrate the mutual dependence of members of the body of Christ (1 Cor. 12:14-17).

Humility begins with self-examination, and it continues with self-denial. Jesus was not suggesting that we maim our bodies, for harming our physical bodies can never change the spiritual condition of our hearts. Rather, He was instructing us to perform "spiritual surgery" on ourselves, removing anything that causes us to stumble or that causes others to stumble. The humble person lives for Jesus first and others next—he puts himself last. He is happy to deprive himself even of good things, if it will make others happy. Perhaps the best commentary on this is Philippians 2:1-18.

### Honesty (18:15-20)

We don't always practice humility. There are times when, deliberately or unconsciously, we offend others and hurt them. Even the Old Testament Law recognized "sins of ignorance" (Num. 15:22), and David prayed to be delivered from "secret faults" (Ps. 19:12), meaning "faults that are even hidden from my own eyes." What should we do when another Christian has sinned against us or caused us to stumble? Our Lord gave several instructions.

*Keep the matter private.* Approach the person who sinned and speak with him alone. It is possible that he does not even realize what he has done. Or, even if he did it deliberately, your own attitude of submission and love will help him to repent and apologize. Above all else, go to him with the idea of winning your brother, not winning an argument. It is possible to win the argument and lose your brother.

We must have a spirit of meekness and gentleness when we seek to restore a brother or sister (Gal. 6:1). We must not go about condemning the offender, or spreading gossip. We must lovingly seek to help him in the same way we would want him to help us if the situation were reversed. The word *restore* in Galatians 6:1 is a Greek medical word that means "to set a broken bone." Think of the patience and tenderness *that* requires!

*Ask for help from others.* If the offender refuses to make things right, then we may feel free to share the burden with one or two dependable believers. We should share the facts as we see them and ask the brethren for their prayerful counsel. After all, it may be that *we* are wrong. If the brethren feel the cause is right, then together we can go to the offender and try once again to win him. Not only can these men assist in prayer and persuasion, but they can be witnesses to the church of the truth of the conversation (Deut. 19:15; 2 Cor. 13:1).

When sin is not dealt with honestly, it always spreads. What was once a matter between two people has now grown to involve four or five people. No wonder Jesus and Paul both compared sin to leaven (yeast), because leaven infects and spreads.

*Ask the church for help.* Remember, our goal is not the winning of a case but the winning of a brother. The word *gained* in verse 15 is used in 1 Corinthians 9:19-22 to refer to winning the lost; but it is also important to win the saved. This is our Lord's second mention of the church (see Matt. 16:18), and here it has the meaning of a local assembly of believers. Our Lord's disciples were raised in the Jewish synagogue, so they were familiar with congregational discipline.

What started as a private problem between two people is now out in the open for the whole church to see. Church discipline is a neglected ministry these days, yet it is taught here and in the epistles (see 1 Cor. 5; 2 Thes. 3:6-16; 2 Tim. 2:23-26; Titus 3:10). Just as children in the home need discipline, so God's children in the church need discipline. If by the time the matter comes to the whole church, the offender has not yet changed his mind and repented, then he must be disciplined. He cannot be treated as a spiritual brother, for he has forfeited that position. He can only be treated as one outside the church, not hated, but not held in close fellowship.

*Keep the local church spiritual* (18-20). It is important that the local assembly be at its best spiritually before it seeks to discipline a member. When a church disciplines a member, it is actually examining itself and disciplining itself. This is why our Lord added these words about authority, prayer, and fellowship. We cannot discipline others if we are not disciplined ourselves. Whatever we bind (permit) in the assembly must first have been permitted by God. (See the comments on Matt. 16:19.)

The church must be under the authority of God's Word. Church discipline does not refer to a group of Christian policemen throwing their weight around. Rather, it means God exercising His authority in and through a local body, to restore one of His erring children.

Not only must there be the authority of the Word, but there must also be prayer (v. 19). The word *agree* in the Greek gives us our English word "symphony." The church must agree in prayer as it seeks to discipline the erring member. It is through prayer and the Word that we ascertain the will of the Father in the matter.

Finally, there must be fellowship (v. 20). The local church must be a worshiping community, recognizing the presence of the Lord in the midst. The Holy Spirit of God can convict both the offender and the church, and He can even judge sin in the midst (Acts 5).

There is a desperate need for honesty in the church today. "Speaking the truth in love" is God's standard (Eph. 4:15). If we practice love without truth, it is hypocrisy. But if we try to have truth without love, it may be brutality. Jesus always taught the truth in love. If the truth hurts, it is because "Faithful are the wounds of a friend . . ." (Prov. 27:6).

But keep in mind that *humility* must come before *honesty*. A proud Christian cannot speak the truth in love. He will use a brother's faults as a weapon to fight with and not as a tool to build with. The result will be only greater disharmony and disagreement.

The first internal problem of the New Testament church was dishonesty (Acts 5). Ananias and Sapphira tried to make the church members believe that they were more spiritual than they really were. They lied to themselves in thinking they could get away with the masquerade; they lied to their fellow Christians and the church leaders; and they tried to lie to the Holy Spirit. The result was judgment and death. God may not kill every hypocrite in the church today, but hypocrisy certainly helps to kill the church.

The second internal problem (Acts 6) had to do with people being neglected. The members and leaders faced this problem with truth and love, and the result was blessing. It takes both truth and love, and both must be used with humility.

### Forgiveness (18:21-35)
When we start living in an atmosphere of humility and honesty, we must take some risks and expect some dangers. Unless humility and honesty result in forgiveness, relationships cannot be mended and strengthened. Peter recognized the risks involved and asked Jesus how he should handle them in the future.

But Peter made some serious mistakes. To begin with, he lacked humility himself. He was sure his brother would sin against him, but not he against his brother! Peter's second mistake was in asking for limits and measures. Where there is love, there can be no limits or dimensions (Eph. 3:17-19). Peter thought he was showing great faith and love when he offered to forgive at least seven times. After all, the rabbis taught that three times was sufficient.

Our Lord's reply, "Until seventy times seven" (490 times) must have startled Peter. Who could keep count for that many offenses? But that was exactly the point Jesus was making: Love "keeps no record of wrongs" (1 Cor. 13:5, NIV). By the time we have forgiven a brother that many times, we are in the habit of forgiving.

But Jesus was not advising careless or shallow forgiveness. Christian love is not blind (Phil. 1:9-10). The forgiveness Christ requires is on the basis of the instructions He gave in verses 15-20. If a brother is guilty of a repeated sin, no doubt he would find strength and power to conquer that sin through the encouragement of his loving and forgiving brethren. If we condemn a brother, we bring out the worst in him. But if we create an atmosphere of love and forgiveness, we can help God bring out the best in him.

The parable illustrates the power of forgiveness. It is important to note that *this parable is not about salvation,* for salvation is wholly of grace and is unconditionally given. To make God's forgiveness a temporary thing is to violate the very truth of Scripture (Rom. 5:8; Eph. 2:8-9; Titus 3:3-7). The parable deals with forgiveness between *brothers*, not between lost sinners and God. The emphasis in this chapter is on brother forgiving brother (vv. 15, 21).

The main character in this parable went through three stages in his experience of forgiveness.

*He was a debtor* (18:23-27). This man had been stealing funds from the king and, when the books were audited, his crime was discovered. The total tax levy in Palestine was about 800 talents a year, so you can see how dishonest this man was. In term's of today's buying power, this was probably equivalent to over $10,000,000.

But this man actually thought he could get out of the debt. He told the king that, given enough time, he could pay it back. We detect two sins here: pride and a lack of sincere repentance. The man is not ashamed because he stole the money; he is ashamed because he got caught. And he actually thought he was big enough to earn the money to repay the king's account. In the economy of that day, a man would have had to work 20 years to earn one talent.

His case was hopeless, except for one thing: The king was a man of compassion. He assumed the loss and forgave the servant. This meant that the man was free and that he and his family would not be thrown into a debtor's prison. The servant did not deserve this forgiveness; it was purely an act of love and mercy on the part of the master.

*He was a creditor* (18:28-30). The servant left the presence of the king and went and found a fellow servant who owed him 100 pence. The average worker earned one penny a day, so this debt was insignificant compared to what the servant had owed the king. Instead of sharing with his friend the joy of his own release, the servant mistreated his friend and demanded that he pay the debt. The debtor used the same approach as the servant: "Have patience with me and I will pay you all of it!" But the unjust servant was unwilling to grant to others what he wanted others to grant to him.

Perhaps he had the *legal* right to throw the man in prison, but he did not have the *moral* right. He had been forgiven himself—should he not forgive his fellow servant? He and his family had been spared the shame and suffering of prison. Should he not spare his friend?

*He became a prisoner* (18:31-34). The king originally delivered him from prison, but the servant put himself back in. The servant exercised justice and cast his friend into prison. "So you want to live by justice?" asked the king. "Then you shall have justice! Throw the wicked servant in prison and torment him! I will do to him as he has done to others." (There is no suggestion that the entire family was sentenced. After all, it was the father who abused the other servant and ignored the king's kindness.)

The world's worst prison is the prison of an unforgiving heart. If we refuse to forgive others, then we are only imprisoning ourselves and causing our own torment. Some of the most miserable people I have met in my ministry have been people who would not forgive others. They lived only to imagine ways to punish these people who had wronged them. But they were really only punishing themselves.

What was wrong with this man? The same thing that is wrong with many professing Christians: They have *received* forgiveness, but they have not really *experienced* forgiveness deep in their hearts. Therefore, they are unable to *share* forgiveness with those who have wronged them. If we live only according to justice, always seeking to get what is ours, we will put ourselves into prison. But if we live according to forgiveness, sharing with others what God has shared with us, then we will enjoy freedom and joy. Peter asked for a just measuring rod; Jesus told him to practice forgiveness and forget the measuring rod.

Our Lord's warning is serious. He did not say that God *saves* only those who forgive others. The theme of this parable is forgiveness between brothers, not salvation for lost sinners. Jesus warned us that God cannot forgive us *if we do not have humble and repentant hearts*. We reveal the true condition of our hearts by the way we treat others. When our hearts are humble and repentant, we will gladly forgive our brothers. But where there is pride and a desire for revenge, there can be no true repentance; and this means God cannot forgive.

In other words, it is not enough to *receive* God's forgiveness, or even the forgiveness of others. We must *experience* that forgiveness in our hearts so that it humbles us and makes us gentle and forgiving toward others. The servant in the parable did not have a deep experience of forgiveness and humility. *He was simply glad to be "off the hook."* He had never really repented.

"And be you kind one to another, tenderhearted, forgiving one another, even as God for Christ's sake hath forgiven you" (Eph. 4:32). "Forbearing one another, and forgiving one another, if any man have a quarrel against any: even as Christ forgave you, so also do you" (Col. 3:13).

# 16

# THE KING'S INSTRUCTIONS

(Matthew 19:1-15)

The King's "retirement" from the crowds was about to come to an end. But the attacks of the enemy would grow more intense, culminating in His arrest and crucifixion. The religious leaders had already tried to ensnare Him with questions about the Sabbath and signs, and they had failed. They tried again, this time with a most controversial issue—divorce.

This subject is both important and controversial today. The divorce rate continues to climb (at this writing, one divorce for every 1.8 marriages), and divorce has invaded even the homes of Christian leaders. Someone has commented that couples "are married for better or for worse, but not for long." We need to examine again what Jesus taught about this subject. He explained four different laws relating to marriage and divorce.

## The Original Creation Law (19:3-6)
Instead of going back to Deuteronomy, Jesus went back to Genesis. What God did when He established the first marriage teaches us *positively* what He had in mind for a man and a woman. If we build a marriage after God's ideal pattern, we will not have to worry about divorce laws.

*The reasons for marriage.* The only thing that was not "good" about Creation was the fact that the man was alone (Gen. 2:18). The woman was created to meet this need. Adam could not find fellowship with the animals. He needed a companion who was equal to him and with whom he could find fulfillment. God's answer to this need was Eve.

Marriage makes possible the continuation of the race. "Be fruitful, and multiply . . ." was God's mandate to the first married couple (Gen. 1:28). From the beginning it was God's command that sex be practiced in the commitment of marriage. Outside of marriage, sex becomes a destructive force; but within the loving commitment of marriage, sex can be creative and constructive.

Marriage is one way to avoid sexual sins (1 Cor. 7:1-6). Of course, a man should not marry simply to legalize lust! If he is lustful outside of marriage, he will no doubt be lustful after he is married. He should not think that getting married will solve all of his personal problems with lust. But marriage is God's appointed way for a man and a woman to share the physical joys of sex.

Paul used marriage as an illustration of the intimate relationship between Christ and the church (Eph. 5:22-23). Just as Eve was taken from the side of Adam (Gen. 2:21), so the church was born from the suffering and death of Christ on the cross. Christ loves His church, nourishes it with His Word, cleanses it, and cares for it. Christ's relationship to His church is the example for all husbands to follow.

*The characteristics of marriage.* By going back to the original Edenic Law, Jesus reminded His listeners of the true characteristics of marriage. If we remember these characteristics, we will better know how to build a happy and enduring marriage.

*It is a divinely appointed union.* God established marriage, and therefore only God can control its character and laws. No court of law can change what God has established.

*It is a physical union.* The man and woman become "one flesh." While it is important that a husband and wife be of one mind and heart, the basic union in marriage is physical. If a man and woman became "one spirit" in marriage, then death would not dissolve the marriage; for the spirit never dies. Even if a man and woman disagree, are "incompatible," and cannot get along, they are still married; for the union is a physical one.

*It is a permanent union.* God's original design was that one man and one woman spend one life together. God's original law knows nothing of "trial marriages." God's Law requires that the husband and wife enter into marriage without reservations.

*It is a union between one man and one woman.* God did not create two men and one woman, two women and one man, two men, or two women. "Group marriages," "gay marriages," and other eccentric variations are contrary to the will of God, no matter what some psychologists and jurists may say.

### The Seventh Commandment (5:27-30)

While Jesus did not refer to the Seventh Commandment in this discussion, He did quote it in the Sermon on the Mount (5:27-32). Let's examine what He said.

Jesus and the New Testament writers affirm the authority of "Thou shalt not commit adultery" (Ex. 20:14). While the word *fornication* seems to cover many kinds of sexual sins (see Mark 7:21; Rom. 1:29; 1 Cor. 6:13), *adultery* involves only married people. When a married person has intercourse with someone other than his or her mate, that is adultery. God has declared that it is wrong and it is sin. There are numerous warnings in the New Testament against sexual sins, including adultery (Acts 15:20; 1 Cor. 6:15-18; Gal. 5:19ff; Eph. 4:17ff; 5:3-12; Col. 3:5; 1 Thes. 4:3-7; Heb. 13:4).

This commandment affirms the sanctity of sex. God created it, God protects it, and God punishes when His law is violated. Nine of the Ten Commandments are repeated in the New Testament for us to heed. (The Sabbath commandment was given only to Israel and does not apply to the church today.) We must not think that because we are "under grace" we can flaunt God's Law and get away with it. "Fornicators and adulterers God will judge" (Heb. 13:4, NASB).

However, Jesus went much deeper in His discussion of adultery. He showed that this can be a sin of the heart as well as a sin of the body. It is not enough simply to control the body; we must also control the inner thoughts and desires. To look at a woman *for the purpose of lusting after her* is to commit adultery in the heart. This does not mean that we cannot admire a beautiful person, or picture; for it is possible to do that and not sin. It is when we look *with the intention* of satisfying lustful desires, that we commit adultery in the heart.

A sanctified sex life begins with the inner desires. Jesus singled out the eye and the hand, because seeing and feeling are usually the first steps toward sexual sin. Of course, He did not command us to perform *physical* surgery, since He was clearly dealing with the *inner* desires. He commanded us to deal drastically with sin, to remove from our lives anything that would pamper our wrong desires. We must "hunger and thirst after righteousness."

Jesus did not alter the original Edenic Law of marriage, nor did He annul the Seventh Commandment. What He taught was based solidly on God's creation and God's moral law.

### The Mosaic Law of Divorce (19:7-8)

Like many people who "argue religion," these Pharisees were not interested in discovering truth. They were interested only in defending themselves and what they believed. This was why they asked about the Jewish law of divorce recorded in Deuteronomy 24:1-4.

I suggest you read this important passage in the New American Standard Bible to distinguish the tenses of the verbs. This translation makes it clear that Moses gave *only one commandment:* The divorced wife could not return to her first husband if she was put away by a second husband. *Moses did not command divorce;* he permitted it. He commanded that the husband give his ex-wife a legal bill of divorcement. But the wife could not return to her first husband after being remarried and divorced.

What a wise law this was. To begin with, the husband would think twice before hastily putting away his wife, since he could not get her back again. Futhermore, it would have taken time to find a scribe (not everyone could write legal documents), and during that time the two estranged people might have been reconciled. The Pharisees were interpreting Moses' Law as though it were a commandment. Jesus made it clear that Moses was only giving *permission* for divorce.

But what did Moses mean by *some uncleanness in her?* The Hebrew means "some matter of nakedness," but this need not refer to sexual sin. That phrase is the equivalent of "some shameful thing" (see Gen. 2:25; 3:7, 10). It is the interpretation of this phrase that divided the two schools of Rabbi Hillel and Rabbi Shammai, famous first-century Jewish scholars. Hillel took a very lax view and said that the husband could divorce his wife for almost any reason, while Shammai took the stricter view and said Moses was speaking only about sexual sin. No matter which side Jesus took, He would surely offend somebody.

There were several laws of marriage given to the Jews, and we must examine them in order to get some perspective. For example, if a man married a woman and discovered that she was not a virgin, he could expose her sin and have her stoned (Deut. 22:13-21). Of course, he had to have proof; and if he did not, he was fined and had to live with the woman all of his life. This law was as much a protection to the woman as to the man.

If a man suspected his wife of unfaithfulness, he followed the procedure outlined in Numbers 5:11ff. We cannot follow that procedure today (which certainly included elements of divine judgment) since there is no priesthood or tabernacle.

Remember that the Law of Moses demanded *the death penalty* for those who committed adultery (Deut. 22:22; Lev. 20:10). Our Lord's enemies appealed to this law when they tried to trap Him (John 8:1). While we have no record in the Old Testament that anyone was stoned for committing adultery, this was the divine law. The experience of Joseph (Matt. 1:18-25) indicates that the Jews used divorce rather than stoning in dealing with an adulterous wife.

Why did God command that the adulterer or adulteress be stoned to death? Certainly as an example to warn the people, for adultery undermines the very fabric of society and the home. There must be commitment in marriage, and faithfulness to each other and to God, if there is to be stability in society and in the church. God had to preserve Israel because the promised Saviour would come through that nation. God opposed divorce in Israel because it weakened the nation and threatened the birth of the Messiah (see Mal. 2:10-16).

But there was another reason for capital punishment: This left the other party free to marry again. Death breaks the marriage bond, since marriage is a physical union (Rom. 7:1-3). It was important that families be continued in Israel that they might protect their inheritance (Num. 36).

We must note one final fact before leaving this section: The divorce that Moses permitted in Deuteronomy 24 *actually severed the original marriage relationship.* God permitted the woman to marry again, and her second marriage was not considered adulterous. The second man she married was called a "husband" and not an adulterer. This explains how the woman of Samaria could have had five *husbands,* and yet be living with a man not her husband (John 4:16-18). Apparently all five of those marriages had been legal and scriptural.

This means that scriptural divorce does sever the marriage relationship. *Man* cannot break this relationship by his laws, but *God can break it*. The same God who gives the laws that join people together can also give laws to put them asunder. God can do it, but man cannot.

Finally, Jesus made it clear that this Mosaic Law of divorce was a concession on God's part. God's original law of marriage left no room for divorce, but that law was laid down before man had sinned. Rather than have two people living together in constant conflict, with one or both of them seeking fulfillment elsewhere and thus commit sin, God permitted divorce. *This divorce included the right to remarriage*. The Pharisees did not ask about remarriage, for this was no problem. They accepted the fact that the parties would seek other mates, and this was allowed by Moses.

## Our Lord's Law of Marriage (19:9-12; 5:31-32)

When Jesus said "And I say unto you," He was claiming to be God; for only God can establish or alter the laws of marriage. He declared that marriage was a permanent union that could only be broken by sexual sin. The word *fornication* in the New Testament covers many kinds of sexual sins. The definition of fornication as "sexual sin between two unmarried persons" would not apply here, for Jesus was talking about married persons. Are we to believe that the 23,000 men who committed fornication under the enticement of Baalam (Num. 25) were all unmarried men? Was the admonition of Acts 15:20, 29 sent only to single church members?

Marriage is a permanent physical union that can be broken only by a physical cause: death or sexual sin. (I would take it that homosexuality and bestiality would qualify.) Man cannot break the union, but God can. Under the Old Testament Law, the sinner was stoned to death. But the church today does not bear the sword (Rom. 13:1-4). Were adultery and fornication more serious under the Law than the same sins are today? Of course not! If anything, such sins are even worse today in the light of the full revelation of God's grace and holiness that we now have in Jesus Christ.

The conclusion seems to be that divorce in the New Testament is the equivalent of death in the Old Testament: It permitted the innocent party freedom to remarry.

Notice that our Lord's new law of marriage and divorce was based on the three previous laws. From the Edenic Law He took the principle that marriage was a physical union that could only be broken by a physical cause, and that only God could permit the breaking of the union. From the Seventh Commandment He took the principle that sexual sin did indeed break the marriage union. From the Mosaic Law of Divorce He took the principle that God could ordain divorce and effectively break the marriage union, and that the freed party could remarry and not be guilty of adultery.

Our Lord's teaching is that there is only one scriptural basis for divorce, and that is sexual sin (fornication). If two people are divorced on any other basis, and marry other mates, they are committing adultery.

Jesus did not teach that the offended mate *had* to get a divorce. Certainly there can be forgiveness, patient healing, and a restoration of the broken relationship. This would be the Christian approach to the problem. But, sad to say, because of the hardness of our hearts, it is sometimes impossible to heal the wounds and save the marriage. Divorce is the *final* option, not the first option.

Happy marriages are not accidents. They are the result of commitment, love, mutual understanding, sacrifice, and hard work. If a husband and wife are fulfilling their marriage vows, they will enjoy a growing relationship that will satisfy them and keep them true to each other. Except for the possibility of sudden temptation, no husband or wife would think of a relationship with another person, so long as their relationship at home is growing and satisfying. And the pure love of a husband or wife is a great protection against even sudden temptation.

The disciples' response to Christ's teaching showed that they disagreed with Him. "If there is no way to get out of a bad marriage, then you are better off staying single!" was their argument. Jesus did not want them to consider divorce as an "out" because then they would not have a serious attitude toward marriage.

In verse 12, Jesus made it clear that each man (and woman) must consider God's will concerning marriage. Some people should not get married because of physical or emotional problems from birth. Others should not get married because of their responsibilities in society; they have been "made eunuchs by man." An only child who must care for aged parents might be an example of this category. Some, like the Apostle Paul, stay single that they might better serve the Lord (1 Cor. 7:7).

It is fitting that our Lord's teaching about marriage should be followed by His blessing of the children for children are the happy heritage of those who are married. Jesus did not look upon the children as a curse or a burden. "Two shall become one flesh" is fulfilled in the birth of children, and the love of the parents is deepened and matured as it is shared with others in the home.

The parents brought the children to Jesus that He might bless them. There is no thought here of baptism or even of salvation. Children who have not reached the age of accountability (Isa. 7:16) are surely covered by the death of Christ (Rom. 5:17-21). Children are born sinners (Ps. 51:5); but if they die before they are accountable, they are regenerated and taken to heaven (2 Sam. 12:23; Ps. 23:6).

The children were certainly privileged to have Jesus take them in His arms and pray for them. Our practice of baby dedication today seeks to follow this example. How happy those children are whose parents are married in the will of God, and who are seeking to obey God, and who bring them to Jesus for His blessing.

# 17

# THE KING'S DEMANDS

(Matthew 19:16—20:34)

We cannot follow the King without paying a price. After all, He went to the cross for us! Have we the right to escape sacrifice and suffering? In this section, our Lord explains the rightful demands that He makes upon those who want to trust Him and be His disciples.

## We Must Love Christ Supremely (19:16-26)

Each of the first three Gospels records this event. When we combine the facts, we learn that this man was rich, young, and a ruler—probably the ruler of a synagogue. We can certainly commend this young man for coming publicly to Christ and asking about eternal matters. He seemed to have no ulterior motive and was willing to listen and learn. Sadly, he made the wrong decision.

The event seems to develop around several important questions.

*"What good thing shall I do, that I may have eternal life?"* (19:16-17) The man was obviously sincere, although his approach to salvation was centered on works and not faith. But this was to be expected among the Jews of that day. However, in spite of his position in society, his morality, and his religion, he felt a definite need for something more.

But our Lord's reply did not focus on salvation. He forced the young man to think seriously about the word *good* that he had used in addressing Jesus. "Only God is good," Jesus said. "Do you believe that I am good and therefore that I am God?" If Jesus is only one of many religious teachers in history, then His words carry no more weight than the pronouncements of any other religious leader. But if Jesus is good, then He is God, and we had better heed what He says.

Why did Jesus bring up the commandments? Did He actually teach that people receive eternal life by obeying God's Law? If anyone *could* keep the commandments, he certainly would enter into life. But no one can keep God's Law perfectly. "Therefore by the deeds of the Law there shall no flesh be justified in His sight: for by the Law is the knowledge of sin" (Rom. 3:20). Jesus did not introduce the Law to show the young man how to be saved, but to show him that *he needed to be saved*. The Law is a mirror that reveals what we are (James 1:22ff).

*"Which commandments?"* (19:18-19) Was the young man being evasive? I don't think so. But he was making a mistake, for one part of God's Law cannot be separated from another part. To classify God's laws into "lesser" and "greater" is to miss the whole purpose of the Law. "For whosoever shall keep the whole Law, and yet offend in one point, he is guilty of all" (James 2:10). The Law represents the authority of God, and to disobey what we may think is a minor law is still to rebel against His authority.

Of course, the young man thought only of external obedience. He forgot about the attitudes of the heart. Jesus had taught in the Sermon on the Mount that hatred was the moral equivalent of murder, and that lust was the equivalent of adultery. We rejoice that this young man had such good manners and morals. But we regret that he did not see his sin, repent, and trust Christ.

The one commandment that especially applied to him, Jesus did not quote: "Thou shalt not covet" (Ex. 20:17). The young man should have pondered *all* of the Commandments and not just the ones that Jesus quoted. Was he looking for easy discipleship? Was he being dishonest with himself? I believe that his testimony was sincere, *as far as he knew*. But he did not permit the light of the Word to penetrate deeply enough. Jesus felt a sudden love for this young man (Mark 10:21), so He continued to try to help him.

*"What lack I yet?"* (19:20-22) Nowhere in the Bible are we taught that a sinner is saved by selling his goods and giving the money away. Jesus never told Nicodemus to do this, or any other sinner whose story is

recorded in the Gospels. Jesus knew that this man was covetous; he loved material wealth. By asking him to sell his goods, Jesus was forcing him to examine his own heart and determine his priorities. With all of his commendable qualities, the young man still did not truly love God with *all* of his heart. Possessions were his god. He was unable to obey the command, "Go and sell . . . come and follow . . ."

The young man went away grieved, but he could have gone away in great joy and peace. We cannot love and serve two masters (Matt. 6:24ff). We can be sure that, apart from Christ, even the material possessions of life give no lasting joy or pleasure. It is good to have the things money can buy provided we do not lose the things that money cannot buy. Unless this rich ruler eventually turned to Christ, he died without salvation, one of the "richest" men in the cemetery.

*"Who then can be saved?"* (19:23-26) The Jewish people of that day believed that riches were an evidence of God's blessing. They based this on the promises God gave the Jewish nation at the beginning of their history. It is true that God *did* promise material blessing if they obeyed, and material loss if they disobeyed (see Deut. 26—28). But in the infancy of the race, the only way God could teach them was through rewards and punishments. We teach young children in the same manner.

However, the highest kind of obedience is not based on a desire for reward or the fear of punishment. It is motivated by love. In His life and His teaching, Jesus tried to show the people that the inner spiritual blessings are far more important than the material gains. God sees the heart, and God wants to build character. Salvation is the gift of God in response to man's faith. Material riches are not a guarantee that God is pleased with a man.

The disciples, being good Jews, were amazed at the Lord's statement about riches. Their question reflected their theology: "If a rich man cannot be saved, what hope is there for the rest of us?" Of course, Jesus did not say that the *possessing* of wealth kept a man from the kingdom. Some manuscripts of Mark 10:24 read, "How hard it is for those who trust in riches to enter the kingdom of God." This is certainly the import of our Lord's teaching. Abraham was a very wealthy man, yet he was a man of great faith. It is good to possess wealth *if* wealth does not possess you.

We cannot follow the King and live for worldly wealth. We cannot serve God and money. The love of money is the root of all kinds of evil (1 Tim. 6:6-10). Jesus Christ demands of all who will follow Him that they love Him supremely.

### We Must Obey Him Unreservedly (19:27—20:16)

Peter was quick to see the contrast between the wealthy ruler and the poor disciples. "We have forsaken all, and followed Thee; what shall we have therefore?" Jesus gave them a marvelous promise of rewards in this life and in the next. They would even share thrones when He established His kingdom. Whatever good things they had forsaken for His sake would be returned to them a hundredfold. In other words, they were not making sacrifices—they were making investments. But not all of the dividends would be received in this life.

However, Jesus detected in Peter's question the possibility of a wrong motive for service. This was why He added the warning that some who were first in their own eyes would be last in the judgment, and some who were last would end up first. This truth was amplified in the parable of the workers in the vineyard.

This parable has nothing to do with salvation. The penny (a day's wages in that time) does not represent salvation, for nobody works for his salvation. Nor is the parable talking about rewards, for we are not all going to receive the same reward. "And every man shall receive his own reward according to his own labor" (1 Cor. 3:8).

The parable is emphasizing *a right attitude in service*. It is important to note that there were actually two kinds of workers hired that day: those who wanted a contract and agreed to work for a penny a day, and those who had no contract and agreed to take whatever the owner thought was right. The first laborers that he hired insisted on a contract.

This explains why the householder paid the workers as he did: He wanted those who were hired first (who insisted on a contract) to see how much he paid the workers who were hired later. It was one way the owner could show those workers how really generous he was.

Put yourself in the place of those workers who were hired first but paid last. They each expected to get a penny, because that was what they agreed to accept. But imagine their surprise when they saw the laborers who were hired *last* each receiving a penny! This meant their own wages should have been 12 pennies each!

But the three o'clock workers also received a penny—for only three hours of work. The men last in line quickly recalculated their wages: four pennies for the day's work. When the men hired at noon also were paid a penny, this cut the salary of the contract workers considerably, for now they would earn only two pennies.

But the owner gave them one penny each. Of course, they complained! But they had no argument, because *they had agreed to work for a penny*. They received what they asked for. Had they trusted the goodness of the owner, they would have received far more. But they insisted on a contract.

The lesson for Christ's disciples is obvious. We should not serve Him because we want to receive an expected reward, and we should not insist on knowing what we will get. God is infinitely generous and gracious and will always give us better than we deserve.

Now we can understand the perils that were hidden in Peter's question in verse 27. For one thing, we must not "suppose" (20:10) that we will get something more if we really do not deserve it. It is possible to do the Father's work and yet not do His will from the heart (Eph. 6:6). If we serve Him only for the benefits (temporal and eternal), then we will miss the best blessings He has for us. We must trust Him unreservedly and believe that He will always give what is best.

There is the danger of pride. "What shall we have?" asked Peter. This parable warned him, "How do you know you will have anything?" Beware of overconfidence when it comes to the rewards God will give, for those first in their own eyes (and in the eyes of others) may end up last! Likewise, do not get discouraged; for those who consider themselves "unprofitable servants" may end up first.

Beware of the danger of watching other workers and measuring yourself by them. "Judge nothing before the time," Paul warns in 1 Corinthians 4:5. We see the worker and the work, but God sees the heart.

Finally, we must beware of criticizing God and feeling that we have been left out. Had the early morning workers trusted the owner and not asked for an agreement, the owner would have given them much more. He was generous, but they would not trust him. They did not rejoice that others received more; instead, they were jealous and complained. The goodness of the owner did not lead them to repentance (Rom. 2:4). It revealed the true character of their hearts: They were selfish! Whenever we find a complaining servant, we know he has not fully yielded to the master's will.

## We Must Glorify Him Completely (20:17-34)

For the third time, Jesus announced His arrest, crucifixion, and resurrection (see 16:21; 17:22). In the previous announcements, He had not specified how He would die. But now He clearly mentioned the cross. He also clearly mentioned His resurrection, but the message did not penetrate the disciples' hearts.

In contrast to this announcement of suffering and death we have the request of James and John and their mother, Salome. Jesus spoke about a cross, but they were interested in a crown. They wanted reserved seats on special thrones! We get the impression that the mother, Salome, was the real inspiration behind this request, and that she was interested in promoting her sons.

Before we criticize what they did, let's notice some commendable features in this event. For one thing, they *did* believe in prayer; and they dared to believe the promise Jesus had given about sitting on thrones (19:28). The word "regeneration" in that verse means "new birth," and refers to the new world over which Jesus and His followers will reign when He returns to earth. It must have taken faith on their part to believe He would establish these thrones, because He had just told them that He was going to die.

But there were several things wrong with their request. To begin with, it was born in ignorance. "Ye know not what ye ask," Jesus replied. Little did Salome realize that the path to the throne is a difficult one. James was the first of the disciples to be martyred, and John had to endure hard days on the Isle of Patmos. These three believers wanted *their* will, not God's will, and they wanted it *their way*.

Another factor was their lack of heavenly direction. They were thinking like *the world:* James and John wanted to "lord it over" the other disciples the way the unsaved Gentile rulers lorded it over their subjects. Their request was *fleshly* (sensual), because they were selfishly asking for glory for themselves, not for the Lord. No doubt they felt relieved that they had gotten to Jesus with this request before Peter did!

Finally, the request was not only of the world and the flesh, but it was of *the devil*. It was motivated by pride. Satan had sought a throne (Isa.

14:12-15) and had been cast down. Satan had offered Jesus a throne and had been refused (Matt. 4:8-11). Satan magnifies *the end* (a throne) but not *the means* to that end. Jesus warned Salome and her sons that the special thrones were available to those who were worthy of them. There are no shortcuts in the kingdom of God.

The result of this request was "indignation" on the part of the other disciples—probably because they had not thought of it first! The wisdom from above always leads to peace; the wisdom of this world leads to war (James 3:13—4:3). Selfishness will only result in dissention and division.

This disagreement gave Jesus the opportunity to teach a practical lesson on leadership. In His kingdom, we must not follow the examples of the world. Our example is Jesus, not some corporation president or wealthy celebrity. Jesus came as a servant; therefore, we should serve one another. He came to give His life; therefore, we should give our lives in service to Him and others.

The word *minister* in verse 26 simply means "a servant." Our English word "deacon" comes from it. The word *servant* in verse 27 means "a slave." Not every servant was a slave, but every slave was a servant. It is sad to note in the church today that we have many celebrities, but very few servants. There are many who want to "exercise authority" (v. 25), but few who want to take the towel and basin and wash feet.

The key to greatness is not found in position or power, but in character. We get a throne by paying with our lives, not by praying with our lips. We must identify with Jesus Christ in His service and suffering, for even He could not reach the throne except by way of the cross. The best commentary on this is Philippians 2:1-18.

To improve our praying we must improve our serving. If we are serving Him and others, then we will not be praying selfishly. If we honestly can say, "Speak, Lord, for Thy servant heareth," then He will say to us, "Speak, servant, for thy Lord heareth." If our prayers do not make us better servants, then there is something wrong with them.

Do our prayers make us easier to live with? The two disciples prayed selfishly and threw the whole fellowship into an uproar! Do our prayers make us more like Jesus Christ? *Do our prayers cost us anything?* Prayer in the will of God does not mean escape; it means involvement. If our prayers do not bring us nearer to the cross, then they are out of God's will.

Salome learned her lesson. When Jesus was crucified, she was standing near the cross (John 19:25, "his mother's sister") and sharing in His sorrow and pain. She did not see two thrones on either side of her Lord—she saw two thieves on two crosses. And she heard Jesus give her son, John, to His mother Mary. Salome's selfishness was rebuked, and she meekly accepted it.

The closing event of Matthew 20 is the healing of Bartimaeus and his friend, both of whom were blind (see Mark 10:46-52). Here Jesus put into practice what He had just taught the disciples. He became a servant to two rejected blind beggars. The crowds around Jesus tried to silence the two men. After all, what claim did they have on the great Teacher? But Jesus had compassion on them and healed them. He was the servant even of beggars.

This chapter contains some hard things for us to receive and practice. If we love the things of this world, we cannot love God supremely. If we are not yielded completely to His will, we cannot obey Him unreservedly. If we seek glory for ourselves, or if we compare ourselves with other believers, then we cannot glorify Him.

We cannot acknowledge Jesus as our King unless we love Him supremely, obey Him unreservedly, and glorify Him completely. But if we do these things, we will share in His life and joy, and one day reign with Him!

# 18

# THE KING'S JUDGMENTS

(Matthew 21:1—22:14)

We now enter the fourth major section of Matthew's Gospel, "The Rejection of the King." In this section (Matt. 21:1—22:14), the Lord Jesus revealed the sins of Israel and explained why the religious leaders rejected Him and His message.

**Spiritual Blindness** (21:1-11)
Since it was Passover, there were probably about 2 million people in and around Jerusalem. This was the only time in His ministry that Jesus actually planned and promoted a public demonstration. Up to this time, He had cautioned people not to tell who He was, and He had deliberately avoided public scenes.

Why did Jesus plan this demonstration? For one thing, He was obeying the Word and fulfilling the prophecy recorded in Zechariah 9:9. This prophecy could apply only to Jesus Christ, for He is the only one with credentials that prove He is Israel's King. We usually do not associate the lowly donkey with kingship, but this was the royal animal of Jewish monarchs (1 Kings 2:32ff). There were actually two animals involved, the mother and the colt (foal). Jesus sat upon the colt with the mother walking beside.

By comparing Matthew's quotation with the original prophecy in Zechariah, we discover some interesting facts. Zechariah's prophecy opens with, "Rejoice greatly" but Matthew omitted this phrase. When Jesus approached the city, He wept! How could He (or the people) rejoice when judgment was coming?

Matthew also omitted "He is just, and having salvation." Our Lord's coming to Jerusalem was an act of mercy and grace, not an act of justice or judgment. He did have salvation for them, but they refused to accept it (John 1:11). The next time Israel sees the King, He will ride in great power and glory (Rev. 19:11ff).

This colt had never been ridden (Mark 11:2), yet he meekly bore his burden. The presence of the mother helped, of course. But keep in mind that his rider was the King who has "dominion over . . . all sheep and oxen, yea, and the beasts of the field" (Ps. 8:6-7). The fact that Jesus rode this beast and kept him in control is another evidence of His Kingship.

There was a second reason for this public presentation: It forced the Jewish leaders to act. When they saw the spontaneous demonstration of the people, they concluded that Jesus had to be destroyed (see John 12:19). The prophetic Scriptures required that the Lamb of God be crucified on Passover. This demonstration of Christ's popularity incited the rulers to act.

The people acclaimed Jesus as their King both by their words and their deeds. They shouted *Hosanna* which means, "Save now!" They were quoting from Psalm 118:25-26, and this psalm is definitely messianic in character. Later that week, Jesus Himself would refer to this psalm and apply it to Himself (Matt. 21:42; Ps. 118:22-23).

Keep in mind that this Passover crowd was composed of at least three groups: the Jews who lived in Jerusalem, the crowd from Galilee, and the people who saw Jesus raise Lazarus from the dead (John 12:17-18). Sharing the news of this miracle undoubtedly helped to draw such a large crowd. The people wanted to see this miracle-worker for themselves.

But the Jews still did not recognize Jesus as their King. What caused Israel's spiritual blindness? For one thing, their religious leaders had robbed them of the truth of their own Word and had substituted man-made traditions (Luke 11:52). The leaders were not interested in truth; they were concerned only with protecting their own interests (John 11:47-53). "We have no king but Caesar!" was their confession of willful blindness. Even our Lord's miracles did not convince them. And the longer they resisted the truth, the blinder they became (John 12:35ff).

## Hypocrisy (21:12-22)

Jesus performed two acts of judgment: He cleansed the temple, and He cursed a fig tree. Both acts were contrary to His usual manner of ministry, for He did not come to earth to judge, but to save (John 3:17). Both of these acts revealed the hypocrisy of Israel: The temple was a den of thieves, and the nation (symbolized by the fig tree) was without fruit. Inward corruption and outward fruitlessness were evidences of their hypocrisy.

*Cleansing the temple* (21:12-16). Jesus had opened His ministry with a similar act (John 2:13-25). Now, three years later, the temple was defiled again by the "religious business" of the leaders. They had turned the Court of the Gentiles into a place where foreign Jews could exchange money and purchase sacrifices. What had begun as a service and convenience for visitors from other lands soon turned into a lucrative business. The dealers charged exorbitant prices and no one could compete with them or oppose them. Historians tell us that Annas, the former high priest, was the manager of this enterprise, assisted by his sons.

The purpose of the Court of the Gentiles in the temple was to give the "outcasts" an opportunity to enter the temple and learn from Israel about the true God. But the presence of this "religious market" turned many sensitive Gentiles away from the witness of Israel. The Court of the Gentiles was used for mercenary business, not missionary business.

When Jesus called the temple "My house," He was affirming that He was God. When He called it "My house of prayer," He was quoting Isaiah 56:7. The entire 56th chapter of Isaiah denounces the unfaithful leaders of Israel. The phrase "den of robbers" comes from Jeremiah 7:11 and is part of a long sermon that Jeremiah delivered in the gate of the temple, rebuking the people for the same sins that Jesus saw and judged in His day.

Why did Jesus call the temple "a den of thieves"? Because the place where thieves hide is called a den. The religious leaders, and some of the people, were using the temple and the Jewish religion to cover up their sins.

What does God want in His house? God wants *prayer* among His people (1 Tim. 2:1ff), for true prayer is an evidence of our dependence on God and our faith in His Word. He also wants *people* being helped (v. 14). The needy should feel welcome and should find the kind of help they need. There should be *power* in God's house, the power of God working to change people. *Praise* is another feature of God's house (vv. 15-16). Here Jesus quoted from Psalm 8:2.

*Cursing the tree* (21:17-22). That Jesus would curse a tree may surprise us. The same power that killed the tree could also have given it new life and fruit. Jesus certainly would not hold a tree morally responsible for being fruitless.

When we consider the time and place of this event, we understand it better. Jesus was near Jerusalem in the last week of His public ministry to His people. The fig tree symbolized the nation of Israel (Luke 13:6-9; Jer. 8:13; Hosea 9:10, 16). Just as this tree had leaves but no fruit, so Israel had a show of religion but no practical experience of faith resulting in godly living. Jesus was not angry at the tree. Rather, He used this tree to teach several lessons to His disciples.

*God wants to produce fruit in the lives of His people.* Fruit is the product of life. The presence of leaves usually indicates the presence of fruit, but this was not the case. In the parable of the fig tree (Luke 13:6-9), the gardener was given more time to care for the tree; but now the time was up. This tree was taking up space and doing no good.

While we can make a useful personal application of this event, the main interpretation has to do with Israel. The time of judgment had come. The sentence was pronounced by the Judge, but it would not be executed for about 40 years. Then Rome would come and destroy the city and temple and scatter the people.

Jesus used this event to teach His disciples a practical lesson about faith and prayer. The temple was supposed to be a "house of prayer," and the nation was to be a believing people. But both of these essentials were missing. We, too, must beware of the peril of fruitlessness.

## Disobedience to the Word (21:23—22:14)

This series of three parables grew out of the demand of the chief priests and elders for Jesus to explain what authority He had for cleansing the temple. As the custodians of the spiritual life of the nation, they had the right to ask this question. But we are amazed at their ignorance. Jesus had given them three years of ministry, and they still would not face the facts. They wanted more evidence.

In taking them back to the ministry of John, Jesus was not trying to avoid the issue. John had prepared the way for Jesus. Had the rulers received John's ministry, they would have received Jesus. Instead, the leaders permitted Herod to arrest John and then to kill him. If they would not accept the authority of John, they would not accept the authority of Jesus; for both John and Jesus were sent by God.

It is a basic principle of Christian living that we cannot learn new truth if we disobey what God has already told us. "If any man is willing to do His will, he shall know of the teaching, whether it is of God . . ." (John 7:17, NASB). The religious rulers had rejected the truth preached by John, and therefore Jesus could not impart new truth. Both He and John were under the same authority.

*They rejected God the Father* (21:23-32). The vineyard, of course, speaks of the nation of Israel (Isa. 5; Ps. 80:8-16). The two sons represent the two classes of people in that nation: the self-righteous religious people, and the publicans and sinners. When John came ministering, the religious crowd showed great interest in his work, but they would not repent and humble themselves and be baptized (Matt. 3:7-12; John 1:19-28). The nonreligious crowd, however, confessed their sins and obeyed John's words and were baptized.

The leaders committed two sins: They would not believe John's message and they would not repent of their sins. Of course, they felt that they had no need to repent (Luke 18:9-14). But when they saw what repentance did for the publicans and sinners, they should have been convinced that John's message was true and salvation was real. Again and again, the religious rulers rejected the clear evidence God gave them.

Their rejection of John was actually a rejection of the Father who had sent him. But God is gracious, and instead of sending judgment, He sent His Son. This leads to the next parable.

*They rejected the Son* (21:33-46). We are still at the vineyard. This parable is based on Isaiah 5:1-7, and in it Jesus reminded the Jews of God's goodness to them as a nation. God delivered them from Egypt and planted them in a rich land of milk and honey. He gave them material and spiritual blessings and asked only that they bear fruit for His glory. From time to time, God sent His servants (the prophets) to the people to receive the fruit. But the people mistreated the servants, and even killed some of them.

What should the householder do? He could have sent his armies to destroy these wicked men. But instead he sent his own son to them. The reference, of course, is to Jesus Christ, the Son of God. He is "the Heir" (Heb. 1:2). Instead of receiving and honoring the son, the men cast him out of the vineyard and killed him. Jesus was crucified "outside the gate" (Heb. 13:12-13, NASB), rejected by His own nation.

The people listening to the parable were caught up in the drama and did not realize that they passed sentence on themselves. Jesus quoted Psalm 118:22-23 to explain that He was that Son and the religious leaders were the husbandmen (v. 45). The crowds had quoted from Psalm 118:26 when they had welcomed Jesus into the city, so this Scripture was fresh in the minds of the rulers.

Often in the Old Testament, God is referred to as a rock or a stone (Deut. 32:4, 18, 30-31; Ps. 18:2, 31, 46). The stone is also a messianic title. To Israel, Jesus was a stumbling stone (Isa. 8:14-15; Rom. 9:32-33; 1 Cor. 1:23). Israel rejected the Messiah, but in His death and resurrection He created the church. To the church, Jesus is the foundation stone, the head of the corner (Eph. 2:20-22; 1 Peter 2:4-5). At the end of the age, Jesus will come as the smiting stone (Dan. 2:34), destroy Gentile kingdoms, and establish His own glorious kingdom.

Of course, the Jewish leaders knew the messianic import of the Scripture Jesus quoted. They were the *builders* who rejected the stone (Acts 4:11). What were the consequences? For one thing, the kingdom would be taken from Israel and given to another nation, the church (1 Peter 2:9, and note the context, vv. 6-10). Those who would attack this stone would be "pulverized"; those whom Christ judges will be crushed to bits.

*They rejected the Holy Spirit* (22:1-14). This parable must not be confused with the parable of the great supper (Luke 14:16-24) even though they have elements in common. Again we meet the Father and the Son; and the Son is alive (in spite of what the husbandmen did) and has a bride. The suggestion is that the Lord Jesus and His church are depicted (Eph. 5:22-33). The period described in this parable must be after His resurrection and ascension and the coming of the Holy Spirit.

The Father is still inviting the people of Israel to come, in spite of what they did to His Son. When we study the first seven chapters of Acts, we discover that the message is going out to none but Jews (Acts 2:5, 10, 14, 22, 36; 3:25; 6:7). "To the Jew first" was God's plan (Rom. 1:16; Acts 3:26). How did the nation's leaders respond to the ministry of the Holy

Spirit through the apostles? They rejected the Word and persecuted the church. The same rulers who permitted John to be killed, and who asked for Jesus to be killed, themselves killed Stephen! Later, Herod killed James (Acts 12:1ff).

How did the king in the parable respond to the way the people treated his servants? He became angry and sent his armies to destroy them and their city. He then turned to other people and invited them to come to the feast. This is a picture of God's dealing with Israel. They rejected the Father when they refused to obey John the Baptist's preaching. Israel rejected the Son when they arrested Him and crucified Him. In His grace and patience, God sent other witnesses. The Holy Spirit came upon the early believers and they witnessed with great power that Jesus was alive and the nation could be saved (Acts 2:32-36; 3:19-26). The miracles they did were proof that God was at work in and through them.

But Israel also rejected the Holy Spirit! This was Stephen's indictment against the nation: "You do always resist the Holy Ghost" (Acts 7:51). With the stoning of Stephen, God's patience with Israel began to end, although He delayed the judgment for almost 40 years. In Acts 8 we read that the message went to the Samaritans, and in Acts 10 we read that it even went to the Gentiles.

This final rejection is, to me, the awful "blasphemy against the Holy Spirit" that Jesus spoke about in Matthew 12:22-32. This was a national sin, committed by Israel. When they rejected John, they rejected the Father who sent him; but there remained the ministry of the Son. When they rejected the Son, *they were forgiven* because of their ignorance (Luke 23:34; Acts 3:17). No sinner *today* can be forgiven for rejecting Christ, for this rejection is what condemns the soul (John 3:16-22).

But there remained the ministry of the Holy Spirit. The Spirit came upon the church at Pentecost, and the apostles performed great signs and wonders (Acts 2:43; Heb. 2:1-4). The rulers rejected the witness of the Spirit, *and this brought final judgment*. They had rejected the Father, the Son, and the Spirit, and there were no more opportunities left.

This "sin against the Holy Spirit" cannot be committed today in the same way as Israel committed it, because the situation is different. The Spirit of God is bearing witness through the Word to the Person and work of Jesus Christ. It is the Spirit who convinces the world of sin (John 16:7-11). The Spirit can be resisted by unbelievers (Acts 7:51), but nobody knows that crisis hour (if there is one) when the Spirit stops dealing with a lost sinner.

Verses 11-14 seem like an appendix to the parable, but they are vitally important. The wedding garment was provided by the host so that everybody was properly attired and the poor did not feel conspicuous. Salvation is personal and individual. We must accept what God gives to us—the righteousness of Christ—and not try to make it on our own. Since these parables had a definite *national* emphasis, this *personal* emphasis at the end was most important.

The nation's leaders were guilty of spiritual blindness, hypocrisy, and deliberate disobedience to the Word. Instead of accepting this indictment from Jesus, and repenting, they decided to attack Him and argue with Him. The result: judgment. We should be careful not to follow their example of disobedience.

# 19

# THE
# KING'S
# DEFENSE

(Matthew 22:15-46)

On Tuesday of Passover week, our Lord's enemies tried to trap Him by using a series of "loaded" questions. These men were still smarting from the treatment they had received in the series of parables He had given. He had exposed their evil intentions and warned them that they were only asking for judgment. The religious leaders did not enjoy being humiliated before the crowds. They were wholeheartedly bent on destroying Jesus, and they hoped to trap Him into saying something that would permit them to arrest Him.

But there was another reason for the questions, one that His enemies did not realize. Jesus was going to die as the Lamb of God, and it was necessary for the lamb to be examined before Passover (Ex. 12:3-6). If any blemish whatsoever was found on the lamb, it could not be sacrificed. Jesus was examined publicly by His enemies, and they could find no fault in Him.

Of course, this personal interchange between our Lord and the religious leaders was also an opportunity for them to believe and be saved. In fact, one Pharisee came very close to the kingdom (Mark 12:32-34). Even at the last minute, there is hope for the lost sinner, if he will receive the truth, repent, and believe.

There are four questions involved in this public discussion, three of them from the enemy, and one from Jesus Christ.

## A Political Question about Taxes (22:15-22)

The Pharisees and the Herodians were enemies; but their common foe brought them together. The Pharisees opposed the Roman poll tax for several reasons: (1) They did not want to submit to a Gentile power; (2) Caesar was revered as a god; and (3) they had better uses for the money than to give it to Rome. Since the Herodians were the party supporting Herod, they were in favor of the tax. After all, Herod's authority was given to him by Caesar; and Herod would have had a difficult time staying in power without Rome's support.

Palestine was an occupied nation, and the Jews had no special love for their conquerors. Every tax the poor people had to pay was another reminder that they were not free. The Zealots, an "underground" organization of fanatical Jews, often staged protests against Rome. They would oppose any Roman tax.

It is easy to see why the Pharisees and Herodians chose the poll tax as the bait for their trap. It appeared that no matter which side Jesus took, He would create problems for Himself and His ministry. If He opposed the tax, He would be in trouble with Rome. If He approved the tax, He would be in trouble with the Jews.

Jesus immediately saw through their scheme. He knew that their real purpose was not to get an answer to a question, but to try to trap Him. They were only acting a part, and this made them hypocrites. On this basis alone, He could have refused to answer them. But He knew the people around Him would not understand. Here was an opportunity for Him to silence His enemies and, at the same time, teach the people an important spiritual truth.

Each ruler minted his own coins and put his own image on them. The "penny" (denarius) had Caesar's image on it, so it belonged to Caesar. "Give back to Caesar what belongs to Caesar," was His reply. "And give back to God what belongs to God." In this simple, but profound reply, Jesus taught several important truths.

*Christians must honor and obey rulers.* This is taught elsewhere in the New Testament (Rom. 13; 1 Peter 2:13-17; 1 Tim. 2:1ff). Christians have a dual citizenship, in heaven (Phil. 3:20) and on earth. We must respect our earthly rulers (or elected leaders), obey the law, pay taxes, and pray for all who are in authority.

*Christians must honor and obey God.* Caesar was not God. While governments cannot enforce religion (Acts 5:29), neither should they restrict freedom of worship. The best citizen honors his country because he worships God.

*Man bears God's image and owes God his all.* Caesar's image was on the coin; God's image is on man (Gen. 1:26-27). Sin has marred that image, but through Jesus Christ, it can be restored (Eph. 4:24; Col. 3:10).

The relationship between religion and government is personal and individual. It is right for the people of God to serve in government (remember Daniel and Joseph). But it is wrong for government to control the church, or for the church to control government.

## A Doctrinal Question about the Resurrection (22:23-33)

In spite of the fact that the Pharisees and Herodians had been worsted, the Sadducees entered the field and tried *their* attack. Keep in mind that this group accepted only the authority of the five Books of Moses. The Sadducees did not believe in a spirit world or in the doctrine of the resurrection (Acts 23:8). They had often challenged the Pharisees to prove the doctrine of the resurrection from Moses, but the Pharisees were not too successful with their arguments.

The Sadducees' hypothetical illustration was based on the Jewish law of "levirate marriage" from Deuteronomy 25:5-10. (The word *levirate* comes from the Latin word *levir* which means "a husband's brother." It has nothing to do with the tribe of Levi.) The purpose of this custom was to preserve a man's name should he die without a male heir. In a nation like Israel, where family inheritance was a major thing, it was important that each family have a male heir. It was considered a disgrace for a man to refuse to raise up a family for his dead brother.

The Sadducees based their disbelief of the resurrection on the fact that no woman could have seven husbands in the future life. Like many people today, they conceived of the future life as an extension of their present life—only better.

But Jesus told them that they were ignorant. They did not know the Scriptures, nor did they know the power of God, which inferred that they really did not know God. There will be no need for marriage in the next life because there will be no death. Therefore it will not be necessary to bear children to replace those who die.

Jesus did *not* say that we would be angels when we are glorified in heaven. He said we would be "*as* the angels" in that we would be sexless and not married or given in marriage. The foolish stories we hear and the cartoons we see about people dying and becoming angels are certainly unbiblical.

Our Lord was not content to refute the Sadducees' foolish views about the future life. He also wanted to answer their claim that there was no resurrection; *and He did it by referring to Moses!* He knew that Moses was the only authority they would accept. He reminded them of Exodus 3:6 where God said to Moses, "I am the God of Abraham, and the God of Isaac, and the God of Jacob." He did not say, "I *was* the God of Abraham . . ." for that would mean that Abraham was no more. By saying "I am," the Lord made it clear that these three men of faith were *at that time alive*. And by repeating "the God of," the Lord was saying that He knew them and loved them personally and individually.

It is a dangerous thing to speculate about the future life. We must rest upon the authority of the Word of God, for only there do we have truth that answers man's questions about the future. The Bible does not tell us everything about the future life, but is does encourage and enlighten us. Jesus answered the foolish, ignorant Sadducees so completely that they were "muzzled" (the word *silence* in v. 34). Even the crowds were astonished and amazed at His answer.

## An Ethical Question about the Law (22:34-40)

The Pharisees probably enjoyed the embarrassment of their enemies, the Sadducees. One of their number showed respect for the Lord and His answer (Mark 12:28) and asked a question of his own: "Teacher, which is the great commandment in the Law?" (Matt. 22:36, NASB). We have every reason to believe that he asked the question in sincerity and with a humble attitude.

This was not a new question, for the scribes had been debating it for centuries. They had documented 613 commandments in the Law, 248 positive and 365 negative. No person could ever hope to know and fully obey all of these commandments. So, to make it easier, the experts divided the commandments into "heavy" (important) and "light" (unimportant). A person could major on the "heavy comandments" and not worry about the trivial ones.

The fallacy behind this approach is obvious: You need only break *one law,* heavy or light, to be guilty before God. "For whosoever shall keep the whole Law, and yet offend in one point, he is guilty of all" (James 2:10).

Jesus quoted the "Shema" (Deut. 6:4), a statement of faith that was recited daily by every orthodox Jew. (The word "Shema" comes from the Hebrew word which means "to hear." The confession of faith begins with, "Hear, O Israel!") The greatest commandment is to love God with all that we are and have—heart, soul, mind, strength, possessions, service. To love God is not to "have good feelings about Him," for true love involves the will as well as the heart. Where there is love, there will be service and obedience.

But love for God cannot be divorced from love for one's neighbor; so Jesus also quoted Leviticus 19:18 and put it on the same level as the Shema. All of the Law and the Prophets hang on *both* of these commandments. We might add that the teachings of the Epistles in the New Testament agree with this statement. If a man really loves God, he must also love his brother and his neighbor (1 John 3:10-18; 4:7-21).

If we have a right relationship with God, we will have no problems with His commandments. Love is the basis for obedience. In fact, all of the Law is summed up love (Rom. 13:8-10). If we love God, we will love our neighbor; and if we love our neighbor, we will not want to do anything to harm him.

But Jesus had a deeper meaning to convey in this marvelous answer. The Jews were afraid of idolatry. When Jesus claimed to be God, they opposed Him because they could not believe it was right to worship a creature. Jesus received worship and did not rebuke those who honored Him. Was this idolatry? No, because He was God! But if the Law commands us to love God *and our neighbor,* then it would not be wrong for the Jews to love Jesus. Instead, they were plotting to kill Him. He had said to them one day, "If God were your Father, you would love Me . . ." (John 8:42). They accepted the authority of the Law, yet they refused to obey it in their lives.

The scribe who had asked the original question seemed to be an honest and sincere man. Not all of the Pharisees were hypocrites. He publicly agreed with Jesus (Mark 12:32-33). This must have given his fellow Pharisees a fright. Jesus discerned that the man's heart was sincere, and He commended him for his intelligence and honesty. Did the man ever get all the way into the kingdom, when he was so very near? We trust so.

Jesus had now answered three difficult questions. He had dealt with the relationship between religion and government, between this life and the next life, and between God and our neighbors. These are fundamental relationships, and we cannot ignore our Lord's teachings. But there is a question more fundamental than these, and Jesus asked it of His enemies.

## A Personal Question about the Messiah (22:41-46)

Jesus did not phrase this question as He had when He asked His disciples, "Whom say you that I am?" (Matt. 16:15) These men who had been arguing with Him were not sympathetic with His cause, nor were they honest in their assessment of His credentials. Jesus had to take an indirect approach with His enemies. He made this sound like another theological question, when in reality it was the most important *personal* question they would ever face.

"Whose Son is the Messiah?" He asked them. As trained experts in the Law, they knew the answer: "He is the Son of David." Had they been asked, they could have referred to numbers of Old Testament Scriptures, including 2 Samuel 7:12-13, Psalm 78:68-72, and Micah 5:2. Once they had given this answer, Jesus asked a second question, this time quoting from Psalm 110:1—"The LORD [Jehovah] said unto my Lord [Hebrew "Adonai"], 'Sit Thou at My right hand, until I make Thine enemies Thy footstool.' "

Every orthodox Jewish scholar interpreted this to refer to the Messiah. Only the Messiah could sit at the right hand of Jehovah God. Jesus believed in the inspiration and accuracy of the Old Testament Scriptures, for He said that David spoke these words "in the Spirit" (v. 43, NASB). Nobody dared to question the accuracy or the authority of the text.

"If Messiah is David's Son," Jesus asked, "then how could Messiah also be David's Lord?" There is only one answer to this question. As God, Messiah is David's Lord; as man, He is David's Son. He is both "the root and the offspring of David" (Rev. 22:16). Psalm 110:1 teaches the deity and the humanity of Messiah. He is David's Lord and He is David's Son.

When He was ministering on earth, Jesus often accepted the messianic title "Son of David" (see Matt. 9:27; 12:23; 15:22; 20:30-31; 21:9, 15). The rulers had heard the multitudes proclaim Him as "Son of David" when He rode into Jerusalem. The fact that He accepted this title is evidence that Jesus knew Himself to be the Messiah, the Son of God. As God, He was David's Lord; but as man, He was David's Son, for He was born into the family of David (Matt. 1:1, 20).

The scholars in that day were confused about the Messiah. They saw two pictures of Messiah in the Old Testament and could not reconcile them. One picture showed a suffering servant, the other a conquering and reigning monarch. Were there two Messiahs? How could God's servant suffer and die? (See 1 Peter 1:10-12.)

Had they listened to what Jesus said, they would have learned that there was only one Messiah, but that He would be both human and divine. He would suffer and die as a sacrifice for sins. He would then rise from the dead in triumph, and one day return to defeat His enemies. However, these religious leaders had their own ideas, and they did not want to change. If they had accepted His teaching, then they would also have to accept Him as the Messiah; and this they were unwilling to do.

The result of this day of dialogue was silence on the part of His enemies. They dared not ask Jesus any more questions, not because they had believed the truth, but because they were afraid to face the truth. "For they did not have courage to question Him any longer about anything" (Luke 20:40, NASB). But neither did they have courage to face the truth and act upon it.

Making a decision about Jesus Christ is a matter of life or death. The evidence is there for all to examine. We can examine it defensively and miss the truth. Or we can examine it honestly and humbly, and discover the truth, believe, and be saved. The religious leaders were so blinded by tradition, position, and selfish pride that they could not—and would not—see the truth and receive it.

We dare not make the same mistake today.

# 20

# THE
# KING'S
# DENUNCIATION

(Matthew 23)

This was our Lord's last public message. It is a scathing denunciation of false religion that paraded under the guise of truth. Some of the common people no doubt were shocked at His words, for they considered the Pharisees to be righteous.

Perhaps we should remind ourselves that not all of the Pharisees were hypocrites. There were about 6,000 Pharisees in that day, with many more who were "followers" but not full members of the group. Most of the Pharisees were middle-class businessmen and no doubt they were sincere in their quest for truth and holiness. The name "Pharisees" came from a word that means "to separate." The Pharisees were separated from the Gentiles, the "unclean" Jews who did not practice the Law ("publicans and sinners," Luke 15:1-2), and from any who opposed the tradition that governed their lives.

Among the Pharisees were a few members who sought for true spiritual religion. Nicodemus (John 3; 7:50-53), Joseph of Arimathaea (John 19:38ff), and the unnamed man mentioned in Mark 12:32-34, come to mind. Even Gamaliel showed a great deal of tolerance toward the newly-formed church (Acts 5:34ff). But for the most part, the Pharisees used their religion to promote themselves and their material gain. No wonder Jesus denounced them. Note the three divisions in this message.

**Explanation to the Crowd** (23:1-12)

In this section, Jesus explained the basic flaws of Pharisaical religion.

*They had a false concept of righteousness* (23:2-3). To begin with, they had assumed an authority not their own. "The scribes and the Pharisees *have seated themselves* in Moses' seat . . ." is the literal translation. There is no record in the Scriptures that God assigned any authority to this group. Their only authority was the Word of God. Therefore, the people were to obey whatever the Pharisees taught *from the Word*. But the people were not to obey the traditions and the man-made rules of the Pharisees.

To the Pharisee, righteousness meant outward conformity to the Law of God. They ignored the inward condition of the heart. Religion consisted in obeying numerous rules that governed every detail of life, including what you did with the spices in your cupboard (vv. 23-24). The Pharisees were careful to say the right words and follow the right ceremonies, but they did not *inwardly* obey the Law. God desired truth in the inward parts (Ps. 51:6). To preach one thing and practice another is only hypocrisy.

*They had a false concept of ministry* (23:4). To them, ministry meant handing down laws to the people and adding to their burdens. In other words, the Pharisees were harder on others than they were on themselves. Jesus came to lighten men's burdens (Matt. 11:28-30), but legalistic religion always seeks to make burdens heavier. Jesus never asks us to do anything that He has not first done. The Pharisees commanded, but they did not participate. They were hypocritical religious dictators, not spiritual leaders.

*They had a false concept of greatness* (23:5-12). To them, success meant recognition by men and praise from men. They were not concerned about the approval of God. They used their religion to attract attention, not to glorify God (Matt. 5:16). This even meant using religious ornaments to display their piety. "Phylacteries" were small leather boxes into which the Pharisees placed portions of the Scriptures. They wore these boxes on their foreheads and arms, in literal obedience to Deuteronomy 6:8 and 11:18. They also increased the size of their "tassels" on the hems of their garments (Num. 15:38; see Matt. 9:20).

The Pharisees also thought that *position* was a mark of greatness, so they sought the best seats in the synagogue and at the public dinners. Where a man sits bears no relationship to what a man is. Albert Einstein wrote, "Try not to become a man of success, but rather try to become a man of value."

They also thought that *titles of honor* were a mark of greatness. The title "rabbi" means "my great one" and was coveted by the religious leaders. (Today religious leaders covet honorary doctor's degrees.) Jesus forbad His disciples to use the title *rabbi* because all of them were brothers, and Jesus alone was their Teacher ("Master" in v. 8). There is a spiritual equality among the children of God, under the Lordship of Jesus Christ.

Jesus also forbad them to use the title *father* with reference to spiritual things. Certainly it is not wrong to call one's biological father by that name, but it is wrong to use it when addressing a spiritual leader. Paul referred to himself as a "spiritual father" because he had begotten people through the Gospel (1 Cor. 4:15). But he did not ask them to use that term when addressing him.

A third title that was forbidden was *master* (v. 10), which means "guide, instructor, leader." This is not the same word that is translated "Master" in verse 8 in the King James Version. That word means "teacher," while this one means "one who goes before and guides." Perhaps a modern equivalent would be "authority." God has placed spiritual leaders in the church, but they must not replace God in our lives. A true spiritual leader directs his people into freedom and a closer fellowship with Christ, not into bondage to his ideas and beliefs.

True greatness is found in serving others, not in forcing others to serve us (John 3:30; 13:12-17). True greatness is not manufactured; it can only come from God as we obey Him. If we exalt ourselves, God will humble us. But if we humble ourselves, in due time God will exalt us (1 Peter 5:6).

### Denunciation of the Pharisees (23:13-36)

We must not read this series of denunciations with the idea that Jesus lost His temper and was bitterly angry. Certainly He was angry at their sins, and what those sins were doing to the people. But His attitude was one of painful sorrow that the Pharisees were blinded to God's truth and to their own sins.

Perhaps the best way to deal with these eight "woes" is to contrast them with the eight beatitudes found in Matthew 5:1-12. In the Sermon on the Mount the Lord described true righteousness; here He described a false righteousness.

*Entering the kingdom—shutting up the kingdom* (23:13; 5:3). The poor in spirit enter the kingdom, but the proud in spirit keep themselves out and even keep others out. The Greek verb indicates people trying to get in who cannot. It is bad enough to keep yourself out of the kingdom, but worse when you stand in the way of others. By teaching man-made traditions instead of God's truth, they "took away the key of knowledge" and closed the door to salvation (Luke 11:52).

*Mourners comforted—destroyers condemned* (23:14; 5:4). While this verse is not in some manuscripts of Matthew, it is found in Mark 12:40 and Luke 20:47. Instead of mourning over their own sins, and mourning with needy widows, the Pharisees took advantage of people in order to rob them. They used their religion as a "cloak of covetousness" (1 Thes. 2:5).

*Meek inherit the earth—proud send souls to hell* (23:15; 5:5). A proselyte is a convert to a cause. The Pharisees were out to win others to their legalistic system, yet they could not introduce these people to the living God. Instead of saving souls, the Pharisees were condemning souls!

A "child of hell" is the equivalent of "child of the devil," which is what Jesus called the Pharisees (John 8:44; Matt. 12:34; 23:33). A "child of the devil" is a person who has rejected God's way of salvation (righteousness through faith in Christ). This person parades his own self-righteousness through whatever religious system he belongs to. The convert usually shows more zeal than his leader, and this "double devotion" only produces double condemnation. How tragic that people can think they are going to heaven, when actually they are going to hell!

*Hungering for holiness—greedy for gain* (23:16-22; 5:6). "Blind guides" is a perfect description, one that must have brought a smile to the lips of the listeners. Jesus had used it before (Matt. 15:14). The Pharisees were blind to the true values of life. Their priorities were confused. They would take an oath and use some sacred object to substantiate that oath—the gold in the temple, for example, or the gift on the altar. But they would not swear by the temple itself or the altar. It was the temple that sanctified the gold and the altar that sanctified the gift. They were leaving God out of their priorities.

Jesus knew that the Pharisees wanted both the gold and the gifts on the altar. This is why the Pharisees practiced "Corban"—anything dedicated to God could not be used for others (Mark 7:10-13; Matt. 15:1-9). These men were not seeking for the righteousness of God; they were greedy for gain. They worked out a "religious system" that permitted them to rob God and others and still maintain their reputations.

*Obtaining mercy—rejecting mercy* (23:23-24; 5:7). The Pharisees majored on minors. They had rules for every minute area of life, while at the same time they forgot about the important things. It is usually the case that legalists are sticklers for details, but blind to great principles. This crowd thought nothing of condemning an innocent man, yet they were afraid to enter Pilate's judgment hall lest they be defiled (John 18:28).

There is no question that the Old Testament Law required tithing (Lev. 27:30; Deut. 14:22ff). Abraham had practiced tithing long before the Law was given (Gen. 14:20), and Jacob followed his grandfather's example (Gen. 28:20-22). The principles of Christian giving under grace are given in 2 Cor. 8—9. We are not content simply to give a tithe (10%), but we also want to bring offerings to the Lord out of hearts filled with love.

Justice, mercy, and faithfulness are the important qualities God is seeking. Obeying the rules is no substitute. While it is good to pay attention to details, we must never lose our sense of priorities in spiritual matters. Jesus did not condemn the practice of tithing. But He did condemn those who allowed their legalistic scruples to keep them from developing true Christian character.

*Pure in heart—defiled in heart* (23:25-28; 5:8). Jesus used two illustrations: the cup and platter, and the sepulchre. They both stated the same truth: it is possible to be clean on the outside and at the same time defiled on the inside. Imagine using dishes that were defiled! Whatever you put into the dish or cup would also become defiled. The Pharisees were careful to keep the outside very clean, because that was the part that men would see; and they wanted the praise of men. But God sees the heart (1 Sam. 16:7). When God looked within, He saw "greed and self-indulgence" (v. 25, NIV).

Jewish people were careful not to touch dead bodies or anything relating to the dead, because this would make them ceremonially unclean (Num. 19:11ff). They would whitewash the tombs lest someone accidentally get defiled, and this was done especially at Passover season. What a graphic picture of the hypocrite: white on the outside, but filled with defilement and death on the inside!

"Blessed are the pure in heart," was our Lord's promise. "Watch over your heart with all diligence, for from it flow the springs of life" (Prov. 4:23, NASB). D. L. Moody used to say, "If I take care of my character, my reputation will take care of itself." The Pharisees lived for reputation, not character.

*Peacemakers and persecuted are God's children—persecutors are the devil's children* (23:29-33; 5:9-12). When Jesus called the Pharisees "serpents . . . generation of vipers," He was identifying them with Satan who is the serpent (Gen. 3:1ff). In His parable of the tares, Jesus made it clear that *Satan has a family* (Matt. 13:38). Satan was a murderer and a liar (John 8:44), and his children follow his example. The Pharisees were liars (v. 30) and murderers (v. 34).

It was traditional for the Pharisees to build, improve, and embellish the tombs of the martyrs. But it was "their fathers" who killed the martyrs! Not their biological fathers, of course, but their "spiritual fathers"—the hypocrites of the past ages.

There have always been counterfeit believers in the world, starting with Cain (Gen. 4:1-15; 1 John 3:10-15). The Pharisees and their kind are guilty of all the righteous blood shed in the name of "religion." The first martyr recorded in Old Testament Scripture was Abel (Gen. 4), and the last one recorded was the prophet Zechariah (2 Chron. 24:20-22—the Hebrew Bible ends with 2 Chronicles, not Malachi).

What will be the result of this long history of murders? Terrible judgment! "This generation" (the "generation of vipers," v. 33) would taste the wrath of God when the cup of iniquity was full (v. 32; Gen. 15:16). Some of this judgment came when Jerusalem was destroyed, and the rest will be meted out in eternity.

As we review these tragic *woes* from the lips of our Lord, we can see why the Pharisees were His enemies. He emphasized the inner man; they were concerned with externals. He taught a spiritual life based on principles, while the Pharisees majored on rules and regulations. Jesus measured spirituality in terms of character, while the Pharisees measured it in terms of religious activities and conformity to external laws. Jesus taught humility and sacrificial service; but the Pharisees were proud and used people to accomplish their own purposes. The holy life of Jesus exposed their artificial piety and shallow religion. Instead of coming out of the darkness, the Pharisees tried to put out the Light; and they failed.

## Lamentation over Jerusalem (23:37-39)

Jesus spoke these words of lamentation as a sincere expression of His love for Jerusalem, and His grief over the many opportunities for salvation that they had passed by. "Jerusalem" refers to the entire nation of Israel. The nation's leaders had been guilty of repeated crimes as they rejected God's messengers, and even killed some of them. But in His grace, Jesus came to gather the people and save them.

"I would have . . . ye would not" summarizes the tragedy of final rejection of the truth. There is no argument here about divine sovereignty and human responsibility, for both are included. God could not force His salvation on the people; neither could He change the consequences of their stubborn rejection. "You will not come to Me that you may have life" (John 5:40).

The image of the mother bird gathering and covering her brood is a familiar one. Moses used it in his farewell sermon (Deut. 32:11), and it is found in other places in the Old Testament (Ruth 2:12; Ps. 17:8; 36:7; 91:4). It is a picture of love, tender care, and a willingness to die to protect others. Jesus did die for the sins of the world, including the nation of Israel; but "His own received Him not" (John 1:11).

"Your house" probably means both the temple and the city, both of which would be destroyed in A.D. 70 by invading Roman armies. The temple was "My house" in Matthew 21:13, but now it has been abandoned and left empty. Jesus left both the temple and the city and went out to the Mount of Olives (Matt. 24:1-3).

Yet, Jesus left the nation with a promise: He would one day return, the nation would see Him and say "Blessed be He that cometh in the name of the Lord!" This is a quotation from Psalm 118:26, that great messianic psalm that was quoted so many times in His last week of ministry. The crowds had used those words on Palm Sunday (Matt. 21:9).

When would this promise be fulfilled? At the end of the age when Jesus Christ returns to earth to deliver Israel and defeat their enemies (Rom. 11:25-27; Zech. 12). The fact that Israel rejected the King would not hinder God's great plan of redemption. Instead of establishing His glorious kingdom on earth, Jesus would build His church (Matt. 16:18; Eph. 2:11-22). When that work is finished, He will return and take His church to heaven (1 Thes. 4:13-18). Then there will be a time of judgment on earth ("the day of the Lord," "the time of Jacob's trouble"), at the end of which He will return to deliver Israel.

We cannot read this severe denunciation without marveling at the patience and goodness of the Lord. No nation has been blessed like Israel, and yet no nation has sinned against God's goodness as has Israel. They have been the channel of God's blessing to the world, for "salvation is of the Jews" (John 4:22). Yet they have suffered greatly in this world.

Jesus was born a Jew, and He loved His nation. We who are Gentiles ought to thank God for the Jews, for they gave us the witness of the one true God, they gave us the Bible, and they gave us Jesus Christ the Saviour. Like Jesus, we ought to love the Jews, seek to win them, pray for the peace of Jerusalem, and encourage them every way we can.

# 21

# THE
# KING'S
# RETURN–PART 1

(Matthew 24:1-44)

The Olivet Discourse grew out of some questions the disciples asked when Jesus told them that the temple would one day be destroyed. First, they wanted to know *when*. This answer is not recorded in Matthew but is given in Luke 21:20-24. Secondly, they asked about the sign of Christ's return. This is answered in Matthew 24:29-44. In their final question, they asked about the sign of the end of the age. Christ's reply is in Matthew 24:4-28.

We must keep in mind that the "atmosphere" of this discourse is *Jewish*. Jesus talked about Judea (v. 16), the Sabbath (v. 20), and the prophecies of Daniel concerning the Jewish people (v. 15). The full truth about the rapture of the church (1 Thes. 4:13-18; 1 Cor. 15:51ff) had not yet been revealed, for it was a mystery (Eph. 3:1-12).

Matthew 24:1-44 indicates that our Lord was discussing events that will take place on earth during the time of Tribulation. (See v. 8, where "birth-pangs" is a symbol of Tribulation; and see also vv. 21, 29.) After the church has been suddenly taken out of the world, there will be a period of "peace and safety" (1 Thes. 5:1-4) followed by a time of terrible suffering. Many Bible scholars believe this period will last seven years (Dan. 9:24-27). It is this period of "tribulation" that Jesus described in the Olivet Discourse. At the end of that period, Jesus will return to the earth, defeat His foes, and establish the promised kingdom.

In the section before us, Jesus explained three different periods in the time of Tribulation.

## The Beginning of the Tribulation (24:4-14)

The events described in this section are "the beginning of birth-pangs" (v. 8). The image of a woman in travail is a picture of the Tribulation period (1 Thes. 5:5; Isa. 13:6-11). Let's consider some of the significant events that will occur at the beginning of this period.

*Religious deception* (24:4-5). The Jews have often been led astray by false prophets and false Christs. The rider on the white horse in Revelation 6:1-2 is the Antichrist, that final world dictator who will lead the nations astray. He will begin his career as a peacemaker, signing a convenant with Israel to protect her from her enemies (Dan. 9:27). Israel will welcome this man as their great benefactor (John 5:43).

*Wars* (24:6). Note that wars are not a sign of the end. There have always been wars in the world, and will be until the very end. Wars of themselves do not announce the end of the age or the coming of the Lord.

*Famines* (24:7a). War and famine usually go together. Revelation 6:6 suggests terribly high prices for staple foods, for a "penny" was a day's wages.

*Death* (24:7b-8). Earthquakes help to create famines, and both help to cause epidemics that take many lives.

*Martyrs* (24:9). Christians have always been hated by the world, but here we have an acceleration of persecutions and murders. All nations will be involved. This certainly was not true in the history of the early church.

*Worldwide chaos* (24:10-13). Those who once were true to each other will betray each other. This suggests that marriages, homes, and nations will be torn asunder because of lack of loyalty. Lawlessness will abound (v. 12), for even the law enforcement agencies will not be able to keep the peace.

Verse 13 has nothing to do with personal salvation in this present age of grace. "The end" does not mean the end of this life; it refers to the end of the age (v. 14). Those believers on earth during this terrible period, who endure in their faith, will be saved when the Lord comes at the end and delivers them.

*Worldwide preaching* (24:14). Revelation 7:1-8 teaches that God will choose and seal 144,000 Jewish evangelists who will carry the kingdom message to the ends of the earth. This verse does not teach that the Gospel of God's grace must be spread to every nation today before Jesus can return for His church. It is the Lord's return *at the end of the age* that is in view here.

### The Middle of the Tribulation (24:15-22)

The midpoint of the Tribulation period is most important, for at that time an event will take place that was prophesied centuries ago by Daniel (9:24-27). Please notice that this prophecy concerns only the Jews and the city of Jerusalem ("thy people and . . . thy holy city," v. 24). To apply it to the church or to any other people or place is to misinterpret God's Word.

The prophecy involves seventy weeks and the Hebrew word "week" means "a week of years," or seven years. Seventy sevens would equal 490 years. But this period of 490 years is broken up into three parts:

(1) During seven weeks (49 years) the city of Jerusalem would be rebuilt and the worship reestablished.

(2) After 62 weeks (434 years) Messiah would come to Jerusalem and die for the sins of the world.

(3) The prince will make an agreement with the Jews for one week (seven years) to protect them from their enemies.

The decree to rebuild Jerusalem was given in 445 B.C. by Cyrus (2 Chron. 36:22-23; Ezra 1). The city was rebuilt in troubled times. Sir Robert Anderson in his classic book *The Coming Prince* (Kregel, 1975) has proved that there were exactly 482 prophetic years (of 360 days each) between the giving of the decree and the day that Jesus rode into Jerusalem as the King.

But we must account for the remaining "week" of seven years. Where does it fit in? Note that the same city that was rebuilt will also be destroyed "by the people of the prince that shall come" (Dan. 9:26), that is, the Romans. ("The prince that shall come" is a name for the Antichrist.) This event took place in A.D. 70. But the Jewish nation would be spared and the city restored again. For at some future date, the prince that shall come (Antichrist) will make a covenant with the Jews *for seven years*. This is where the missing "week" fits in. He will agree to protect them from their enemies and permit them to rebuild their temple. (Daniel

9:27 talks about a restoration of the sacrifices, and this would demand a temple.)

The logical place for this seven-year period is after the Rapture of the church. "The time of Jacob's trouble," the Tribulation period, will be seven years long. Second Thessalonians 2:1-12 indicates that the Antichrist cannot be revealed until the *restrainer* is taken out of the midst. That restrainer is the Holy Spirit in the church. Once the church is out of the world, then Satan can produce his masterpiece, the Antichrist.

He will make the agreement for seven years, but after three-and-one-half years ("in the midst of the week") he will break that agreement. He will then move into the Jewish temple himself and proclaim that he is God (2 Thes. 2:3-4; Rev. 13).

The Antichrist will cause a living statue of himself to be put into the temple, and his associate (the false prophet, Rev. 20:10) will cause the whole earth to worship it. Satan has always wanted the world's worship, and in the middle of the Tribulation he will begin to receive it (Matt. 4:8-11). Jesus called this statue "the abomination of desolation" (v. 15; Dan. 9:27).

An interesting parenthesis occurs at the end of Matthew 24:15—"whoso readeth, let him understand." This statement indicates that what Jesus was teaching would have greater significance for people reading Matthew's Gospel in the latter days. By reading the Prophet Daniel and the words of Jesus, these believers will understand the events and know what to do. This is another evidence that the Olivet Discourse applies to people during the Tribulation period.

Prophetic scholars have speculated as to why the Antichrist would break his covenant with the Jews after three-and-one-half years. It has been suggested that the invasion of Israel by Russia, prophesied in Ezekiel 38—39, would occur at that point. Certainly Israel will be at ease and dwelling in safety at that time, for she will be protected by the Antichrist (Ezek. 38:11). At that time, he will be the ruler of a 10-nation alliance, "The United States of Europe" (Rev. 17:12-13). Russia, of course, will be soundly beaten, not by Israel, but by Almighty God. When the Antichrist sees that his great enemy, Russia, has been beaten, he will take advantage of the opportunity and move into Israel, breaking his covenant and taking over the temple.

The readers of this prophecy in the latter days will know what to do:

Get out of Judea! These instructions are similar to those given in Luke 21:20ff, but they refer to a different time period. Luke's instructions apply to the siege of Jerusalem in A.D. 70, and the "sign" was the gathering of the armies around the city. Matthew's instructions apply to Jewish believers in the middle of the Tribulation, and the "sign" is the desecration of the temple by the image of the Antichrist. Those who have confused those two "sign events" have ended up believing that Jesus Christ returned in A.D. 70!

This entire paragraph relates only to Jews, for no Christian believer would worry about breaking a Sabbath law. This event ushers in "the Great Tribulation," the last half of Daniel's 70th week, when tha judgments of God will be hurled upon the earth. During the first three-and-one-half years of the Tribulation, the judgments were natural: wars, famines, earthquakes, etc. But during the last half, the judgments will be supernatural and devastating.

During this period, God will care for His elect (v. 22), referring to Jews and Gentiles who believe and are converted. "The elect" here does not refer to the church since the church will have been raptured at least three-and-one-half years previously.

### The End of the Tribulation (24:23-44)
World conditions will be so terrible that men will wonder if any relief will come, and this will give false christs opportunities to deceive many. Satan is capable of performing "lying wonders" (2 Thes. 2:9-12; Rev. 13:13-14). The fact that a religious leader performs miracles is no assurance that he has come from God. Many Jews will be deceived, for "the Jews require a sign" (1 Cor. 1:22). Jesus performed true signs in His Father's name, and the nation rejected Him (John 12:37ff). Satan's miracles they will accept.

Verse 27 indicates that the return of Jesus to the earth will be sudden, like a stroke of lightning. The event that precedes His return is the gathering of the Gentile nations at Armageddon (Rev. 16:13-16; 19:11ff). The eagles flying around the carcass picture the awful carnage that will result from this great battle (Rev. 19:17-19). The cosmic changes mentioned in Matthew 24:29 precede the return of Jesus Christ to the earth.

We are not told what "the sign of the Son of man in heaven" is, but the people on earth at that time will recognize it. When Jesus comes for the church, He will come in the air and His people will be caught up to meet Him in the air (1 Thes. 4:17). But our Lord's second coming at the end of the Tribulation will be a great public event, with every eye seeing Him (Rev. 1:7).

This event will have special meaning for Israel. Jesus will return at that hour when Israel is about to be defeated by the Gentile armies (Zech. 12). He will rescue His people, and they will see Him and recognize that He is their Messiah (Zech. 12:9-14). There will be a national repentance, national cleansing, and national restoration under the gracious leadership of their Messiah.

We must not confuse the trumpet of Matthew 24:31 with the "trump of God" mentioned in 1 Thessalonians 4:16. "His elect" in Matthew 24:31 refers to people on earth, Jews and Gentiles, who have trusted Christ and been saved. In the Old Testament, Israel's movements were announced by trumpet signals (Num. 10; Joel 2:1ff). Israel has been a scattered people for many centuries. The angels will gather Israel with trumpets just as the priests did in Old Testament times (Lev. 23:23-25).

Scholars of prophecy do not agree on all the details of future events. But the following summary is a fair representation of what many prophetic scholars believe as to the order of events:

1. The rapture of the church (1 Thes. 4:13-18; 1 Cor. 15:51-58). This can occur at any time.

2. The leader of the 10 European nations makes a 7-year agreement with Israel (Dan. 9:26-27).

3. After three-and-one-half years, he breaks the agreement (Dan. 9:27).

4. He moves to Jerusalem and sets up his image in the temple (2 Thes. 2:3-4; Rev. 13).

5. The Antichrist begins to control the world and forces all people to worship and obey him. At this time God sends great tribulation upon the earth (Matt. 24:21).

6. The nations gather at Armageddon to fight the Antichrist and Israel, but see the sign of Christ's coming and unite to fight Him (Zech. 12; Rev. 13:13-14; 19:11ff).

7. Jesus returns to the earth, defeats His enemies, is received by the Jews, and establishes His kingdom on earth (Rev. 19:11ff; Zech. 12:7—

13:1). He will reign on earth for 1,000 years (Rev. 20:1-5).

The purpose of prophecy is not to entertain the curious, but to encourage the consecrated. Jesus closed this section of His discourse with three practical admonitions, built around three illustrations: a fig tree, Noah, and a thief in the night. Verse 36 makes it clear that no one will know the day or the hour of the Lord's coming. But they can be aware of the movements of events and not be caught by surprise.

*The fig tree* (vv. 32-35). Luke 21:29 reads, "Behold the fig tree and all the trees" (NASB). The fig tree in the Bible is often a picture of Israel (Luke 13:6-10; Hosea 9:10); and the other trees would picture the nations of the world. Perhaps our Lord was suggesting that increased nationalism will be one of the signs of the end times. Certainly future events cast their shadows before them. "And when these things *begin* to come to pass . . ." (Luke 21:28a, italics mine) suggests that a sign need not be full-blown before it is important to God's people.

The budding of the trees indicates that summer is near. The beginning of these signs indicates that the Lord's coming is near. The generation alive on earth at that time will see these events take place. Our generation sees a foreshadowing of these signs. We do not look for signs as such; we look for the Saviour (Phil. 3:20). Jesus can come for His church at *any* time.

*The days of Noah* (vv. 36-42). Here the emphasis is on the fact that the people did not know *the day* when judgment would strike. Noah and his family in the ark are a picture of God's miraculous preservation of Israel during the awful time of the Tribulation. (Enoch is a picture of the church which is raptured before the Tribulation—Gen. 5:21-24; Heb. 11:5; 1 Thes. 5:1-10; 1:10).

What kept the people from listening to Noah's message and obeying? The common interests of life—eating, drinking, marrying, giving in marriage. They lost the *best* by living for the *good*. It is a dangerous thing to get so absorbed in the pursuits of life that we forget Jesus is coming.

The verb "taken" in verses 39-41 means "taken away in judgment." *Do not apply these verses to the Rapture of the church* when believers are caught up in the air to meet the Lord. During the Tribulation, a division will take place: Some people will perish in judgment (be taken away), while others will remain to enter into the kingdom. The use of "took them all away" in verse 39 makes this clear.

*The thief in the night* (vv. 42-44). Jesus used Noah to warn that men will not know *the day*, and He used the picture of the burglar to warn that they will not know *the hour*. After the Rapture of the church, there will be a time of peace and safety on earth (1 Thes. 5:1ff). Then suddenly God's judgments will fall (2 Peter 3:10ff).

People alive on earth during the Tribulation period will be able, from the Scriptures, to tell the drift of events; but they will not be able to calculate the exact day or hour of Christ's return. Added to this is the fact that the days will be "shortened . . . for the elect's sake" (Matt. 24:22). This may mean fewer days of tribulation, or it may mean fewer hours so that the people on earth suffer a bit less (Rev. 8:12).

When we combine the exhortations found in these three pictures, we end up with: "Know that He is near! Watch therefore! Be ye also ready!" Believers alive during that period of history will certainly find great comfort in the promises of the Word of God.

While the interpretation of this section relates to Israel during the Tribulation, we may apply the Word to our own hearts. We do not know when our Lord will return for His church. Therefore, we must be alert, watchful, and faithful. Jesus dealt with this in detail in the next section of the Olivet Discourse (24:45—25:30).

How grateful we ought to be that God has not appointed us to wrath, but to obtain salvation when Jesus Christ appears. He has saved us from the wrath to come (1 Thes. 1:10; 5:9-10). As the people of God, we will certainly go through tribulation (John 16:33; Acts 14:22), but not *the* Tribulation.

# 22

# THE
# KING'S
# RETURN–PART 2

(Matthew 24:45—25:46)

We noted that the "atmosphere" of the first section of the Olivet Discourse was definitely Jewish. A careful reading of this section indicates that the "atmosphere" has changed. Jesus had been describing the sign-events of the Tribulation period, and had named one judgment after another, culminating in His return to earth. But in this section, the emphasis is on *the Lord delaying His return* (24:48; 25:5, 19).

It seems reasonable to assign Matthew 24:45—25:30 to our present age of the church, during which time it appears that the Lord is delaying His return (2 Peter 3). The closing section (25:31-46) describes the judgment the Lord will execute when He returns to earth. In general, the teachings in the Olivet Discourse relate to the Jews (24:4-44), the professing church (24:45—25:30), and the Gentile nations (25:31-46). This corresponds with the threefold division of mankind mentioned by Paul in 1 Corinthians 10:32. We have already studied in detail our Lord's coming as it relates to Israel, so let us look at it in the two remaining relationships.

**Christ's Coming and the Professing Church** (24:45—25:30)
We must not be surprised that our Lord suddenly changed from discussing His return as it relates to Israel to His return as it relates to the church. It is not uncommon in Scripture for a speaker or writer to change emphasis right in the middle of a sentence. For example, the entire church

age occurs in the time period between the words *given* and *and* in Isaiah 9:6. A similar "leap" is seen in Isaiah 61:2, where the church age takes place in the period between the "year of the Lord" and the "day of vengeance."

In the section devoted to Israel, Jesus described primarily the outward events of the period; in this section, He described inward attitudes. While everyone who has trusted Jesus Christ as Saviour is going to heaven (John 3:16-18; 17:24), not every believer is ready to meet the Lord.

When Jesus Christ returns and takes His church to heaven, He will sit upon His judgment seat and judge His own people (Rom. 14:10-12; 2 Cor. 5:8-11). He will not judge our sins, because these have already been judged on the cross (Rom. 8:1-4). But He will judge our works and will give rewards to those who have earned them (1 Cor. 3:9-15). These parables suggest that Jesus will judge three different groups of professed believers.

*Obedient and disobedient servants* (24:45-51). God's people on earth are called a household (Gal. 6:10; Eph. 2:19). God has put servants over each household to feed the members. This suggests to us the local church family with its spiritual leaders. The purpose of spiritual leadership is that the leaders feed the people, not that the people feed the leaders! The Apostle Peter caught this truth and emphasized it in his first letter (1 Peter 5:1-4).

It is a serious thing to be a pastor or other officer in a local church. We must take care that our motives are right and that we serve Christ and His people in love. Both in word and deed, we must lead the family in the right way (Heb. 13:7-8). The members of the family should submit to spiritual leadership, because one day both people and leaders will face the judgment seat of Christ (Heb. 13:17).

The servant's task is not to be popular, but to be obedient. He must feed the family the food that it needs, when it needs it. He should bring out of his "spiritual cupboard" things new and old (Matt. 13:52). Some Bible teachers, in their search for something new and exciting, forget the nutrition of the old truths of the Word. But other ministers are so wrapped up in the old that they fail to discover new insights and new applications of the old truths. The new grows out of the old, and the old is made more meaningful by the new.

If the spiritual leader is obediently doing his job when the Lord returns, he shall be rewarded. But if that leader is not doing his job when the Lord returns, he will be dealt with in a severe way. I prefer to translate verse 51: "And shall punish him severely and appoint him his portion with the hypocrites. . . ." (Even in that day of despotic rule, it would be unthinkable for a master to cut his servant in half.) The whole picture is one of pain and loss. This does not suggest punitive measures at the judgment seat of Christ, because there we will have glorified bodies. But it does suggest loss of reward and loss of opportunity.

Jesus did not amplify the truth here, but from other Scriptures we learn that one reward for obedient service will be ministry in the kingdom that He will establish on earth (Luke 19:11ff). The reward for obedient service is the capacity for greater service. Not to have a place of ministry in His kingdom would, to me, be a tremendous loss.

What caused this servant's downfall? *Something went wrong in his heart:* He ceased to expect his Lord to return (v. 48). He lived like the world and mistreated his fellowservants. Whenever God's servants cannot work together, it is often because somebody has forgotten that the Lord will return. Looking for His appearing, and loving His appearing, should motivate us to be faithful and loving (1 John 2:28; 1 Thes. 2:19-20).

*Wise and foolish witnesses* (25:1-13). A wedding in that day had two parts. First, the bridegroom and his friends would go from his house to claim the bride from her parents. Then the bride and groom would return to the groom's house for the marriage feast. The suggestion here is that the groom has already claimed his bride and is now on his way back home. However, we must not press the image of the church as a bride too far, because much of this truth was not revealed until the ministry of Paul (Eph. 5:22ff).

The church has known for 2,000 years that Jesus is coming again, and yet many believers have become lethargic and drowsy. They are no longer excited about the soon-coming of the Lord. As a result, there is little effective witness given that the Lord is returning.

The oil for burning reminds us of the special oil used in the tabernacle services (Ex. 27:20-21). Oil is usually a symbol of the Spirit of God, but I wonder if this particular oil is not also a symbol of the Word of God? The church should be "holding forth the word of life" in this dark and wicked world (Phil. 2:12-16). We need to keep the word of His patience (Rev.

3:10) and keep witnessing of the return of Jesus Christ.

When the bridegroom and bride appeared, half of the bridesmaids were unable to light their lamps because they had no oil. "Our lamps are going out!" they cried. The bridesmaids who had oil were able to light their lamps and keep them shining bright. It was they who entered into the wedding feast and not the foolish girls who had no oil. This suggests that not every professing Christian will enter heaven, for some really have not trusted Jesus Christ sincerely. Without the Spirit of God and the Word of God, there can be no true salvation.

Jesus ended this parable with the warning He had uttered before: "Watch" (24:42; 25:13). This does not mean standing on a mountaintop gazing at the heavens (Acts 1:9-11). It means "to stay awake and be alert" (Matt. 26:38-41).

*Profitable and unprofitable servants* (25:14-30). This parable must not be confused with the parable of the pounds (Luke 19:11-27) although the two parables do have similarities. Please note that each servant in this parable was given money (a talent was worth about 20 years' wages) according to his ability. The man with much ability was given five talents; the man with average ability received two talents; the man with minimal ability received one talent.

The talents represent opportunities to use our abilities. If five talents were given to a person with minimal ability, he would be destroyed by the heavy responsibility. But if only one talent were given to a man of great ability, he would be disgraced and degraded. God assigns work and opportunity according to ability. We are living in the period of time between verses 18 and 19. We have been assigned our ministries according to the abilities and gifts God has given us. It is our privilege to serve the Lord and multiply His goods.

The three servants fell into two categories: faithful, and unfaithful. The faithful servants took their talents and put them to work for their Lord. The unfaithful servant hid his talent in the earth. Instead of using his opportunities, he buried them! He did not purposely do evil. But by doing nothing, he was committing sin and robbing his Lord of service and increase.

The two men who put their money to work each received the same commendation (vv. 21, 23). It was not the *portion* but the *proportion* that made the difference. They started as servants, but their Lord promoted them to rulers. They were faithful with a few things, so the Lord trusted them with many things. They had worked and toiled, and now they entered into joy. Their faithfulness gave each of them a capacity for greater service and responsibility.

The third servant was unfaithful and therefore was unrewarded. Because this man was afraid he might fail, he never tried to succeed. He feared life and his responsibilities. This paralyzed him with anxiety, so he buried the talent to protect it. The least he could have done was put the money in a bank and collect some interest. There was no real risk in that.

What we do not use for the Lord, we are in danger of losing. The master reprimanded the unfaithful, unprofitable servant, and then took his talent from him. The man with the most talents received the extra talent.

Some feel that this unprofitable servant was not a true believer. But it seems that he *was* a true servant, even though he proved to be unprofitable. The "outer darkness" of verse 30 need not refer to hell, even though that is often the case in the Gospels (Matt. 8:12; 22:13). It is dangerous to build theology on parables, for parables illustrate truth in vivid ways. The man was dealt with by the Lord, he lost his opportunity for service, and he gained no praise or reward. To me, that is outer darkness.

It is possible that the one-talent man thought that his one talent was not really very important. He did not have five talents, or even two. Why worry about one? *Because he was appointed as a steward by the Lord.* Were it not for the one-talent people in our world, very little would get accomplished. His one talent could have increased to two and brought glory to his Master.

These three parables encourage us to love His appearing, look for His appearing, and labor faithfully until He comes. We should be watching, witnessing, and working. We may not be successful in the eyes of men, or even popular with others. But if we are faithful and profitable, we shall receive our reward.

## Christ's Coming and the Gentile Nations (25:31-46)

This section explains to us how Jesus Christ will judge the Gentile nations. The word *nations* in verse 32 means "Gentiles," and it is in the neuter gender in the Greek. The word *them* in that same verse is in the masculine. This means that the nations will be gathered before Jesus

Christ, but He will judge them *as individuals*. This will not be a judgment of groups (Germany, Italy, Japan, etc.) but of individuals within these nations.

We must not confuse this judgment with the Great White Throne judgment described in Revelation 20:11-15. Some scholars merge both passages and call this "the general judgment." The Bible knows nothing of a "general judgment." This judgment takes place on earth immediately after the battle of Armageddon. The White Throne judgment takes place in space somewhere ("the earth and the heaven fled away," Rev. 20:11). The judgment here in Matthew 25 takes place *before* the kingdom is established on earth, for the saved are told to 'inherit the kingdom" (v. 34). The white throne judgment will take place *after* the 1,000 year reign of Christ (Rev. 20:7ff).

There is another error we must avoid. We must not force this passage to teach salvation by good works. A superficial reading would give the impression that helping one's neighbor is sufficient to earn salvation and go to heaven. But this is not the message of this passage. Nobody at any time in the history of the world was ever saved by good works.

The Old Testament saints were saved by faith (Heb. 11); the New Testament saints were saved by faith in Jesus Christ (Eph. 2:8-10). People today are saved the same way. The gospel of "do good" is not a scriptural message. It is right for *believers* to do good (Heb. 13:16; Gal. 6:10), but this is not the way unbelievers can be saved.

If we keep in mind the three groups in the account, it will help to solve this problem: There were sheep, goats, and brethren. Who are these people that the King dares to call "My brethren"? It seems likely that they are the believing Jews from the Tribulation period. These are people who will hear the message of the 144,000 and trust Jesus Christ. Since these believing Jews will not receive the "mark of the beast" (Rev. 13:16-17), they will be unable to buy or sell. How, then, can they survive? Through the loving care of the Gentiles who have trusted Christ and who care for His brethren.

The interesting thing about this judgment is that the *sheep* individuals are surprised at what they hear. They will not remember having seen the Lord Jesus Christ and ministering to His needs. But just as they lovingly ministered to the believing Jews, they did it to Christ. Their motive was not reward, but sacrificial love. In fact, these Gentiles took their own lives in their hands when they welcomed the homeless Jews and cared for them. "He that receiveth you receiveth Me," Jesus said to His disciples (Matt. 10:40); and surely this would also apply to His brethren.

The individuals designated *goats* were judged because they did not trust Jesus Christ and give evidence of that faith by caring for His brethren. They apparently received the mark of the beast and took care of themselves and their own, but they had no time for the Jewish remnant that was suffering on earth (Rev. 12:17). There are sins of omission as well as sins of commission (James 4:17). Not doing good is the moral equivalent of doing evil.

When we compare the two judicial sentences (vv. 34, 41), we discover some interesting truths. To begin with, the sheep were blessed of the Father; but it does not say that the goats were "cursed of the Father." The sheep *inherit* the kingdom, and inheritance is based on birth. Because they had been born again through faith, they inherited the kingdom.

This kingdom was prepared for these saved individuals, but verse 41 does not state that the everlasting fire was prepared for the goats. It was prepared for the devil and his angels (Rev. 20:10). God never prepared hell for people. There is no evidence from Scripture that God predestines people to go to hell. If sinners listen to Satan, and follow his ways, they will end up where he ends up—in the torments of hell. There are only two eternal destinies: everlasting punishment for those who reject Christ or eternal life for those who trust Him.

The sheep will be ushered into the kingdom to share in Christ's glory. The church will be reigning with Christ, and Israel will enjoy the fulfillment of the promises made through the prophets. All of creation will share in the glorious liberty of God's children (Rom. 8:19-21). Jesus Christ will rule from David's throne in Jerusalem (Luke 1:30-33), and peace will reign for 1,000 years (Isa. 11).

As we look back over the Olivet Discourse, we should review several facts. To begin with, God is not finished with the people of Israel. Jesus made it clear in this sermon that Israel would be purified and brought to faith in the Messiah. God has not cast away His people (Rom. 11:1ff).

Second, the Old Testament promises of the kingdom will be fulfilled. The Tribulation period will be a very difficult time for people on the earth. But it will be "travail" in preparation for the birth of the kingdom. The suffering will lead to glory.

Third, God is going to judge this world. He is not sending cataclysmic judgments today because this is a day of grace when His message is, "Be you reconciled to God" (2 Cor. 5:14ff). The heavens are silent because man's sins have already been judged at the cross. God has spoken once and for all through His Son, and He will not speak to this earth again until He sends His judgments during the Tribulation.

Fourth, we as Christians and members of His church are not looking for signs. "The Jews require a sign" (1 Cor. 1:22). There will be no signs given prior to the sudden return of Christ in the air for His church. However, as we see some of these Tribulation signs *beginning* ("When these things begin to take place . . ." Luke 21:28, NASB), we feel that the end is not far away. It seems that international tensions and problems are increasing to the point where the world will cry out for a dictator, and Satan will have his candidate ready.

Finally, no matter what view of prophecy we take, we know that Jesus is coming again. As Christians, we must be alert and ready. We must not waste our opportunities. We may not have a great deal of ability or a great many gifts, but we can still be faithful in the calling He has given us.

# 23

# THE
# KING'S
# PREPARATION

(Matthew 26:1-56)

Events were now moving to a climax. The King was preparing to suffer and die. This preparation was in three stages and at three different locations. As we examine these stages, we can see the growing conflict between Christ and the enemy.

### At Bethany: Worship versus Waste (26:1-16)
Matthew does not claim to give us a chronological account of the events of the last week. At this point he inserted a flashback to describe the feast in Bethany and the beautiful act of worship that Mary performed. The religious leaders were meeting to plot against Jesus, but His friends were meeting to show their love and devotion to Him. Also, by joining these two accounts, Matthew showed the connection between Mary's worship and Judas' betrayal. It was after the feast in Bethany that Judas went to the priests and offered his help (Mark 14:10-11). The Lord's rebuke triggered Judas' response.

The feast at Bethany took place "six days before the Passover" (John 12:1) in the house of Simon the leper. Apparently he had been healed by the Lord Jesus. There were at least 17 people at this dinner: Simon, Mary, Martha, Lazarus, Jesus, and the Twelve Apostles. True to her character as the "doer" in the family, Martha did the serving (Luke 10:38-42). The three key persons in this event are Mary, Judas, and Jesus.

*Mary* (26:7). Only John identifies this woman as Mary, sister of Martha and Lazarus. She is found only three times in the Gospels, and in each instance she is at the feet of Jesus. She sat at His feet and listened to the Word (Luke 10:38-42); she came at His feet in sorrow after the death of Lazarus (John 11:28-32); and she worshiped at His feet when she anointed Him with the ointment (John 12:1ff). Mary was a deeply spiritual woman. She found at His feet her blessing, she brought to His feet her burdens, and she gave at His feet her best.

When we combine the Gospel records, we learn that she anointed both His head and His feet, and wiped His feet with her hair. A woman's hair is her glory (1 Cor. 11:15). She surrendered her glory to the Lord and worshiped Him with the precious gift that she brought. It was an act of love and devotion that brought fragrance to the whole house.

Because she had listened to His word, Mary knew that soon Jesus would die and be buried. She also knew that His body would not need the traditional care given to the dead because His body would not see corruption (Ps. 16:10; Acts 2:22-28). Instead of anointing His body *after* His death, she did so *before* His death. It was an act of faith and love.

*Judas* (26:8-9). The disciples did not know the true character of Judas. His criticism of Mary sounded so "spiritual" that they joined him in attacking her. We know the real reason Judas wanted the ointment sold: The money would go into the treasury and he would be able to use it (John 12:6).

Judas is a tragic figure. He was called to be one of Christ's disciples and was named an apostle along with the others (Mark 3:13-19). He received power to heal (Matt. 10:1-4), and he probably used this power. It is not the power to do miracles that is proof of salvation (Matt. 7:21-29), but obedience to God's Word.

In spite of his affiliation with the band of disciples, and his association with Christ, Judas was not a true believer. When Jesus washed the disciples' feet, He made it clear that one of them (Judas) was not cleansed (John 13:10-11). Like many professing Christians today, Judas was "in" the group of believers but not "of" them.

Notice that every time Mary sought to do something for Jesus, she was misunderstood. Her sister Martha misunderstood her when Mary sat at Jesus' feet to hear Him teach the Word. Judas and the other disciples misunderstood her when she anointed Jesus. Her friends and neighbors misunderstood her when she came out of the house to meet Jesus after Lazarus had been buried (John 11:28-31). When we give Jesus Christ first place in our lives, we can expect to be misunderstood and criticized by those who claim to follow Him.

Why did Judas follow Jesus for three years, listen to His Word, share His ministry, and then turn traitor? One thing is certain: Judas was not the victim of circumstances or the passive tool of providence. It was prophesied that one of Messiah's close associates would betray Him (Ps. 41:9; 55:12-14). But this fact does not relieve Judas of responsibility. We must not make him a martyr because he fulfilled this prophecy.

While we can never fully understand the mind and heart of Judas, we do know that he had every opportunity to be saved. He was often warned by Jesus; in the Upper Room, Jesus even washed Judas' feet. Probably, Judas saw in Jesus the hope for Israel's political freedom. If Jesus established His kingdom, Judas, as treasurer, would have had an important position. When Jesus repeatedly refused to become a political Messiah, Judas turned against Him. Satan found a willing tool in Judas. Satan put the ideas into Judas' mind (John 13:2) and then entered into Judas to use him to betray Jesus to the enemy (John 13:27).

Judas' life is a warning to those who pretend to serve Christ but whose hearts are far from God. He is also a warning to those who waste their opportunities and their lives. "Why this waste?" asked Judas when he saw that expensive ointment poured out upon Jesus. Yet Judas wasted his opportunities, his life, and his soul! Jesus called him *son of perdition* (John 17:12) which literally means "son of waste."

*Jesus* (26:10-16). He immediately came to the defense of Mary, for He always protects His own. He rebuked Judas and the other disciples and praised Mary for her loving act of devotion. *Nothing given to Jesus in love is ever wasted.* Her act of worship not only brought joy to the heart of Jesus and fragrance to the house, but also blessing to the whole world. Her devotion encourages us to love and serve Christ with our very best. Such service brings blessings to others that perhaps we will know nothing about until we see Him.

Jesus did not criticize the disciples because they were concerned about the poor. He was concerned about the poor, and we should be, too. He was cautioning them against missing their opportunity to worship Him. They would always have opportunities to help the poor. But they would

not always have the opportunity to worship at His feet and prepare Him
for burial.

### In the Upper Room: Faithfulness versus Betrayal (26:17-30)

*Preparation for Passover* (26:17-19). It was necessary to purchase and
prepare the materials needed for the Passover feast. It was also necessary
to find a place in crowded Jerusalem where the feast could be held. Jesus
sent Peter and John to make these important preparations (Luke 22:8).
They were to follow a man who was carrying a pitcher of water and he
would show them a large upper room. It would be most unusual for a *man*
to be carrying water, for this was usually done by the women.

Peter and John would have had to secure the bread and bitter herbs, as
well as the wine, for the feast. They would have had to find a perfect
lamb, and then have had the lamb slain in the court of the temple and the
blood put on the altar. The lamb would be roasted whole, and then the
feast would be ready.

*Announcement of a betrayer* (26:20-25). Up to the very end, the
disciples did not realize that one of their own number, Judas, was the
traitor. They did not see any difference in the way Jesus treated Judas,
which is a remarkable testimony to our Lord's patience and love. It was
during the Passover feast, as they were eating, that Jesus announced the
presence of a traitor. The disciples looked at one another, wondering who
the traitor might be. Then they asked Jesus, "It is not I, is it?" The
construction of the question indicates they expected *No* as the answer.

Judas was reclining to our Lord's left; this was a place of honor at a
feast. (This may explain why the disciples *again* started arguing over who
was the greatest. See Luke 22:24-30.) John was reclining at our Lord's
right, and thus was able to rest on His breast (John 13:23). It was an act of
friendship to eat bread together, especially bread that had been dipped
into the dish of herbs. It was also an honor to be given a morsel of bread
by your host. Jesus gave the bread to Judas (Ps. 41:9), and Judas accepted
it *knowing full well that he was betraying his Lord*. For Jesus, giving the
bread was a gracious act of hospitality; for Judas, accepting the bread was
an evil act of treachery.

Verse 24 presents both the human and the divine sides of this event.
From the divine point of view, Judas' treachery was predicted in Scripture and was part of the plan of God. But from the human point of view,

Judas was guilty of a base crime and was completely responsible for what he did. Divine sovereignty and human responsibility are not in conflict, even though we may not be able to understand how they work together to fulfill God's will.

After Judas took the morsel of bread, Satan entered into him (John 13:27). He then went out to keep his promise to the religious leaders in delivering Jesus into their hands; and even then, the other disciples did not know what he was doing. "He went immediately out; and it was night" (John 13:30). For Judas, it is still night.

*Institution of the Lord's Supper* (26:26-30). It was after Judas had left the room that Jesus instituted something new, the Lord's Supper (1 Cor. 11:23-34). He took two elements from the Passover feast, the unleavened bread and the cup, and He used these to picture His own death. The broken bread pictured His body given for the sins of the world. The "fruit of the vine" (v. 29) pictured His blood, shed for the remission of sins. The text does not indicate that anything special or mysterious happened to these two elements. They remained bread and the "fruit of the vine" but they now conveyed a deeper meaning: the body and the blood of Jesus Christ.

The Lord's Supper reminds us to *look ahead* for Christ's return. We will observe this supper until He comes (1 Cor. 11:26). The Passover pointed ahead to the Lamb of God who would take away the sins of the world (John 1:29). The Lord's Supper announces that this great work has been accomplished.

In verse 29, Jesus added the note of future glory in the kingdom. Jesus did eat bread, fish, and honey after His resurrection (Luke 24:41-43; John 21:9-15). But there is no record that He drank the fruit of the vine. Even as He faced the rejection of His nation and the suffering of the cross, He was looking ahead to the kingdom that would be established because of His sacrifice. There were traditionally four cups drunk at the Passover feast, each cup relating to one of the four promises in Exodus 6:6-7. The third cup ("I will redeem you") was the one Jesus used for the Lord's Supper, a picture of the redemption He would accomplish. The fourth cup will not be fulfilled until the kingdom is established.

The hymn that Jesus and His disciples sang before they left the Upper Room was part of the traditional Hallel, Psalms 116—118. Read those psalms in the light of Christ's death and resurrection and see how they take on new meaning. Imagine our Lord being able to sing praises to God in the face of rejection, suffering, and death.

### Gethsemane: Submission versus Resistance (26:31-56)
At the Mount of Olives was a private garden which Jesus often had used as a retreat (John 18:2). *Gethsemane* means "oil press," a significant name in the light of our Lord's agony in that garden.

*The disciples' failure announced* (vv. 31-35). This announcement was probably made as the band of men made their way to the garden. We usually point to Peter as the one who failed the Lord, but *all* of the disciples were involved. Jesus referred to Zechariah 13:7 in warning His disciples, but He also added a word of promise: He would rise again and meet them in Galilee. Unfortunately, the men paid little attention to the promise of His resurrection. On resurrection day, the angels reminded them of the meeting in Galilee (Matt. 28:7, 10).

When Peter disagreed with the Lord, this was the beginning of his sin of denying the Lord. Peter was unwilling to apply the word "all" to himself. Instead of reassuring Peter, the Lord gave him a personal warning: He would deny Christ three times! Peter thought he was *better* than the other men, and Jesus told him he would be even more cowardly than the others.

Peter's response was to deny Christ's word even more fervently, and the other disciples joined in this protest. Had Peter listened to the word and obeyed it, he would not have denied his Lord three times.

*Jesus' surrender accomplished* (vv. 36-46). He left eight of the disciples at the entrance to the garden, while He and Peter, James, and John went further into the garden. This was the third time He had taken these three men with Him. They were with Him on the Mount of Transfiguration (Matt. 17:1ff) and in the home of Jairus where He raised Jairus' daughter from the dead (Luke 8:49ff). He wanted them to watch and pray. He was entering into a difficult time, and the presence of His disciples would be an encouragement to Him.

We must not think that it was the fear of death that made our Lord so agonize in the garden. He did not fear death, but faced it with courage and peace. He was about to "drink the cup" that His Father had prepared for Him, and this meant bearing on His body the sins of the world (John 18:11; 1 Peter 2:24). Many godly people have been arrested, beaten, and slain because of their faith. But only Jesus experienced being made sin and a curse for mankind (2 Cor. 5:21; Gal. 3:13). The Father has never forsaken any of His own, yet He forsook His Son (Matt. 27:46). This was the cup that Jesus willingly drank for us.

Jesus was not wrestling with God's will or resisting God's will. He was yielding Himself to God's will. As perfect man, He felt the awful burden of sin, and His holy soul was repelled by it. Yet as the Son of God, He knew that this was His mission in the world. The mystery of His humanity and deity is seen vividly in this scene.

Peter and his fellow disciples had promised to be faithful to death, *and yet they went to sleep!* They needed to pray for themselves, because danger was around the corner. And how much it would have meant to their Lord if they had watched and prayed with Him. They had failed, but their Lord had succeeded.

*The arrest achieved* (vv. 47-56). Jesus knew that Judas and the arresting officers were near, so He awakened the sleeping disciples and prepared them for what was coming. The fact that this band of soldiers and temple guards carried weapons and lanterns shows that Judas did not really understand Jesus. Judas thought they would have to search for Him in the garden and fight off His disciples in order to arrest Him. But Jesus came to them and calmly surrendered. It would not even have been necessary for Judas to betray Jesus with a kiss, for Jesus told the soldiers who He was.

It is tragic to see how Judas cheapened everything that he touched. His name means *praise* (Gen. 29:35), yet who would name a son "Judas" today? He used the kiss as a weapon, not as a sign of affection. In that day, it was customary for disciples to kiss their teacher. But in this case, it was not a mark of submission or respect. The Greek verbs indicate that Judas kissed Jesus repeatedly.

At this point, some of the other disciples asked, "Shall we strike with the sword?" When He was with them in the Upper Room, Jesus had talked to them about swords (Luke 22:31-38). Jesus was preparing them for a different kind of life. They would need to use whatever means He provided for their care and safety. They would be in a hostile world, and He would not always perform miracles to help them.

The problem was, the disciples misunderstood what He taught them. As usual, they took Him literally. " 'Lord, look, here are two swords.'

And He said to them, 'It is enough' " (Luke 22:38, NASB). Peter had argued with the Word, denied the Word, and disobeyed the Word (when he went to sleep). Now he ran ahead of the Word. In his zeal to help Jesus, Peter cut off Malchus' ear with a sword. He did not wait for the Lord to tell him what to do, but (like Moses in Egypt, Ex. 2:11-15) Peter rushed ahead and trusted the arm of flesh. Had Jesus not healed the ear of Malchus, there probably would have been *four* crosses on Calvary!

The fact that the guards had not arrested Him in the temple indicates that there was a divine timetable controlling His life. These things were not happening by accident, but by appointment. It was all part of God's plan, yet evil men were responsible for the deed. "This Man, delivered up by the predetermined plan and foreknowledge of God, you nailed to a cross by the hands of godless men and put Him to death" (Acts 2:23, NASB).

Of course, they had no right to arrest Jesus. He had broken no laws, He had committed no crimes. They were treating Him like a common thief—and yet it was *Judas* who was the thief! The disciples who bravely promised to deliver Him, deserted Him. "Behold, the hour cometh, yea, is now come, that you shall be scattered, every man to his own, and shall leave Me alone; and yet I am not alone, because the Father is with Me" (John 16:32). Later, even the Father would leave Him!

Each of us must decide: Will it be the sword or the cup? Will I resist God's will or submit to God's will? The cup usually involves suffering, but that suffering ultimately leads to glory. We need not fear the cup, for it has been prepared by the Father especially for us. He knows how much we can take, and He mixes the contents in wisdom and love.

# 24

# THE KING'S TRIAL

(Matthew 26:57—27:26)

After Jesus was arrested, He was taken to the house of Annas, the former high priest who was the father-in-law of Caiaphas, the high priest (John 18:13ff). Annas, a shrewd politician, was something of a "godfather" in the temple establishment. Jesus then was taken to Caiaphas and, in the morning, to the meeting of the Sanhedrin. They turned Him over to Pilate who tried to put Him under Herod's jurisdiction (Luke 23:6-12). But Herod sent Him back to Pilate.

Matthew centered his attention on four persons who were involved in the trial and suffering of the Lord.

**Caiaphas** (26:57-68)
According to Old Testament Law, the high priest was to serve until death. But when the Romans took over the nation of Israel, they made the high priesthood an appointed office. This way they could be certain of having a religious leader who would cooperate with their policies. Annas served as high priest from A.D. 6 to A.D. 15, and five of his sons, as well as Caiaphas his son-in-law, succeeded him. Caiaphas was high priest from A.D. 18-36, but Annas was still a power behind the throne (see Luke 3:2).

Both Annas and Caiaphas were Sadducees, which meant they did not believe in the resurrection, the spirit world, or the authority of any of the Old Testament except the five Books of Moses. It was the high priestly family that managed the "temple business" which Jesus had overthrown twice during His ministry. Of course, these men were most happy to lay hands on their enemy. Caiaphas had already made it clear that he intended to sacrifice Jesus in order to save the nation (John 11:47-54).

The high priest hastily assembled the Sanhedrin, composed of the chief priests, the elders, and the scribes (Mark 14:53). While the men were gathering, Caiaphas and his assistants were seeking for witnesses who could testify against the prisoner. They had already determined that He was guilty, but they wanted to go through the motions of a legal trial.

Since no honest witnesses could be found (which in itself proves our Lord's innocence), the leaders arranged for false witnesses to testify. The Law of Moses warned against false witnesses (Deut. 19:15-21), but even the religious leaders twisted God's Word to accomplish their selfish purposes. That there were *two* witnesses fulfilled the letter of the law. But that they deliberately lied broke both the letter and the spirit of the Law. These witnesses cited a statement Jesus had made early in His ministry: "Destroy this temple, and in three days I will raise it up" (John 2:19). It was a serious matter to speak against the temple; this very charge later led to the death of Stephen (Acts 6:12-14; 7:45-50).

When confronted with this charge, Jesus remained silent. This was a fulfillment of Isaiah 53:7. Jesus could not deny that He made the statement, and yet neither could He explain the spiritual meaning of the statement to this group of worldly-minded men. In His attitude toward His enemies, Jesus set an example for us to follow (1 Peter 2:18-23).

When Caiaphas saw that the false charges were not incriminating Jesus, he took another approach. He put Jesus under oath. In our day of repeated perjury and carelessness with the truth, we cannot appreciate the solemn importance that the Jews gave to oaths. This, of course, was according to their Law (Num. 30:2; Ex. 20:7; Lev. 19:12). Caiaphas knew that Jesus claimed to be the Son of God (John 10:30-33), so he put Him under oath to declare this. The clever priest knew that Jesus could not avoid replying.

Jesus *did* affirm that He was the Son of God. He applied to Himself Psalm 110:1 and Daniel 7:13, both of which are messianic passages. In these two quotations, Jesus predicted His resurrection and ascension and His return in glory. This would mean salvation to those who trust Him, but for Caiaphas it would mean condemnation.

Without even considering the evidence, Caiaphas passed the sentence. The treatment given Jesus after the verdict had been reached was certainly illegal and inhumane. Of course, all of this only revealed the wickedness of the priest's heart. At the same time, it fulfilled the messianic prophecies (Isa. 50:6).

### Peter (26:69-75)

Peter has been criticized for following "afar off" (v. 58); but that was not his mistake. His mistake was that he followed at all. He was supposed to get out! Jesus had warned Peter that he would deny Him. Jesus had also quoted Zechariah 13:7 which states that the "sheep shall be scattered." Finally, Jesus had expressly commanded the disciples not to follow: "Let these go their way" (John 18:8-9). If Peter had listened to the word and obeyed it, he would never have failed the Lord in such a humiliating way.

The Apostle John was also a part of this failure, for he had followed with Peter and gotten both of them entrance into the high priest's house (John 18:15-16). Jesus had warned them to "watch and pray" lest they enter into temptation (Matt. 26:41). But they had gone to sleep instead. Consequently, they entered into temptation, and Peter fell.

Peter's denial of Christ was the climax of a series of failures. When the Lord first warned Peter that he would be tested by Satan, Peter affirmed his faith and his ability to remain true to the Lord. In pride, Peter argued with the Word of God! He even dared to compare himself to the other disciples and affirm that, though they might fall, *he* would remain true.

The fact that Peter was standing by the enemy's fire, warming himself, indicates how defeated he was. The denial was even more humiliating because two of the interrogators were servant girls. The third challenge came from a man, one of the bystanders; but Peter failed again. This man was a relative of Malchus, the man Peter had wounded (John 18:26). So Peter's impulsive deed caught up with him even after Jesus had repaired the damage.

Mark's account of this event indicates that the cock would crow twice (Mark 14:30). After the third denial, the cock crowed for the second time (Mark 14:72). This means that the first cock-crowing was a warning to Peter, and he should have left the scene immediately. The third denial and the second cock-crow climaxed the test, and Peter had failed.

The crowing of the cock reminded Peter of the word of Jesus. Had

Peter remembered and obeyed the word, he would never have denied his Lord. It was at that time that Jesus turned and looked at Peter (Luke 22:61), and that look of love broke the apostle's heart. Peter went out and wept bitterly.

After His resurrection, Jesus met privately with Peter and restored him to his discipleship (Mark 16:7; 1 Cor. 15:5). Jesus also restored him publicly (John 21:15-19). Peter learned some important lessons during that difficult experience. He learned to pay attention to the Word, to watch and pray, and to put no confidence in his own strength.

### Judas (27:1-10)

The Jewish council reconvened in the morning and delivered the official verdict against Jesus, so that people could not say that their hastily-called night meeting was unlawful. Now *all* were able to attend. It is likely that Nicodemus and Joseph of Arimathaea either did not attend or abstained from voting (John 19:38-42). But the Jews did not have the authority to exercise capital punishment (John 18:31), so the prisoner went to Pilate, the Roman procurator. Only he could sentence the prisoner to death.

At this point, Judas returned to the scene. He witnessed the official trial and sentencing of Jesus and realized that He was condemned to die. Judas' response was one of remorse and regret. The Greek word translated "repented himself" in verse 3 indicates, not a sorrow for sin that leads to a change of mind and action, but a regret at being caught, a remorse that leads to despair. Peter truly repented, and Jesus restored him. But Judas did not repent, and this led him to suicide.

Judas had sold Jesus for the price of a slave (Ex. 21:32). In desperation, he threw the money on the temple floor and left. The Law would not permit the use of this kind of *tainted* money for temple purposes (Deut. 23:18). The leaders were careful to observe the Law even while they were guilty of breaking it. They used the money to buy a "potter's field" where Jewish strangers who died could be buried properly.

Acts 1:18-19 adds to our understanding of the event. Judas went off by himself, brooded over his terrible crime, and finally hanged himself. Apparently his body was not discovered for some days, because it became bloated and his bowels gushed out. Perhaps the tree limb on which he was hanging also broke and helped to cause this.

Acts 1:18 does not say that Judas committed suicide in the field that the priests bought with the money. That act would have defiled the land and the priests would never have purchased it. Matthew 27:7 states that the priests bought a field; Acts 1:18 states that the money Judas acquired was used to buy it. Judas could not have purchased a field with that money because he gave the money back to the priests. The priests called the cemetery "the field of blood" because it was purchased with "blood money." Judas' suicide added more "blood" to the name, since it was he who contributed the money.

But, why did Matthew relate this event to a prophecy in Jeremiah, when the prophecy is found in Zechariah 11:12-13? One possible solution is that this prophecy was *spoken* by Jeremiah (note Matt. 27:9) and became a part of the Jewish oral tradition. It was later *written* by Zechariah. The Prophet Jeremiah definitely was involved in the purchase of a field (Jer. 32:6ff), and also with a potter's house (18:1ff), and a burial ground (19:1-12). Matthew may have been referring to these general facts as background for the specific prophecy written by Zechariah.

## Pilate (27:11-26)

Pontius Pilate was the sixth Roman procurator to serve in Judea. He was not liked by the Jews because he did things that deliberately violated their Law and provoked them. He was not above killing people to accomplish his purposes (Luke 13:1). Pilate's position was always rather precarious because of his bad relationship with Israel and because of Rome's changing policy with the Jews.

The Jewish leaders accused Jesus of three crimes. They claimed that He was guilty of misleading the nation, forbidding the paying of taxes, and claiming to be a king (Luke 23:2). These were definitely political charges, the kind that a Roman governor could handle. Pilate focused on the third charge—that Jesus claimed to be a king—because this was a definite threat to Rome. If he could deal with this "revolutionary" properly, Pilate could please the Jews and impress the Emperor at the same time.

"Are You the king of the Jews?" Pilate asked. Jesus gave him a clear reply: "It is as you say." However, Jesus then asked Pilate a question about his question (John 18:34-37). Was Pilate thinking of "kingship" in the Roman sense? If so, then Jesus is not that kind of a king. Jesus explained to the governor that His kingdom was not of this world, that He had no armies, that His followers did not fight. Rather, His kingdom was a reign of truth.

This conversation convinced Pilate that Jesus was not a dangerous revolutionary. "I find no fault in Him," was Pilate's decision. But the Jewish rulers were insistent that Pilate condemn Jesus. They repeated their charges and, as they enlarged upon them, mentioned that Jesus was from Galilee. When Pilate heard that, he saw a way out of his dilemma, since Galilee was under Herod's jurisdiction. It is possible that Herod was displeased with Pilate because Pilate had slain some of Herod's citizens (Luke 13:1). This would have been an opportunity for Pilate to become reconciled to Herod.

Matthew did not record the trial held before Herod Antipas (Luke 23:6-12). Herod was the one who had murdered John the Baptist and had threatened to kill Jesus (Luke 13:31-32). Jesus was silent before Herod, for Herod had silenced the voice of God. All the king could do was mock Jesus and send Him back to Pilate. If Pilate had hoped to get rid of the problem, he was disappointed. However, this maneuver did patch up the quarrel between the two rulers.

Pilate wanted to solve the problem but not make any definite decision about Jesus. As a Roman governor, he was pledged to uphold the law. But as a politician, he knew he had to get along with the people. Every decision Pilate made forced him to make another decision, until he was the prisoner of his own evasions. He questioned Jesus further, but He made no reply.

Pilate had one more scheme: He would follow the tradition of releasing a prisoner. Instead of selecting some unknown prisoner, Pilate deliberately chose the most notorious prisoner he had, Barabbas. This man was a robber (John 18:40) and a murderer (Mark 15:7). Pilate reasoned that the crowd would reject Barabbas and ask for Jesus to be released, for who wants a convicted murderer and robber turned loose into society?

But Pilate was wrong. In spite of the fact that Jesus had ministered by healing the sick and even raising the dead, the people rejected Him and chose a murderer to be released. Pilate realized that a riot was in the making, and he could not afford to let this happen. The very thing the rulers wanted to prevent—a riot at Passover season (Matt. 26:5)—they engineered themselves in order to force Pilate to act. The governor *did* act, purely out of expediency and not on the basis of integrity. He released a guilty man and condemned an innocent Man, and that innocent Man was the Son of God.

Pilate took three steps in an attempt to exonerate himself. First, he washed his hands and declared that he was innocent of any guilt. Second, he stated clearly that Jesus was a just person, that is, not worthy of death. Third, he offered to punish Jesus and then release Him, but the rulers would accept no compromise. Finally, the religious rulers used the one weapon against which Pilate had no defense: "If you release this Man, you are no friend of Caesar; everyone who makes himself out to be a king opposes Caesar" (John 19:12, NASB). At this, Pilate capitulated, had Jesus scourged, and delivered Him to be crucified.

Since the Jews could not execute criminals, it was necessary for the Roman officials to assist; and Pilate issued the order. Of course, all of this was in fulfillment of prophecy. The Jews did not crucify; they used stoning to execute criminals. Psalm 22, written by a Jew, is a vivid picture of crucifixion. "They pierced my hands and my feet" (Ps. 22:16). Jesus was made a curse for us, for "Cursed is everyone who hangs on a tree" (Deut. 21:23; Gal. 3:13). But still God was at work in fulfilling His divine purposes.

Pilate knew what was right, but refused to do anything about it. He was "willing to please the people" (Mark 15:15). Judas yielded to *the devil* in his great sin (John 13:2, 27); Peter yielded to *the flesh* when he denied his Lord; but Pilate yielded to *the world* and listened to the crowd. Pilate looked for the easy way, not the right way. He has gone down in history as the man who condemned Jesus.

# 25

# THE KING'S SUFFERING AND DEATH

(Matthew 27:27-66)

Matthew and the other Gospel writers recorded the historical facts of our Lord's suffering and death. It remained for the writers of the New Testament Epistles to explain the theological meaning of this event. History states that "Christ died," but theology explains, "Christ died for our sins . . ." (1 Cor. 15:3). Let's consider the various kinds of suffering that our Lord endured that day.

**Mocked by the Soldiers** (27:27-30)
The official indictment against Jesus was that He claimed to be the King of the Jews (v. 37). The soldiers took advantage of this accusation and paid "homage" to the king. It was a cruel way to treat an innocent prisoner who had already been scourged. But Pilate did nothing to restrain them. He was glad to get the prisoner off of his hands.

First, the soldiers disrobed Jesus and dressed Him in an old "soldier's cloak." Imagine attiring the Prince of Peace (Isa. 9:6) in a discarded military uniform! Matthew described the robe as *scarlet*, while Mark used the word *purple*. There is no contradiction; "reddish-purple" would be a good description of an old faded garment. Imagine how our Lord must have felt when this robe was thrown on His bleeding body.

A king must have a crown, so they wove together the thorny twigs of a plant, and pushed it upon His head. They gave Him a reed as a scepter, and then bowed before Him, saying, "Hail, King of the Jews!" They repeated this mock homage not realizing that the One they were mocking was indeed King of kings and Lord of lords.

Then they did something that no subject would ever do to his king: They spat upon Him and hit Him with the reed. While some of the soldiers were bowing before Him, others were hitting Him on the head or spitting upon Him (Isa. 50:6). Jesus took all of this humiliation and pain without speaking or fighting back (1 Peter 2:18ff). His submission was not a sign of weakness; it was a sign of strength.

### Crucified (27:31-38)

Crucifixion was the most shameful and painful way to execute a criminal. Jesus did not simply die; He died ". . . even the death of a cross" (Phil. 2:8). Roman citizens ordinarily were not crucified. In fact, crucifixion was never mentioned in polite society, so degrading was this form of capital punishment.

Jesus was led outside the city to the place of execution (Heb. 13:12-13). It was required that the prisoner carry his own cross (or at least the crossbeam), and that he wear a placard around his neck announcing his crime. That placard was then hung over his head on the cross for all to see.

While the record does not state so expressly, it appears that Jesus was unable to carry the cross, and this was slowing down the progress of the group. When we remember that He had been awake all night, scourged, and abused by the soldiers, we can conclude that He was exhausted. Jesus started out bearing His cross (John 19:17). Mark 15:22 says, "And they bring Him to Golgotha" (literal translation). This suggests that the soldiers had to assist Jesus in the procession, for the word "bring" has the meaning of "to carry, to bear."

There was to be no delay in this execution. The Passover was about to be celebrated, and the Jewish leaders did not want their holy day desecrated by the dead bodies of criminals (John 19:31). In order to hasten the procession, the soldiers drafted a visitor to Jerusalem, Simon from Cyrene. He had come to Jerusalem to celebrate Passover, and now he was humiliated by being forced to carry the cross of an unknown criminal! Roman soldiers had the authority to draft citizens (Matt. 5:41).

Mark referred to Simon as though the people reading his Gospel would recognize him: "the father of Alexander and Rufus" (Mark 15:21).

Apparently these two sons were well-known members of the church. It seems likely that this humiliating experience resulted in Simon's conversion as well as in the conversion of his family. Simon came to Jerusalem to sacrifice his Passover lamb, and he met the Lamb of God who was sacrificed for him.

It was customary to give a narcotic drink to those about to be crucified, for this would help to ease the pain. Jesus refused this drink; He did the will of God in complete control of His faculties. Also, this act fulfilled Psalm 69:21.

It was customary for the soldiers to share the loot at an execution. This was a fulfillment of Psalm 22:18. After they had finished gambling for His clothing (John 19:23-25), they sat down and "guarded Him there" (v. 36). After all, this Jesus was known to be a miracle-worker. Nobody knew how many followers He had, and perhaps they were even then preparing to rescue Him. He had one man in His band of disciples who had been a Zealot (Matt. 10:4—"Simon the Zealot"), and that fanatical group stopped at nothing when it came to opposing Roman authority.

By combining the Gospel records, we arrive at the full accusation that was put over His head: "This is Jesus of Nazareth the King of the Jews." The Jewish rulers did not approve of what Pilate wrote, but for once the governor did not vascillate (John 19:21-22). In one sense, this title proved to be the first "Gospel tract" ever written. It announced to one of the thieves crucified with Him that He was a Saviour and a King. He dared to believe this message and asked Jesus to save him!

### Mocked by the Jews (27:39-44)

Jesus was not executed in a quiet building, away from the city's noise and activity. He was executed on a public highway, on a day when perhaps hundreds of people were traveling. The fact that His indictment was written in three languages—Greek, Hebrew, and Latin—indicates that a cosmopolitan crowd passed by Golgotha, "the place of the skull." This in itself was humiliating, for the passersby could stare and shout bitter mockery at the victims. Again, this mockery from the crowd had been predicted (Ps. 22:6-8).

It was bad enough that the common rabble mocked Him, but even the Jewish leaders joined the attack. They reminded Him of His promise to rebuild the temple in three days (John 2:19; Matt. 26:61). "If You can do that, You can come down from the cross and prove to us that You are God's Son!'' In reality, it was the fact that He *stayed* on the cross that proved His divine Sonship.

The Jewish rulers mocked His claim to be the Saviour. "He saved others; He cannot save Himself" (v. 42, NASB). He *had* saved others. But if He saved Himself, then nobody else could be saved! He did not come to save His life, but to give it as a ransom for sinners.

### Rejected by the Father (27:45-56)

Jesus was crucified at nine o'clock in the morning; and from nine until noon, He hung in the light. But at noon, a miraculous darkness covered the land. This was not a sandstorm or an eclipse, as some liberal writers have suggested. It was a heaven-sent darkness that lasted for three hours. It was as though all of creation was sympathizing with the Creator. There were three days of darkness in Egypt before Passover (Ex. 10:21-23); and there were three hours of darkness before the Lamb of God died for the sins of the world.

Jesus had spoken at least three times before this darkness fell. While they were crucifying Him, He repeatedly prayed, "Father, forgive them, for they know not what they do" (Luke 23:34). He had spoken to the repentant thief and assured him a place in paradise (Luke 23:39-43). He had also given His mother into the care of His beloved disciple, John (John 19:18-27). But when the darkness came, Jesus was silent for three hours.

After three hours, the darkness left. Then Jesus cried, "My God, My God, why hast Thou forsaken Me?" This was a direct quotation from Psalm 22:1. It was during the time of darkness that Jesus had been made sin for us (2 Cor. 5:21). He had been forsaken by the Father! That darkness was a symbol of the judgment that He endured, when He was "made a curse" for us (Gal. 3:13). Psalm 22:2 suggests a period of light and a period of darkness; and Psalm 22:3 emphasizes the holiness of God. How could a holy God look with favor on His Son who had become sin?

Jesus spoke these words in Hebrew, and the spectators did not understand Him. They thought He was calling for Elijah to help Him. Had they listened carefully and consulted Psalm 22 in its entirety, they would have understood the truth.

In rapid succession, the Lord spoke three more times. He said,

"I thirst" (John 19:28); and this fulfilled Psalm 69:21. Someone took pity on Him and moistened His lips with some sour wine. The others waited to see if perhaps Elijah would come to His rescue.

Then Jesus shouted, "It is finished! Father, into Thy hands I commit My spirit!" The fact that He shouted with a loud voice indicates that He was in complete control of His faculties. Then He voluntarily yielded up His spirit and died.

Though He was "crucified through weakness" (2 Cor. 13:4), He exercised wonderful power when He died. Three miracles took place simultaneously: The veil of the temple was torn in two from top to bottom; an earthquake opened many graves; some of the saints arose from the dead. The rending of the veil symbolized the wonderful truth that the way was now open to God (Heb. 10:14-26). There was no more need of temples, priests, altars, or sacrifices. Jesus had finished the work of salvation on the cross.

The earthquake reminds us of what happened at Mount Sinai when God gave the Law to Moses (Ex. 19:16ff). The earthquake at Calvary signified that the demands of the Law had been met and the curse of the Law forever abolished (Heb. 12:18-24). The torn veil indicates that He conquered sin; the earthquake suggests that He conquered the Law and fulfilled it; and the resurrections prove that He defeated death.

We are not told who these saints were; they were simply believers who had died. The King James Version suggests that they did not come out of the graves until *after* His resurrection; the *New American Standard Bible* agrees with this. It is difficult to believe that they were given life on Friday afternoon and yet remained in their tombs until Sunday. The *New International Version* suggests that these saints were resurrected immediately and came out of their tombs, but that they did not visit in Jerusalem until after Jesus had been raised from the dead. It is not likely that many Jews would be in the cemetery on Passover, since they might be defiled by the dead. These resurrections could have taken place with nobody finding out at that time.

The result of all of this was the testimony of the centurion and those watching. "Truly this was the Son of God." Did this indicate saving faith? Not necessarily. But certainly it indicated hearts that were open to the truth.

The only disciple at the cross when Jesus died was John (John 19:35).

But many women were watching from a distance, undoubtedly those who had assisted Him in His ministry (Luke 8:2). Three women were named: Mary Magdalene, who had been delivered of seven demons (Luke 8:2); Mary the mother of James and Joses, who also was at the tomb on Resurrection morning (Matt. 28:1; Mark 16:1); and Salome, the mother of James and John. Salome had asked Jesus for special thrones for her sons. We wonder how she felt as she saw Him hanging on a cross.

### His Guarded Tomb (27:57-66)

Were it not for the intervention of Joseph of Arimathaea and Nicodemus (John 19:38), the body of Jesus might not have had a decent burial. Joseph and Nicodemus had come to believe in Jesus, even though they had not openly testified of their faith. God kept them hidden, as it were, that they might care for the body of Jesus. Since Joseph was a rich man, and he prepared the new tomb, he helped in the fulfillment of prophecy, Isaiah 53:9—"He was assigned a grave with the wicked, and with the rich in His death . . ." (NIV).

It is not likely that Joseph prepared that tomb for himself. He was a wealthy man and certainly would not want to be buried so near a place of execution. He prepared that tomb for Jesus, and he selected a site near Golgotha so that he and Nicodemus could bury Christ's body quickly. Joseph and Nicodemus could very well have been in the garden waiting for Jesus to die. When they took Him from the cross, they defiled themselves and were not able to eat the Passover. But, what difference did it make? They had found the Lamb of God!

In contrast to the loving care given by Jesus' friends, notice the plottings and maneuvering of the Jewish leaders. The disciples had forgotten that Jesus promised to rise from the dead on the third day, but His enemies remembered. Pilate permitted the leaders to set a guard at the tomb. This guard put an official Roman seal on the stone. All of this was of God, for now it was impossible for anyone—friend or foe—to steal the body. Without realizing it, the Jewish leaders and the Roman government joined forces to help prove the resurrection of Jesus Christ.

# 26

# THE KING'S VICTORY

(Matthew 28)

If anything proves the Kingship of Jesus Christ, it is His resurrection from the dead. The final chapter in Matthew's Gospel is a record of victory. It is a thrilling fact that believers today share in that victory.

Notice the various stages in the experience of the believers with reference to His resurrection.

### They Thought He Was Dead (28:1)

The women who had lingered at the cross came early to the tomb, bringing spices that they might anoint His body. They thought He was dead. In fact, they wondered how they would move the huge stone that blocked the entrance to the tomb (Mark 16:3). It is remarkable that they did not believe in His resurrection when He had taught this truth repeatedly (Matt. 16:21; 17:23; 20:19; 26:32).

We must never underestimate the importance of the resurrection of Jesus Christ. The world believes that Jesus died, but the world does not believe that He arose from the dead. Peter's message at Pentecost emphasized the resurrection. In fact, it is emphasized throughout the Book of Acts. What is the significance of the Resurrection?

*It proves that Jesus is God's Son.* Jesus stated that He had authority to lay down His life and to take it up again (John 10:17-18).

*It verifies the truth of Scripture.* Both in the Old Testament and in the teaching of Jesus, His resurrection is clearly taught (see Pss. 16:10; 110:1). If Jesus had not come out of the tomb, then these Scriptures would not be true.

*It assures our own future resurrection.*Because Jesus died and rose again, we shall one day be raised to be like Him (1 Thes. 4:13-18). In fact, the entire structure of the Christian faith rests upon the foundation of the Resurrection. If we do away with His resurrection, we have no hope.

*It is proof of a future judgment.* "Because He hath appointed a day, in the which He will judge the world in righteousness by that man who He hath ordained; whereof He hath given assurance unto all men, in that He hath raised Him from the dead" (Acts 17:31).

*It is the basis for Christ's heavenly priesthood.* Because He lives by the power of an endless life, He is able to save us "to the uttermost" (Heb. 7:23-28). He lives to intercede for us.

*It gives power for Christian living.* We cannot live for God by our own strength. It is only as His resurrection power works in and through us that we can do His will and glorify His name.

*It assures our future inheritance.* Because we have a living hope, we can experience hopeful living. A dead hope grows weaker and weaker before it eventually dies. But because Jesus Christ is alive, we have a glorious future.

Whenever God's people gather on the Lord's Day they bear witness that Jesus is alive and that the church has received spiritual blessings. When the followers of the Lord gathered that first Lord's Day, they were discouraged and defeated.

### They Heard He Was Alive (28:2-8)

"And behold, a severe earthquake had occurred" (v. 2, NASB). Two angels had appeared (Luke 24:4) and one of them had rolled the stone away from the door. Of course, the soldiers on duty were greatly frightened by this sudden demonstration of supernatural power. The stone was not rolled away to permit Jesus to come out, for He had already left the tomb. It was rolled back so that the people could see for themselves that the tomb was empty.

One of the angels spoke to the women and calmed their fears. "He is not here! Come, and see!" Keep in mind that these women, as well as the disciples, did not expect Jesus to be alive.

What did they see in the tomb? The graveclothes lying on the stone shelf, still wrapped in the shape of the body (John 20:5-7). Jesus had passed through the graveclothes and left them behind as evidence that He was alive. They lay there like an empty cocoon. There was no sign of struggle, the graveclothes were not in disarray. Even the napkin (which had been wrapped around His face) was folded carefully in a place by itself.

We cannot examine this evidence in the same way the believers did that first Easter Sunday. But we do have the evidence of the Word of God. Jesus was not held by the bonds of death (Acts 2:24). He had promised to arise from the dead, and His Word was never broken.

The remarkable change in the early believers is another proof of His resurrection. One day they were discouraged and hiding in defeat. The next day they were declaring His resurrection and walking in joyful victory. In fact, they were willing to die for the truth of the resurrection. If all of this were a manufactured tale, it could never have changed their lives or enabled them to lay down their lives as martyrs.

There were over 500 witnesses who saw Jesus alive at one time (1 Cor. 15:3-8). These appearances of the risen Christ were of such a nature that they could not be explained as hallucinations or self-deception. The people who saw Him were surprised. It would have been impossible for over 500 people to suffer hallucinations at the same time. Even the Apostle Paul, who was an enemy of the church, saw the risen Christ; that experience transformed his life (Acts 9).

The existence of the church, the New Testament, and the Lord's Day add further proof that Jesus is alive. For centuries, the Jews had been God's people, and they had honored the seventh day, the Sabbath. Then a change took place: Jews and Gentiles united in the church and became God's people; they met on the first day of the week, the Lord's Day. The New Testament is a lie if Jesus is dead, for every part of it points to a risen Christ.

Of course, Christians have experienced His resurrection power in their own lives. While the inward, subjective experience *alone* would not prove our Lord's historic resurrection, when combined with the other evidences, it adds great weight to the case. Still it is possible for people to be self-deluded. "Believers" in all kinds of cults will claim their way is true because of what they have experienced. But Christians have the weight of church history, Scripture, and dependable witnesses to back up their own personal experiences of faith.

"Come and see!" was followed by "Go and tell!" We must not keep the Resurrection news to ourselves. The angel sent the women to tell (of all people) Christ's own disciples. They should have been expecting the news, but instead, they questioned it even when they heard it.

### They Met the Living Christ Personally (28:9-15)
It is when we are obeying God's Word that He comes to us. Jesus had already appeared to Mary Magdalene in the Garden (John 20:11-18; Mark 16:9). Notice that our Lord's first two resurrection appearances were to believing women. These faithful women were not only the last to leave Calvary, but they were also the first to come to the tomb. Their devotion to Jesus was rewarded.

"All hail!" can be translated, *Grace*. What a marvelous greeting for the Resurrection day! The women fell at His feet, took hold of Him, and worshiped Him. There must have been some fear in their hearts, for He immediately assured them with His typical, "Be not afraid!"

Not only had the angel commissioned them, but the Lord also commissioned them. The phrase "My brethren" revealed the intimate relationship between Christ and His followers. Jesus had spoken similar words to Mary Magdalene earlier that morning (John 20:17). Jesus reinforced the instructions of the angel that the disciples meet Him in Galilee (see 28:7). In the garden, Jesus had told His disciples that He would rise from the dead and meet them in Galilee; but they had forgotten (Matt. 26:31-32).

While the believers were worshiping the living Christ, the unbelievers were plotting to destroy the witness of the resurrection of Jesus Christ. By now, some of the soldiers had realized that they were in a desperate plight. The Roman seal had been broken, the stone had been rolled away, and the body was not in the tomb. For a Roman soldier to fail in his duty was an offense punishable by death (Acts 12:19; 16:27-28). But the soldiers were shrewd: They did not report to Pilate or to their superior officers; they reported to the Jewish chief priests. They knew that these men were as anxious to cover up the miracle as were the soldiers themselves! Between the chief priests, the elders, and the soldiers, they put together a story that would explain the empty tomb: The body was stolen.

By examining this story, we see that it actually *proves* the resurrection of Jesus Christ. If Jesus' body was stolen, then it was taken either by His friends or His enemies. His friends could not have done it since they had left the scene and were convinced that Jesus was dead. His enemies would not steal His body because belief in His resurrection was what they were trying to prevent. They would have defeated their own purposes if they had removed His body. And, if they had taken it, why did they not produce it and silence the witness of the early church?

Anyone who stole the body would have taken the body *in the grave-clothes*. Yet the empty graveclothes were left in the tomb in an orderly manner. This was hardly the scene of a grave robbery.

The religious leaders had given money to Judas to betray Jesus. They also gave money to the soldiers to say that the body had been stolen. These Romans would have demanded a large price, for their lives were at stake. If their superiors heard that these soldiers had failed, they could have been executed. Even if the story got to Pilate, he was not likely to do much about it. He was sure that Jesus was dead (Mark 15:43-45), and that was all that mattered to him. The disappearance of Jesus' body created no problems for Pilate.

Mark Twain once wrote that a lie can go around the world while truth is still lacing up her boots. There is something in human nature that makes it easy for people to believe lies. It was not until the coming of the Spirit at Pentecost, and the powerful witness of the apostles, that the Jews in Jerusalem discovered the truth: Jesus Christ was alive! Any sincere person who studies this evidence with an open heart will conclude that the resurrection of Jesus Christ is an historic fact that cannot be refuted.

Our Lord also appeared to the two Emmaus disciples that day (Luke 24:13-32), and also to the 10 disciples in an upper room in Jerusalem (John 20:19-25). A week later, He appeared to the 11 disciples and dealt with Thomas' unbelief (John 20:19-25). On that first Easter Sunday, Jesus also made a special appearance to Peter (Luke 24:33-35; 1 Cor. 15:5).

That day began with the disciples and the women thinking Jesus was dead. Then they were told that He was alive. Following that announcement, they met Him personally. There was one more stage in their experience.

### They Shared the Good News with Others (28:16-20)

Some Bible scholars equate this "mountain meeting" in Galilee with the appearance of the Lord to "more than 500 brethren at one time" (1 Cor. 15:6). The fact that some of the people present doubted His resurrection would suggest that more than the 11 apostles were present, for these men were now confirmed believers. Our Lord's ascension did not take place at this time, but later, after He had ministered to His disciples in Jerusalem (Luke 24:44-53).

Matthew 28:18-20 is usually called "The Great Commission," although this statement is no greater than that in any of the other Gospels, nor is it the last statement Jesus made before He returned to heaven. However, this declaration does apply to us as believers, so we should understand the factors that are involved.

*An authority* (28:18). In this verse, the word *power* means "authority," the right to use power. The entire Gospel of Matthew stresses the authority of Jesus Christ. There was authority to His teaching (7:29). He exercised authority in healing (8:1-13), and even in forgiving sins (9:6). He had authority over Satan, and He delegated that authority to His apostles (10:1). At the close of his Gospel, Matthew made it clear that Jesus has ALL authority.

Since Jesus Christ today has all authority, we may obey Him without fear. No matter where He leads us, no matter what circumstances we face, He is in control. By His death and resurrection, Jesus defeated all enemies and won for Himself all authority.

Christianity is a missionary faith. The very nature of God demands this, for God is love and God is not willing that any should perish (2 Peter 3:9). Our Lord's death on the cross was for the whole world. If we are the children of God and share His nature, then we will want to tell the good news to the lost world.

When we read the Book of Acts, we see that the early church operated on the basis of the Lord's sovereign authority. They ministered in His name. They depended on His power and guidance. They did not face a lost world on the basis of their own authority, but on the authority of Jesus Christ.

*An activity* (28:19-20a). The Greek verb translated *go* is actually not a command but a present participle (going). The only command in the entire Great Commission is "make disciples" ("teach all nations"). Jesus said, "While you are going, make disciples of all the nations." No matter where we are, we should be witnesses for Jesus Christ and seek to win others to Him (Acts 11:19-21).

The term "disciples" was the most popular name for the early believers. Being a disciple meant more than being a convert or a church member. *Apprentice* might be an equivalent term. A disciple attached himself to a teacher, identified with him, learned from him, and lived with him. He learned, not simply by listening, but also by doing. Our Lord called 12 disciples and taught them so that they might be able to teach others (Mark 3:13ff).

A disciple, then, is one who has believed on Jesus Christ and expressed this faith by being baptized. He remains in the fellowship of the believers that he might be taught the truths of the faith (Acts 2:41-47). He is then able to go out and win others and teach them. This was the pattern of the New Testament church (2 Tim. 2:1-2).

In many respects, we have departed from this pattern. In most churches, the congregation pays the pastor to preach, win the lost, and build up the saved—while the church members function as cheer leaders (if they are enthusiastic) or spectators. The "converts" are won, baptized, and given the right hand of fellowship, then they join the other spectators. How much faster our churches would grow, and how much stronger and happier our church members would be, if each one were discipling another believer. The only way a local church can "be fruitful and multiply" (instead of growing by "additions") is with a systematic discipleship program. This is the responsibility of *every* believer, and not just a small group who have been "called to go."

Jesus had opened the minds of His disciples to understand the Scriptures (Luke 24:44-45). They knew what He wanted them to teach to their own converts. It is not enough to win people to the Saviour; we must also teach them the Word of God. This is also a part of the Great Commission.

*An ability* (28:20b). Jesus is not only "in the midst" when His people gather together (Matt. 18:20), but He is also present with them as they scatter into the world to witness. Had He remained on earth, Jesus could not have fulfilled this promise. It was when the Spirit came, that Jesus could be with His people no matter where they were.

Dr. G. Campbell Morgan told about an experience in his life that involved this statement. Early in his Christian life, Morgan used to visit several elderly ladies once a week to read the Bible to them. When he came to the end of Matthew's Gospel, Morgan read, "Lo, I am with you always, even unto the end of the age." He added, "Isn't that a wonderful promise?" One of the ladies quickly replied, "Young man, that is not a promise—it is a fact!"

There are no conditions for us to meet, or even to believe; for *Jesus*

*Christ is with us*. Paul discovered this to be true when he was seeking to establish a church in the difficult city of Corinth. Obeying this commission, Paul came to the city (Acts 18:1), won people to Christ and baptized them (v. 8) and taught them the word (v. 11). When the going was tough, Paul had a special visit from the Lord: "Be not afraid . . . for I am with thee . . ." (vv. 9-10).

The phrase "the end of the age" indicates that our Lord has a plan; He is the Lord of history. As the churches follow His leading and obey His Word, they fulfill His purposes in the world. It will all come to a climax one day; meanwhile, we must all be faithful.